High Sierra SUV Trails

Volume I

The East Side

A guide to 35 interesting and scenic four-wheeling excursions in the High Sierra

Roger Mitchell

Two roads diverged in a wood, and I-
I took the one less traveled by,
And that has made all the difference.

Robert Frost

High Sierra SUV Trails

Volume I

The East Side

A guide to 35 interesting and scenic four-wheeling excursions in the High Sierra

Roger Mitchell

All photos by the author except where noted

Track & Trail Publications
Oakhurst California

Published by Track & Trail Publications
P.O. Box 1247
Oakhurst CA 94644

First Edition 2002

Cover photo: The Wheeler Crest Road

Other related Track & Trail Publications:
Death Valley SUV Trails
High Sierra SUV Trails II – The Western Slope

Other titles currently in preparation:
Inyo-Mono SUV Trails
Western Nevada SUV Trails
Mohave Desert SUV Trails
Grand Canyon SUV Trails
High Sierra SUV Trails III – The North Country

Library of Congress Cataloging-in-Publication data:

Mitchell, Roger, 1938-
High Sierra SUV Trails, Vol. I, The East Side, 1st ed.
bibliographic references (p.) and index
Includes ISBN Number 0-9707115-1-4
Guidebook- Sierra Nevada mountains (Calif. And Nev.) – (2) History
– Mines and mining

Ansel Adams 1902-1984

This book is dedicated to the memory of Ansel Adams, a friend, a teacher, an accomplished musician and, perhaps most of all, a great master of the photographic arts. His gentle humor and keen eye for beauty have been missed for nearly twenty years.

The author and publisher of this guide make no representations as to the safety of any of the routes described in this publication. At the time of this printing all route descriptions were reasonably up to date. However, conditions change, sometimes very rapidly. Backroad travelers should enter the mountains with their vehicles in good mechanical condition, carrying extra clothing, water, and food should an unexpected emergency occur. It is recommended that each vehicle carry a detailed map, and that drivers first inquire about current road conditions at the local Ranger Station before attempting any of these routes.

It should also be noted that administrative actions by the U.S. Forest Service can impact the visitor's use of the forest. Roads which are open to motor vehicles one day can be closed the next day. Always obey any posted sign, and, if in doubt, check with the nearest Ranger Station.

Contents

Acknowledgements 1
Introduction 2
Acronyms 4
Rules of the Road, Written and Otherwise 5
Warnings 6
The Mitchell Scale 8
Chapter I: Trails Out of Reno 11
1. Poeville, Poedunk and Peavine Peak 12
2. Verdi Peak Lookout 17
3. The Hunter Lake Corridor 22
Chapter II: Trails Out of Truckee 27
4. Mount Watson 29
5. Martis Peak 32
Chapter III: Trails Out of South Lake Tahoe 39
6. Descending Kings Canyon 41
7. Genoa Peak 45
8. The Barker Pass Circuit 49
9. Ellis Peak, the Easy Way 54
10. Ellis Peak, the Hard Way 57
11. The McKinney-Rubicon Trail to the PCT 61
Chapter IV: Trails Out of Markleeville 65
12. Scotts Lake 67
13. Crater Lake and the Alpine Mine 69
14. Red Lake to Blue Lakes 73
15. The Mokelumne Corridor 77
16. Loope Canyon Loop 81
17. The 'Lost' Pennsylvania Mine 86
Chapter V: Trails Out of Bridgeport 93
18. Fremont's Lost Cannon 95
19. Backroad to Sonora Pass 99
20. The Tamarack Trail 106
21. Munckton Memories 109
Chapter VI: Trails Out of Lee Vining 115
22. High on Copper Mountain 116
23. The Disaster at Jordan 121
24. Beartrack Canyon 125
Chapter VII: Trails Out of Mammoth Lakes 129
25. Inyo Craters and Crater Flat 131
26. Deadman Pass 137
27. Laurel Lakes 142

Chapter VIII: Trails Out of Bishop 149
28. The Wheeler Crest 150
29. The Buttermilk Country 154
30. Coyote Creek 160
31. Baker Creek 164
Chapter IX: Trails Out of Big Pine 167
32. Glacier View 169
Chapter X: Trails Out of Independence 175
33. Armstrong Canyon 177
34. Valley Viewpoint 185
Chapter XI: Trails Out of Lone Pine 189
35. The Haiwee Pass Trailhead 191
Appendix A: Glossary of Geologic Terms Used in the Text 195
Appendix B: Geologic Time Chart 200
Appendix C: The Plio-Pleistocene Ice Age 201
Appendix D: Common Flowers Found Along the Sierra Nevada SUV Trails 202
Appendix E: Collecting and using wild berries 204
Appendix F: Collecting and using Piñon nuts 206
Appendix G: Tea for the taking 208
Appendix H: Equipment checklist for backcountry vehicles 210
Appendix I: Fuel Safety 213
Appendix J: Some useful addresses 214
References 218
Index 221

Acknowledgments

I would like to thank my wife, Loris, who has been my traveling companion, my scribe, my secretary and my proofreader. Without her support and assistance, this book would never have gone to press. Thanks, too, are in order to Glenn Harmelin, who was always there with technical support when I needed him.

In the preparation of this book, I consulted with many folks in the U.S. Forest Service. Although I am under no obligation to do so, I always submit the appropriate portions of the manuscripts to the relevant District Ranger for their staff to review prior to publication. In this way, hopefully, any policy or resource problems can be worked out ahead of time. In the Humboldt-Toiyabe National Forest, Laura Williams of the Carson Ranger District was very helpful. In the Lake Tahoe Management Unit, Civil Engineer Garrett Villanueva kept me up to date on recent road "improvements". In the Inyo National Forest, ORV Coordinator Julie Molzahn and Recreation Specialist Rod Ellis of the Lone Pine Ranger District kindly provided their suggestions. My thanks go to you all.

My hat also goes off to the hundreds of men and women in four-wheel drive clubs up and down the state, whose organizations have entered into cooperative agreements with the U.S. Forest Service to maintain many of the jeep trails I describe. I hesitate to list these clubs individually for fear of leaving someone out. Nevertheless without them, many of these enjoyable routes would simply no longer exist.

Lake Tahoe Hi-Lo 4WD Club	Lake Tahoe	McKinney-Rubicon Trail
North Tahoe Trailbusters 4WD Club	Lake Tahoe	Ellis Peak and Blackwood Trails
Reno Jeepers	Reno NV	Barker Creek Trail

I'm sure I have overlooked someone. Please forgive me. Your efforts have not gone unnoticed and are very much appreciated.

Introduction

If you are a rock crawler who simply likes to take his four-wheel drive rig out to push it to the limit, this guide may not be for you. If, however, you are interested in broadening your knowledge and appreciation of nature while enjoying wholesome outdoor activity, then, hopefully, this guide will be of some assistance. It was not the author's intent to simply make this guide an inventory of off-road vehicle trails. The outings I describe have some interesting historical, natural, or scenic feature.

Today there are few places where you can drive and hope to have the place all to yourself. But the quest is made somewhat easier if you have an SUV or other kind of four-wheel drive vehicle. By selecting backroads and jeep trails such as those described herein, you will find that you have left most of the masses behind. While you may not find complete solitude, a campsite in the wild is often more enjoyable and meaningful than crowded public campgrounds.

I wrote *Eastern Sierra Jeep Trails* in 1971, followed by *Western Sierra Jeep Trails* in 1976. A lot has happened in those last twenty five to thirty years, so when I decided to update these guides I was uncertain what changes I might find. As I expected, some of the trails I described in the 1970s no longer exist today. However, in rechecking these routes, I was pleasantly surprised to find some of my favorite trails were virtually unchanged, and a few new ones had been opened. Surprisingly, perhaps, after thirty years of use, some of these roads have gotten worse, not better. Several times I found roads previously rated at Class II, were now Class III.

This publication is designed to introduce the four-wheeler to some very pretty high country scenery that most folks never see. These trails will take you off the well-beaten tourist routes, sometimes far off. You must have a high clearance vehicle for most of these backroads, although not all absolutely require four-wheel drive. Indeed, a few of these jeep trails are so difficult that only the most dedicated rock-crawling four-wheelers will attempt them. However, I have also included many routes that any novice four-wheeler should be able to handle with any SUV.

Many of these backcountry areas have a confusing labyrinth of roads and jeep trails. For this reason I describe the distances down to tenths of a mile so the reader can more easily find the correct way to go. You may wish to reset your trip odometer to zero when you leave the pavement at the start of each of these trails. Keep in mind, too, that **not all odometers read alike, particularly if you have added larger tires. Your distances may vary somewhat from mine.**

The trails described herein were all rechecked between the years 1999 and 2001. The trail information was current at the time the book was published. Things change, however, and the reader must use common sense and adapt to post-publication changes. Trails may wash out, be covered by rockslides, have trees fall on them and otherwise become totally impassable. They may also come under the blade of a forest service bulldozer and suddenly get much better, perhaps too good! Old mines and historic buildings deteriorate. What you see may not be the same thing that I saw a year or two earlier when I wrote this guide. The U.S. Forest Service and Bureau of Land Management administrative policies change as well. What was once an approved *Designated Route* may be changed and administratively withdrawn from use by motorized vehicles. Once in a while new trails open. That does happen too, although not very often. **Before embarking on any of these trails, be sure to stop at the nearest Forest Service Ranger Station to obtain the most current road information.**

Off-roaders have become understandably defensive as they see more and more of their favorite trails disappear. Some long established trails have been put off limits when Congress has passed laws creating new wilderness areas. The passage of the *California Wilderness Act of 1984* had a profound and adverse impact on four-wheelers. In the Sierra Nevada this act closed the road into Summit City Canyon by the creation of the Mokelumne Wilderness, the road to Spanish Lake by the Monarch Wilderness, the road to Chain Lakes by the expansion of the John Muir Wilderness, the road to Woodpecker Meadow by the expansion of the Domeland Wilderness, the road to Heitz Meadow by the Ansel Adams Wilderness, the route to Summit Meadows by the South Sierra Wilderness, and the route into Casa Vieja Meadows by the Golden Trout Wilderness. Those are clear and undeniable truths. Admittedly, it could have been even worse. Congress exempted small corridors through a few wilderness areas, thus allowing off-roaders to continue to use their favorite trails. This saved the Ershim-Dusy Trail when the Dinkey Lakes Wilderness was established, and the Clover Valley-Deer Valley route when the Mokelumne Wilderness was created.

In the past, some four-wheel drive routes have been lost to logging, for new high-standard roads often accompany timber sales. The once beautiful Wolf Creek Trail in Toiyabe National Forest is now a wide oiled road thanks to a timber sale. Sequoia National Forest has so cut up the Kern Plateau that many miles of jeep trails were turned into graded and even paved roadways.

Outside of the Sierra Nevada, losses involving new wilderness areas have been even greater with passage of the *California Desert Protection Act of 1994.* That single piece of legislation closed more jeep trails in California than all the previous closures combined! In general, recent years have been a net loss for off-road recreation. Four-wheelers have been fighting in retreat and losing!

Acronyms

In order to economize in the use of words, I have resorted to the use of initials in certain frequently used word groups. Hopefully, these initials will not sound foreign to the reader as we tend to use them this way in everyday speech.

BLM Bureau of Land Management, a federal agency under the Department of the Interior responsible for the multiple use management of millions of acres of federal land outside of our national parks, national forests, and natural wildlife preserves.

DFG Department of Fish and Game, a State of California agency responsible for managing the state's wildlife.

DWP City of Los Angeles, Department of Water and Power.

EDNF El Dorado National Forest.

HTNF Humboldt-Toiyabe National Forest.

INF Inyo National Forest.

JEEP A registered trademark of a specific auto manufacturer, but I use the term, both upper and lower case, in a generic sense, to include all four-wheel drive vehicles.

NPS National Park Service, a federal agency under the Department of the Interior.

PCT The Pacific Crest Trail, a 2600-mile long trail for backpackers which goes from Canada to Mexico.

PG&E Pacific Gas and Electric Company.

TNF Tahoe National Forest.

TRT Tahoe Rim Trail, a 150-mile long footpath that completely encircles Lake Tahoe.

SCE Southern California Edison Company.

SUV Sport utility vehicle.

USFS United States Forest Service, a federal agency under the Department of Agriculture responsible for the multiple use management of millions of acres of federally owned forest lands.

USGS United States Geological Survey, a federal agency under the Department of the Interior responsible for mapping and geological studies.

Rules of the Road
Written and Otherwise

This guide is written specifically for drivers of four-wheel drive vehicles. Obviously, mountain bikes can go everywhere a 4x4 can go, and then some. By implication then, this book might also guide mountain bikes. Whether you rely on a gasoline engine or pedal power, here are a few common sense rules you need to remember:

1. Follow established jeep trails or "designated routes." Don't make new ones of your own. Respect the boundaries of designated Wilderness Areas and other places posted *No Vehicles*. There is a place for feet and a place for wheels. *Tread lightly on the land.*
2. Some of these trails may cross private property. Please respect the owners' wishes and heed *No Trespassing* signs.
3. **Be very fire conscious**. Smoke only in cleared areas or where it is safe to do so. Carry an ax, a shovel, and a bucket in your 4x4. Be sure your muffler is an effective spark arrester. Don't park in tall grass where your catalytic converter can come in contact with vegetation. Obtain a *campfire permit* every year. Make sure your campfire is dead out when you leave it.
4. For safety, it is always best to travel with at least one other vehicle. Go prepared for sudden severe weather.
5. Grant hikers and horsemen the right of way.
6. Do not deface or destroy objects of historical interest. Save them for the next person to enjoy. Please remember the *National Antiquities Act of 1906* and the *Archeological Resources Act of 1979* prohibit the disturbing or collecting of Indian artifacts.
7. Leave the land as you would like to find it. Whenever possible, camp in existing campsites. Otherwise, *leave no trace* when you break camp and leave. Camp at least one hundred feet back from streams and lakes. Pack out all litter, even if it isn't yours. Don't drive across wet meadows, and don't drive in streams unnecessarily.
8. **Consider any mineshaft or tunnel to be unsafe. Do NOT enter!**

Please pick up any litter you might find along the trail.

Warning

Although the author has used most of the roads and trails described herein for the last thirty or more years, they have all been re-scouted between 1999 and 2001. The route descriptions were accurate at that time this publication went to press. Conditions change however, sometimes in a matter of minutes. Bad roads become graded, and good roads can become flooded, washed out, or buried by landslides. A section of trail that has been Class I or II for the last fifty years may deteriorate to Class V very suddenly. A single thunderstorm may make a road suddenly dangerous or impassable. **The reader must exercise great caution and use common sense when traveling any of these routes. Do not attempt to ford streams if you are uncertain as to the water depth, strength of current, and firmness of the bottom. Never drive anyplace where you cannot see ahead. When in doubt always stop and scout the route ahead on foot. If possible have a passenger slowly guide you through difficult places. Remember, if your vehicle gets stuck or breaks down, you are on your own. Help may be a very long distance away.**

In addition to the physical hazards of the trail, one must be aware that public land management agencies such as the U.S. Forest Service and the Bureau of Land Management can administratively close a road or area with little or no advance notice. One must always heed the signs placed by these agencies.

In summary then, be vigilant, be cautious, and be safe. Remember, no guarantee is made that the reader will find the trail as described.

A Rather Unusual Warning

At first I was reluctant to include this caveat in this guide, because in my five decades in the Sierra, I have never encountered the problem I am about to describe. Nevertheless, I am assured by U.S. Forest Service personnel that this situation can and does occur. If it happens to you, you will not think it so funny.

Our old friend the porcupine, *Erethizon dorsatum*, has a widespread habitat throughout the Sierra Nevada. Although not usually around in any great numbers, they can be found anywhere there are trees, from 4,000 feet up to 10,000 feet. These guys are the largest of all terrestrial rodents and like their smaller distant relatives, mice, they like to roam about at night looking for tasty tidbits.

OK, so why should this revelation be of any interest to the four-wheeler? Well, it seems that porcupines have developed a taste for neoprene or butyl brake lines, fan belts, and radiator hoses. Why any porcupine would want to eat your car when some perfectly yummy tree bark may be nearby I cannot say. Nevertheless, these critters have been known to snack on automotive parts at night, while the owners were blissfully asleep in a tent a few feet away.

So what is the solution? You might keep a dog in camp, although dogs will only take on a porcupine once! (The second time porky rambles through camp old Fido probably won't let out a peep.) The Forest Service suggests surrounding your car with 3-foot high chicken wire. Yea sure, every off-roader needs to carry a roll of chicken wire in his rig. Some people have piled loose rocks under their car to prevent access, but that too seems like a lot of work. Handle the potential problem however you want; just don't say that I didn't warn you!

The Mitchell Scale

Everything seems to have its standard of measurement. Earthquakes have their Richter scales. Temperature has its degrees. Sound has its decibels. Thus it is that I have attempted to quantify the degree of difficulty to the various jeep trails described. This scale, which I modestly call *The Mitchell Scale,* was blatantly stolen from rock climbers and mountaineers who have their own peculiar brand of madness. It goes from Class I, the easiest, to Class VI, the most difficult.

CLASS I: This includes just about any kind of semi-improved, not normally maintained road, over which you can safely maneuver a standard passenger car.

CLASS II: This road is a bit more rough than Class I. The road may have a high center, large rocks or deep ruts and potholes, requiring vehicles with a greater degree of under-chassis clearance. While four-wheel drive is not absolutely necessary, this is not a road recommended for standard passenger cars.

CLASS III: Here both high clearance and four-wheel drive are the minimum requirements necessary, and perhaps low range gears as well. Drivers of most SUVs should have no trouble with this road if due care is taken.

CLASS IV: Here the going gets rougher. An experienced four-wheeler in a short wheelbase vehicle should take this trail in stride, although a passenger might disembark and be utilized as a "spotter" to guide the driver over tight places. To avoid damage, drivers of SUVs should attempt these areas with extreme caution.

CLASS V: This very difficult route is for heroes only. It is highly questionable whether the abuse your vehicle is taking is really worth the effort. Vehicle damage is always a possibility. Skidpans under everything are a must. Don't try this trail alone! Portions of the famous Rubicon Trail are certainly in this category (see *High Sierra SUV Trails Volume II - The Western Slope*).

Class VI: This route is so extreme that a winch is usually required, along with feats of creative engineering and road building. There are no Class VI routes described in this book.

Special Note: Weather conditions are an additional factor. A Class I or II road when it is dry in the summer may become Class III a few months later when it has a few inches of snow on it.

It should also be noted that most of the routes described herein are well over 7,500 feet in elevation and, as such, can be expected to be buried in deep snow during the winter and spring months. The exceptions are Excursions 23, 34, and 35, which may be open most of the winter, except after storms. The rest of the roads should be snow free by early June and remain that way through October.

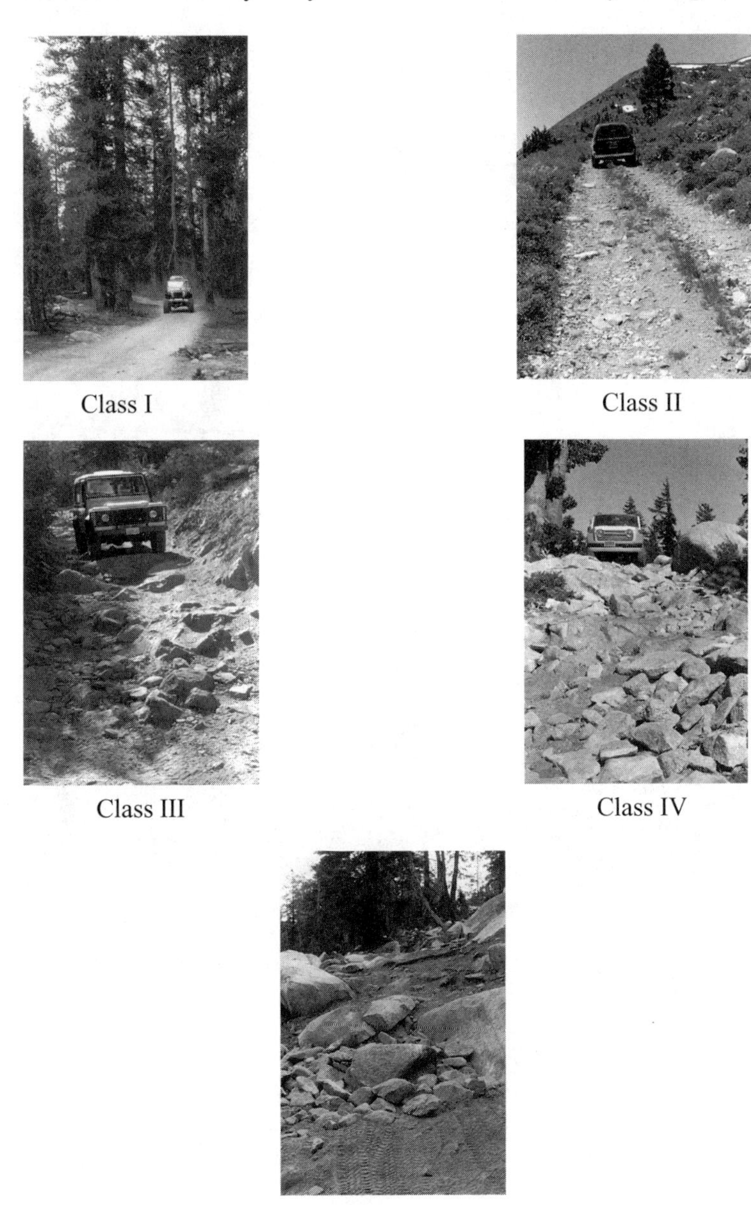

Class I

Class II

Class III

Class IV

Class V

Early summer travelers should carry a
bucksaw or a chainsaw to clear downed snags.

Early summer travelers should also carry a
shovel to dig paths through lingering snow banks.

Chapter I
Trails Out of Reno Nevada
(Humboldt-Toiyabe National Forest)

Reno started as *Fuller's Crossing,* named after C.W. Fuller, who built a toll bridge over the Truckee River and a hotel here in 1859. The name changed to *Lake's Crossing* in 1863, when Myron C. Lake bought the property. The Central Pacific Railroad brought its tracks to the north bank of the Truckee in 1868. Lake gave forty acres to the railroad so that they would place a station here. Thus Reno was born on May 9th, 1868, with a post office established four days later. Railroad officials named the station after Jesse Lee Reno, an American Army officer killed in the Civil War.

With a population of 150,000 today, Reno is the second largest city in Nevada, and the county seat of Washoe County. Together with its neighbor, Sparks, the Reno area offers a full range of goods and services. While entertainment is certainly the principal industry here, behind all the glitter of the gambling casinos there are a lot of people living here who have nothing to do with the gaming industry. Reno and Sparks are the state center for many governmental offices, utilities, warehousing, and light manufacturing. In addition, the University of Nevada has a large campus here.

Backroad explorers in particular may wish to visit the National Automobile Museum displaying more than 200 classic, vintage, or specialty automobiles. Others may find the Nevada Historical Museum of interest.

Reno is an extraordinary place in that, within a few minutes' drive of downtown, you can be in low gears climbing steadily upward on your favorite dirt road high above the city. The three routes described in this chapter all offer spectacular views of the entire Reno-Sparks area.

1

Poeville, Poedunk, and Peavine Peak

Primary Attraction:	The site of an old mining camp founded in 1863, coupled with an ascent of a 8,200' mountain top with a marvelous view of the Reno area.
Time Required:	If you take time to explore all the side roads this excursion has to offer, the outing will take the entire day.
Miles Involved:	From the intersection of I-80 and U.S. Highway 395 to the top of Peavine Peak is 16 miles. The return trip to Reno is another 16 miles.
Degree of Difficulty:	Most of the route is Class I or II, with only a little Class III.
Remarks:	The 1982-revised edition of the Verdi, Nevada 1:24,000 topographic map shows the roads and various jeep trails very well.

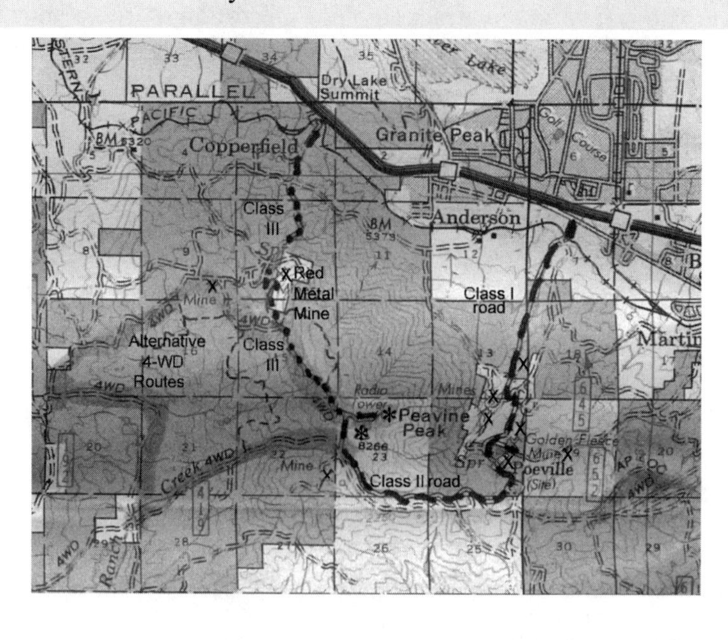

From the intersection of I-80 and Highway 395, go north on Highway 395 for eight miles, getting off at Stead Ave., Exit 76. Turn left going under the freeway, and then after 0.1 miles turn right again onto this extension of Virginia Street. Go west 0.6 miles to where an unmarked graded dirt road takes off to the left. If you pass a house on the left, and you can see a green municipal water tank on the right a quarter of a mile away, you know you are at the right place. Note your odometer reading as you leave the pavement. The elevation here is 5,200 feet. In the next 6.7 miles you will climb 3,000 feet.

The rough graded road crosses the railroad and begins to climb the hillside to the south. Peavine Peak is straight ahead on the horizon. Today's outing will take us up and around this highpoint.

At a point 1.7 miles from the pavement, the tailings dumps of the Fravel Mine are passed on the left. When the Peavine Mining District was laid out in 1863, it was a box twenty miles from east to west by ten miles north to south. The Fravel Mine goes back to those early days, although none of the original structures has survived.

A short distance up the road on a bench to the right is the Paymaster Mine, the site of private property. The road makes a sweeping switchback and continues to climb. Three miles from the pavement, several Class II roads go down into a draw to the left. This is the site of the Golden Fleece Mine, and a small mining camp called Poeville that grew up around it.

Early in 1863 brightly colored veins of copper were discovered on the eastern side of what would be called Peavine Peak. (The mountain was so-named from the wild peas found growing near its summit.) Assays of the copper revealed gold was also present. News of the find spread by word of mouth throughout the saloons and dancehalls of Virginia City, and within a year several hundred would-be miners had pitched tents in the flat below the diggings. Originally the camp was called Peavine, then Poe City after John Poe, who surveyed a town site and sold lots. When a post office was established, the name again changed and it became Poeville. A few called the camp "Podunk".

In 1864 specimens of colorful copper ore were put on display at the Nevada State Fair in Carson City, but the remoteness of the site cooled the fever of potential investors. Copper requires many tons of ore, and that requires a railroad to carry those tons to the smelter. There was no railroad anywhere near Poe City. That situation was to change, however, when the Central Pacific Railroad started laying tracks eastward from Sacramento in January of 1863. On Thanksgiving Day in 1866, those tracks were extended as far to the east as Cisco. For the first time, the ores of Poeville could be taken by wagon to a railhead. Indeed, it was ore from Poeville that the Central Pacific first carried to the smelter in Sacramento. Unfortunately, winter storms closed the wagon road and halted the eastward march of the rails. The tracks finally entered Nevada on December 13,1867. The tracks were now only ten miles from the mines, stimulating further development, and by 1868 nearly a dozen mines were working the veins of Peavine Mountain. Those mines included the Paymaster, with a 125-foot incline shaft leading to a 1700-foot drift tunnel that drained the workings. The Emma Mine had a 400-foot shaft. The Golden Fleece, Cleopatra, and Golden Eagle Mines had tunnels 900 feet, 800 feet, and 700 feet in length respectively.

Growth was slow, but steady. Mining activity reached its peak in 1873 and 1874. By this time the camp is said to have a population of some 1500 people, with scores of substantial houses made of logs and brick. The town had the usual saloons, dance halls, bawdy houses, general stores, and livery stables. The constant pounding of a 10-stamp amalgamation mill could be heard throughout the area. As the shafts became deeper, however, the veins pinched out. One by one, the mines closed, and by 1880 Poeville had been reduced to a dozen or so residents.

Interestingly however, the camp did not completely die. The *Reno Evening Gazette* on June 7, 1909, reported that two partners by the names of Lynch and Faber had dug four more inches in an old tunnel to find fresh ore that had assay values of $50 to $2,000 per ton in silver. They and several others had reopened old mines and were producing ore. Optimism was in great abundance, with claims being made that Poeville might yet become another Butte, Tonopah, or Goldfield. In looking at the site today, one gets no idea of the activity that once went on here. Little remains save the tailings dump of the Golden Fleece and several other mines.

In 1909 H.H. Fravel took this photo of his father and others at Poeville. (Photo courtesy of Nevada Historical Society.)

Today only barren tailings dumps mark the site of Poeville.

The graded road swings up the mountainside above Poeville and turns to the west. As the road gains elevation, the predominate vegetation becomes Desert Mahogany, *Cercocarpus ledifolius,* a shrub which grows to almost tree-like proportions. To the left two side roads drop down to Peavine Creek and the site of the old Nevada Central Mine. The Class I road, still rough, eventually swings to the north. Six miles from the pavement, a Class III side road to the left goes west down Bull Ranch Creek to enter national forest lands. Several of these trails eventually descend to the Truckee River Canyon, where I-80 can be reached.

The Class I road to Peavine Peak continues north 0.4 miles, where roads go off in several directions. We are going to go to the left, but first, lets see the sights to the right. To the sharp right, behind you, a road climbs to an 8,266' summit that was once a forest fire lookout. The summit is not crowded with electronics equipment. Also to the right is the road to Peavine Peak, another 8,250' summit festooned with radio and television antennae. The view from the top is marvelous, with all of Reno laid out at your feet to the southeast.

The rocks of Peavine Mountain are mostly very old metamorphic rocks, primarily schist, that have been intruded by quartz monzonite. This is a silica-rich form of granite associated with the Sierra Nevada Batholith of Cretaceous age. The mineral deposits are found near where these two rock masses come in contact with each other.

Peavine Peak north summit, elevation 8260 feet.

Peavine Peak south summit, elevation 8266 feet.

Back 0.4 miles at the intersection, Road 642 heads off to the northwest. The road is Class II at first, and then becomes Class III as it starts a steep descent down to the Red Metal Mine. The early history of this mine remains a little obscure, but it is thought to have been first worked well over a century ago. We know it was in limited operation in 1912, with ore being sent 7½ miles by wagon down to the rail siding in Purdy, California. The mine gets its name from the important copper mineral bornite, which was found here. This sulphide of copper and iron displays a peculiar reddish color upon a fresh fracture and brilliant peacock colors on weathered surfaces. A careful search of the mine dumps may still reveal specimens of the copper minerals bornite, the bright green malachite, and, perhaps, a little blue azurite. **Warning: these old workings are dangerous. Stay well clear of areas where rocks may fall from up above.**

Beyond the Red Metal Mine the road continues as an easy Class III, but the downgrade becomes exceedingly steep. At a point 4.3 miles from the summit of Peavine Peak, your 3,000 foot descent of the mountain is complete, as you once again cross the railroad tracks. Turn right along the highway frontage road, and in a little less than three miles you will be back at Exit 76, your starting point.

2

Verdi Peak

Primary Attraction:	This backroad leads to a fire lookout, perched high above I-80 and having a great view overlooking the Reno Basin to the east and the lake country to the west. Along the way, the devastating effects of forest fire can be seen close at hand.
Time Required:	If your time is very limited, this excursion can be done in half a day. Consider making the excursion in the early evening so you can watch the lights of Reno come on.
Miles Involved:	The one way distance from downtown Reno to the summit of Verdi Peak is only 23 miles.
Degree of Difficulty:	Eleven of those miles are over paved roads and the remaining twelve miles of dirt roads are mostly Class I or II, with only a very little Class III. The road is usually kept open in the summer, but during the winter months, the United States Forest Service locks the gate on the access road.

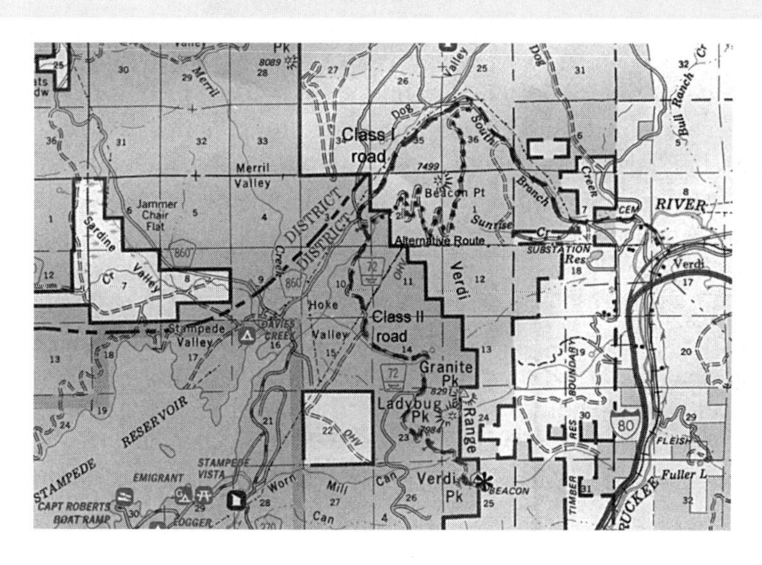

Our starting point for this backroad adventure is Virginia Street (Exit #13) and I-80 near downtown Reno. Go west on I-80 nearly eight miles to Exit #5 at Verdi. Note your odometer reading as you leave the interstate highway.

Stay right on the I-80 Business Route which goes through Verdi. Today Verdi is a bedroom suburb of Reno, but it was not always that way. When the Central Pacific Railroad's tracks reached this point in 1868, the place was named O'Neil's Crossing after a man who had built a bridge here eight years earlier. As early as 1864, the abundance of ponderosa pine on the nearby slopes had encouraged the construction of a sawmill nearby. The rowdy lumber camp that sprang up around the sawmill was called Crystal Peak. Central Pacific Railroad officials built a siding to service the sawmill and renamed the place Verdi after Giuseppe Verdi, the famous Italian opera composer. A station was also constructed, and until the CPRR rails were extended to Reno, the stagecoach from Virginia City came to Verdi so that its passengers could connect with the railroad. In driving through town, you may notice the post office on the left. It, too, has a long history. By November of 1869 so many people had left Crystal Peak to move to nearby Verdi that even the post office moved with them. The Verdi postal facility closed briefly in October of 1873, but reopened three months later and has served the residents ever since.

At a point 2.5 miles from Exit #5, turn right onto Bridge Street. The turnoff is well signed. Bridge Street takes you past the fire station on the left and the elementary school on the right. Shortly after crossing a couple of one-lane bridges, turn right onto Dog Valley Road. This is slightly more than three miles from Exit #5. The road enters California, the pavement ends, and Humboldt-Toiyabe National Forest is entered. The Dog Valley Road is also known as Forest Road 002.

The blackened forest along the roadsides occurred during the Crystal Fire, which started on August 6, 1994. Firefighting agencies typically give forest fires names of geographic features near the point of origin. In this case the fire got its name from the site of Crystal Peak, a rowdy lumber camp of the 1860s just a half mile northwest of Verdi. On that tinder dry August day, this fire quickly moved uphill, and eventually burned 7,310 acres. As forest fires go, the Crystal Fire was a relatively small one. Nevertheless it cost $5 million dollars to extinguish, plus another half million in post-fire erosion control expenses. Even all these years after the fire, the devastating effects of the forest fire are readily apparent. Everyone using the forest needs to be super careful with fire.

Our road of graded dirt is wide and well maintained as it climbs 1,100 feet up the south fork of Dog Creek. As you ascend this gulch today in the air-conditioned comfort of your SUV, think of the early emigrants who struggled to move their wagons up this grade. The hardships they had faced during the last weeks were nothing compared to what still lay ahead of them.

The devastating effects of the 1994 Crystal Fire
will be seen for many years to come.

The top of the ridge is reached at a point 6.5 miles from Exit #5 and, here, the road forks. Forest Road 002 goes right to Dog Valley, a customary resting point on the old Emigrant Trail. Go left on Forest Road 027, also known as the Henness Pass Road. It heads south towards Stampede Reservoir, and eventually comes out at Boca, just east of Truckee.

Shortly after leaving the intersection, views open to the west where a series of terraces can be seen contouring around the mountainside below Crystal Peak. These scars on the landscape were made necessary for erosion control purposes after another devastating forest fire many years ago.

Go south on Forest Road 027 for 2.5 miles. Here, on a small rise, those traveling west on the Emigrant Trail got their first look at the high peaks of the Sierra Nevada Range and a new understanding of the hardships that still awaited them. Today this point is the administrative boundary between Humboldt-Toiyabe National Forest and Tahoe National Forest, as well as a crossroads and a key intersection. For Verdi Peak, you will want to turn left here, but be careful, for two roads go to the left. The first is Forest Road 074. This Class II road switchbacks up the ridge, circles under Beacon Point, and after five miles, returns to Forest Road 002 near the intersection of Roads 002 and 027. This is not the road you want, although it does offer an alternative route back to Verdi, and it does offer some nice views down into the Reno basin.

For Verdi Peak, take the second road left, a Class I dirt road. There should be a forest service sign indicating the way. After 0.3 miles stay right at the fork.

Soon you will be passing Upper Hoke Meadow on the right. At a point 1.2 miles in from the Henness Pass Road, a forest service sign announces the hillside to the left is part of a Penny Pines Project. In this old burned area, reforestation has taken place, with money for the young seedlings donated by private citizens and various organizations. In this tract, funding was provided by a number of women's clubs, garden clubs, and as memorials to deceased persons.

As it climbs higher, the road becomes more narrow, and occasionally has short sections of Class II, where rocks sticking up in the roadway require high clearance vehicles. Three miles in from the Henness Pass Road, there is an unimproved but nice campsite in the aspens to the right. A tiny trickle of water comes down here, fed by Verdi Spring, just 0.3 miles farther up the road.

A half-mile beyond Verdi Spring, there is a major fork in the road. The right fork descends the mountainside to rejoin the Henness Pass Road; stay left at this road junction. In another half-mile there will be nice views west of Stampede Reservoir down in the valley to the right. Soon Boca Reservoir can be seen to the south. Even farther to the south across the Truckee River Valley, swathes cut through forested slopes mark the site of the Northstar Ski Area.

Five miles in from the Henness Pass road, the last of three gates is encountered. Presumably, if you have gotten this far, all will have been standing open. The bedrock geology now becomes volcanic, and with it, the road becomes steeper and more rough. While technically only Class II, many drivers will feel more comfortable engaging their four-wheel drive for the last mile and a half.

Five and a half miles in from Henness Pass, a windswept ridgetop is reached, where a handful of Sierra junipers have gained a foothold and have thrived in conditions too spartan for other species of trees. Just beyond, a short spur road to the left dead-ends after only 0.4 miles.

Finally 6.0 miles in from the Henness Pass Road, the road ends at the small parking area at the base of Verdi Peak. An easy walk of five minutes and an ascent of 43 stairs take you to the Verdi Peak Lookout. From here there is a grand view of the surrounding countryside. To the northeast, the communications antennae on top of the twin summits of Peavine Peak clearly stand out (see Excursion #1). To the east is the Reno-Sparks urban area. Looking downwards to the south, I-80 can be seen in the Truckee River Canyon. In the valley to the west is Stampede Reservoir, one of three important reservoirs in the upper Truckee River basin.

In this age of government downsizing, many fire lookout towers have been closed as a cost cutting measure. Those that do remain open are likely to be staffed with a volunteer spotter. It takes a special person to spend their daylight hours vigilantly scanning the forest for those first telltale wisps of smoke. But the job is not as lonely as it might seem. There is a steady stream of radio traffic on the forest service radio net, and, if encouraged, local denizens of the forest often come by for a handout. In readily accessible lookouts like Verdi Peak, human visitors also come up for the view.

The Verdi Peak Lookout is one of those that budget cuts have closed. One must wonder, however, if this move might have been penny wise, but pounds foolish. Had an observer been stationed on Verdi Peak at 12:04 p.m. on the afternoon of June 17, 2001, the very beginnings of the Martis Fire would have been seen and reported early. Prompt suppression might have spared 14,500 acres of forest from being burned. As it was, the fire spread rapidly and was not contained until two weeks later, and at a cost to the taxpayers of more than 15 million dollars! In the case of the Martis Fire, the public was lucky, because although the Martis Fire threatened houses at the edge of Reno and Incline Village, firefighters lost only one mobile home.

In the unlikely event that you visit Verdi Peak when the lookout is actually open and staffed, ask the lookout to show you how they spot smokes and triangulate the location on the map. Ask too, why the four-legged stool has heavy glass insulators on its feet.

Once you return home, if you have access to the Internet and you are interested in keeping track of forest fires, punch in http://www.nifc/information.html and you will get the Current Wildland Fire Information page, updated daily by the National Interagency Fire Center in Boise, Idaho. The web page summarizes current fires by geographic area, often contains photos, and even includes a glossary of wildland fire terms.

3

The Hunter Lake Corridor

Primary Attraction:	A moderately challenging road crosses the Carson Range with fine views of the Reno Basin, coupled with nice backcountry scenery.
Time Required:	You had better plan on taking the entire day for this excursion. Hunter Lake also offers some primitive, but otherwise very nice, campsites for those wanting a weekend outing.
Miles Involved:	The total loop from Exit #10 on I-80 past Hunter Lake and back to Exit #10 is about 23 miles. Of this eleven miles are on rough Class II dirt roads, and nine miles are rough Class III roads.
Degree of Difficulty:	From the city limits of Reno to Big Meadow the steep grades, coupled with rocks, roots, and ruts in the road, make this route Class II at best, but with many miles of Class III where low range gears are advisable. This excursion involves many miles of rough, rocky roads, unsuitable for the "city tires" which most SUVs come with.
Remarks:	The roads described cross private property at the beginning and end of this excursion. At the time this trail was last scouted in 2001, there were no locked gates and no *Keep Out* signs posted, thus suggesting implied consent to use the access road. However, this situation could change overnight. The reader is urged to respect the owner's property rights should conditions change.

When Congress established the 28,000-acre *Mount Rose Wilderness Area*, a narrow corridor along an existing jeep trail was intentionally left out of the *Wilderness* classification in order to get the bill passed. While environmentalists did not like the wilderness area being bisected into two portions, off-roaders rejoiced that they could still drive into Hunter Lake. This excursion takes the reader through that narrow corridor in the wilderness and across the ridge into the Truckee River Canyon.

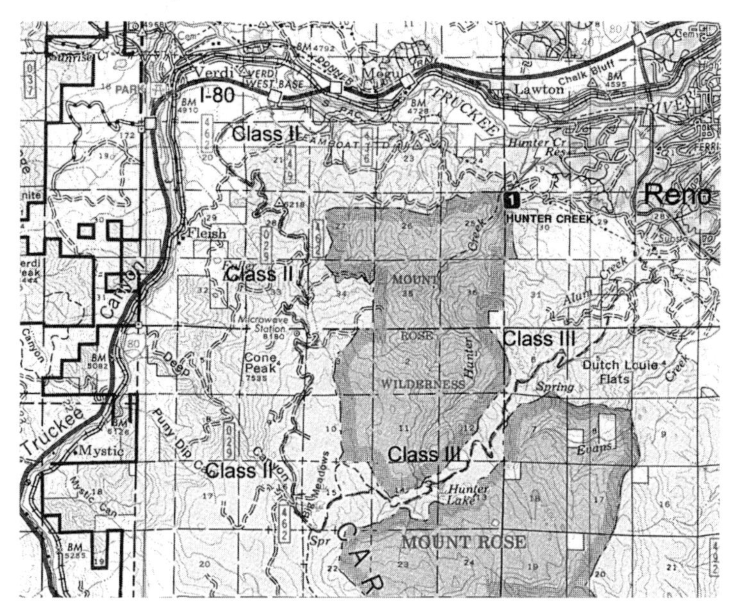

Reno residents can approach the trailhead from any number of directions, but for our purposes we will start on I-80 at Exit #10 on McCarran Blvd., just west of downtown Reno. Proceed south on McCarran Blvd. 3.4 miles to the Caughlin Parkway. You will first encounter Caughlin and McCarran at a point 1.7 miles south of I-80, but do not turn here. Continue on yet another 1.7 miles to the second intersection of these two major streets. Turn right onto Caughlin Parkway and note your odometer reading as you do so. All distances along the way are measured from McCarran Blvd.

You are now entering the Caughlin Ranch Subdivision. Pass a shopping center on the left and, at the end of it, turn left onto Village Green Parkway. Turn left again at a point one half mile from McCarran, this time onto Pinehaven. Just up the block a sign reads:

Hunter Lake Access Road
Road Crosses Private Property
Permission To Pass Is Revocable At Any Time

Here an access road of graded dirt leads a quarter of a mile to an electrical substation. Before reaching the gate, however, just 0.2 miles off the pavement, turn left onto the Class II road, heading west up into the mountains. This is the start of the road through the Hunter Lake Corridor.

It should be noted that this road has many local variations along the way, several possible routes that diverge, and soon come together again. The first of these choices comes at a point 1.1 miles from McCarran. Here a steep side road right climbs up to the ridgetop. Try it if you feel adventuresome, but my recommendation would be to continue straight ahead in a southerly direction. You may wish to engage your four-wheel drive here. It will provide the extra traction and pulling power for the steep grades ahead.

The road forks at the 1.2 mile-point from McCarran; go to the right. The road, now Class III, climbs steeply up the forested ridge of ponderosa pine. It is a rutted and rocky 1.4 miles across rough volcanic rocks to the next intersection. Here roads seem to go everywhere. This time stay to the left. When your odometer indicates you are 2.8 miles from McCarran, stop for a moment and look at Reno spread out below. There are not many places where you can be so near the bright lights of the city, yet be deep in the forest.

That forest is soon left behind as the road steeply climbs up onto a dry ridgetop covered with desert mahogany. From this lofty vantage point, more fine views can be had of the Reno basin. The road now re-enters the forest, and the first of several nice campsites is passed on the left 4.5 miles from McCarran. There are more such campsites just ahead in the aspen groves that line a little stream.

If you have not yet dropped your transmission down into low range, you may wish to do so at this time. While the road remains only Class III, the road now switchbacks up a south-facing ridge where the road is rocky, rutted, and steep. Simply drop down into "Granny" and take it slow and easy.

At a point 5.7 miles from McCarran Blvd., the road forks again; stay to the right. A sage-covered meadow area is crossed, but the road generally continues ever upward. Somewhere about eight miles above McCarran Blvd., the bedrock geology changes from relatively younger volcanic rocks to very old metamorphic rocks, which make up the ancestral core of the Sierra Nevada Range. Here one can clearly distinguish layers of banded slate. The volcanic rocks may only be ten million years old, while the metamorphic rocks may be well over 150 million years old.

Finally, 8.8 miles from McCarran Blvd. at an elevation of 8,200 feet, a series of unimproved campsites to the left announce that Hunter Lake is in the meadow just south of the trees. Perhaps "lake" is a misnomer; Hunters Pond might be a more accurate description. Nevertheless, the small body of water is home to the wily trout, although their size matches the size of the body of water. Hunter Lake gets its name from nearby Hunter Creek, which flows into the Truckee River near the site of Hunter's Crossing. There, one John M. Hunter operated a toll bridge over the Truckee River in the late 1860s.

Looking south from Hunter Lake are 10,243' Sunflower Mountain (slightly to the right) and 9,038' Alpine Walk Peak (slightly to the left). Both are within the Mt. Rose Wilderness. Indeed, the wilderness boundary is within a half mile on either side of the road here.

An angler tries his luck at Hunter Lake.

One might hope that the road improves beyond Hunter Lake. It does not; it remains Class III for nearly five more miles. Beyond Hunter Lake the road crosses the tiny stream draining Hunter Lake, and enters a forest almost entirely of lodgepole pine. Soon the upper waters of Hunter Creek are crossed. Nearby, the roadside is littered with the remains of vehicles that made it in here, but never took their operators out.

At a point 11.2 miles from McCarran Blvd., a low divide is crossed, marking the crest of the Carson Range. The elevation here is 8,700 feet. Just a quarter of a mile on the other side one begins to get glimpses of Big Meadow. Ironically, early in the summer, Big Meadow has a body of water standing in it that is larger than Hunter Lake, yet Hunter is a "lake" and the lake at Big Meadow is not!

Big Meadow

Our road skirts around the east and south sides of Big Meadow, passing the remnants of an old log dam which once spanned the meadow at its narrowest point. At the 12.5 mile-point, a side road left (spur road 392G) contours around the hillside a mile and a half to reach Davis Meadow, in the headwaters of Bronco Creek. Should you elect to visit Davis Meadow, you will come face to face with the devastation left in the wake of the 14,500 acre Martis Fire that burned through here in June of 2001. This fire started west of Floriston just after noon on June 17, 2001. Strong winds caused the fire to jump across I-80, and start up the steep slopes east of the Interstate Highway. Within days the fire had moved several miles west, skirting Davis Meadow, and into the Mt. Rose Wilderness.

A quarter of a mile beyond the road to Davis Meadow, nearly thirteen miles from McCarran Blvd., we come to the intersection of our jeep trail and Forest Road 462. By turning left one can rejoin I-80 just over the state line at Floriston. To return to Reno, turn right. From here it is eleven miles of rough, but mostly downhill, Class II road to Boomtown, at Exit #4 on I-80. It is but another five miles by freeway back to the starting point at McCarran Blvd., Exit #10.

Chapter II
Trails Out of Truckee
(Lake Tahoe Basin Management Unit)

Truckee was born of necessity, the railroad's necessity. It was the Central Pacific Railroad that pushed its tracks eastward out of Sacramento in January of 1863, in a great race with the Union Pacific to complete the first transcontinental railroad. (The two lines eventually met at Promontory Point, Utah on May 11,1869.) By April 3, 1868, the CP tracks had crossed Donner Pass and descended 2,400 feet to a flat meadow area, where the Gray and Coburn families had been living in log cabins for the past several years. The railroad needed a point where engines could be doubled up for the steep grades crossing Donner Summit and where train crews could be exchanged. By 1870 Truckee had become the largest town on the railroad between Sacramento and Ogden, Utah. One of the first commercial structures built was the American Hotel, which opened its door a few months later. With the nearest county sheriff many miles away to the west, Truckee soon gained the reputation of being a lawless timber and railroad town. By 1871 the problem was so bad that a *Vigilance Committee* was formed to deal with undesirable persons of ill repute. 1871 was also the year in which Mrs. Derr set fire to her husband's favorite saloon. Unfortunately the resulting conflagration was not limited to the saloon, and 67 other buildings in town burned as well.

Truckee had things going for it other than the railroad, not the least of which was lumber from the surrounding slopes. The Comstock mines had an insatiable appetite for timber, and Truckee's several sawmills were in operation to fill this need. Ice also proved to be a very profitable export. Ponds were created where ice would form, to be later cut into blocks and shipped to markets in Sacramento and San Francisco, and as far away as New York City. In 1876 a large and very successful brewery operated in nearby Boca until it accidentally burned in 1893. The winter of 1893-94 also gave birth to an artificially created 60-foot icicle, the brainchild of one local resident, Charles McGlashan. Train travelers were so delighted with it that within two years Truckee had developed an "Ice Palace" and "Winter Carnival" to attract tourists. This soon expanded into other related winter sports such as skiing, tobogganing and dogsled racing, all made easily accessible by rail.

With a population of about 3,000 people, present day Truckee no longer depends on the railroad. Indeed, one eastbound and one westbound Amtrak train stops here daily, but only for a few minutes. Today there are two Truckees. There is the charming old historic Truckee, which stretches for several blocks across the street from the old railroad depot built in 1896. A ten-minute walk along Commercial Row will take you past dozens of structures more than a century old. Merchants have made a special effort to restore these buildings and retain the Old West atmosphere. While strolling along Commercial Row, pay particular attention to The Capitol Building built in 1870, and the I.O.O.F. Hall built in 1871. At the corner of Spring and Jibboom Streets is the old jail, used from 1875 to 1964.

There is also the modern Truckee at the western edge of town. Its service stations and national chain fast food outlets cater to the travelers along busy I-80. This is the Truckee where local residents shop for their daily needs. In the winter, many skiers find Truckee's room rates more appealing than those a few minutes away in the Lake Tahoe Basin. More than just a few of Truckee's residents commute daily to jobs in Tahoe City and Incline Village.

Tahoe National Forest has a ranger station in Truckee, where current road information can be obtained. It is at the eastern edge of town where State Route 89 crosses I-80. There are a number of campgrounds nearby, including the forest service's 74-unit Granite Flat Campground.

Many of the buildings along Truckee's Commercial Row
date back to the 1870s and 1880s.

4

Mount Watson

Special Features: At the south end of Lake Tahoe, Mount Watson can be easily ascended by a high clearance vehicle. From the road's end it is an easy scramble on foot to the summit block, where there are outstanding views of the Lake Tahoe Basin.

Time Required: This backroad excursion can be done in a few hours out of Truckee, or it can be combined with the following excursion to Martis Peak for a full day of backroad fun in the forest.

Miles Involved: From Commercial Row in downtown Truckee, it is only nine miles up State Route 267 to the turnoff at Brockway Summit. From there it is another eight and a half miles to the summit.

Degree of Difficulty: Only the last two miles are unpaved dirt and they are an easy Class II and III.

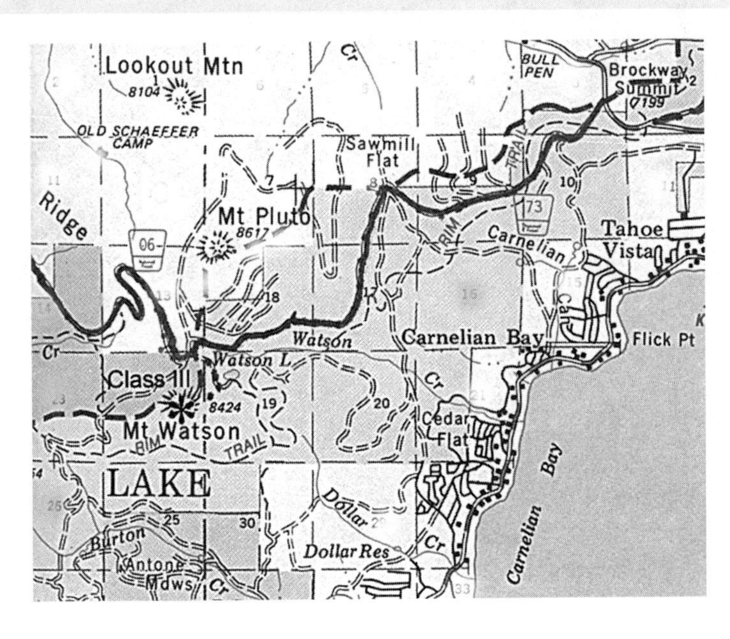

From Truckee, take State Route 267 southbound in the direction of Kings Beach. At a point nine miles out of downtown Truckee, you will reach Brockway Summit at an elevation of 7,179 feet. The turnoff to Mount Watson is on the right, just a few hundred feet on the other side of this low pass. A sign announces it is the Mount Watson Road, Forest Highway 73. Turn right and note your odometer reading as you leave State Route 267.

The paved road gently climbs through a mixed forest of fir and pine, with occasional glimpses of Lake Tahoe being offered through the trees. A post announces each mile that is passed. At a point 5.8 miles from State Route 267, a side road left, 16N50, goes 0.7 miles to Watson Lake. At one time this pretty little lake was accessible only by a jeep trail, but in the summer of 2001, the U.S. Forest Service paved the access road.

Seven miles in from State Route 267, Forest Road 16N73E goes off to the left. This is the road to Mount Watson and we leave the pavement here. As you leave the highway, notice that the rocks are the typical Sierra Nevada granite; that will soon change.

Follow this dirt road through the forest of predominately red fir. The road heads south at first, but soon turns to the east. Although the road starts at Class II, it soon becomes an easy Class III, where water bars cut diagonally across the roadway to divert runoff make this road unsuitable for passenger cars or motorhomes. The road forks at a point 1.3 miles from the pavement. The left fork soon comes to a dead-end at a campsite on the ridgetop overlooking Lake Tahoe. The right fork immediately ascends a steep Class IV pitch, and it too comes to a sudden end. Short wheelbase bobtail rigs should have no trouble making it to the end of the road. Drivers of other vehicles may wish to park at the fork and walk the last 300 yards.

Where the road ends, there is a waterless, but otherwise nice campsite on the ridgetop overlooking Lake Tahoe. As nice as the view might be from here, this is not the summit of Mount Watson. Leave your vehicle and scramble up the rocky high point a few hundred yards to the west. The view from this rocky spire of volcanic andesite is grand, but the elevation is only 8,408 feet. The true summit of Mount Watson is sixteen feet higher and a quarter mile further west along the ridge. It is an easy, but trailless hike that takes only a few minutes.

From either summit block, there are fine views south of Lake Tahoe and the surrounding countryside. To the west, the Alpine Meadows ski area can also be seen. A trek to Mt. Watson is certainly worthy of the small effort.

Incidently, for those who wonder how places are named, Mount Watson seems to have gotten its name from one Robert Montgomery Watson who moved to the Lake Tahoe area in 1875. Later he purchased and operated the Tahoe House, one of the North Shore's finest hostelries.

Lake Tahoe from the summit of Mount Watson

5

Martis Peak

Primary Attraction:	A fire lookout tower overlooking the Lake Tahoe Basin and north into the Truckee River Canyon.
Time Required:	From Truckee allow two or three hours for this outing.
Miles Involved:	From downtown Truckee it is only nine miles up State Route 267 to the turnoff on the south side of Brockway Summit. From there it is another six miles to the Martis Peak fire lookout.
Degree of Difficulty:	The dirt road portion of the route is mostly Class II or better, but there is one mile of Class III.
Remarks:	The countless timber sales in the Martis Peak area over the years have resulted in a labyrinth of roads. For getting around, the 1973 upgrade of the 1969 revision of the 1955 Martis Peak 7.5 minute topographic sheet is recommended over any of the various U.S. Forest Service maps.

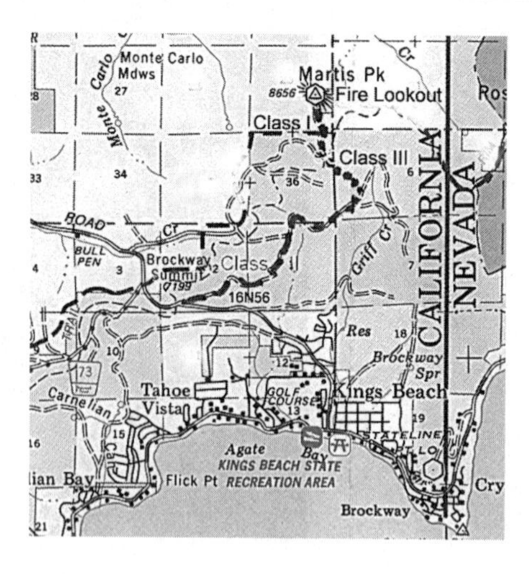

From Truckee, take State Route 267 southbound in the direction of Kings Beach. At a point 8½ miles out of Truckee, note your odometer as you cross Brockway Summit. Our route is just a half-mile on the other side of this low pass.

There may be some confusion over the Forest Service Road numbering designation. On the 1997 Forest Service Lake Tahoe Management Unit map, the road is identified as 16N34. That designation is incorrect. The sign actually posted on the road is 16N56 and that is correct. A second sign reads *Road Not Suitable for Passenger Cars*.

Our route to Martis Peak begins here, on State Route 267 on the south side of Brockway Summit.

Whatever the correct designation, our backroad adventure begins here. This portion of the Tahoe National Forest has been, and still is being, heavily logged for its timber, and there is a confusing myriad of dirt roads and logging spurs going everywhere. But if you reset your trip odometer to zero, or otherwise note your mileage, when you leave Highway 267, and follow these directions carefully, you should be able to find Martis Lookout.

The beginning of this dirt road is also a trailhead for access to the Tahoe Rim Trail, a popular 150-mile long hiking and equestrian trail that circles all around Lake Tahoe. The trail was funded by public contributions and built with volunteer labor. The final three miles of the system were completed in September of 2001.

Upon leaving State Route 267, the forest service road heads eastward through the forest which has thickets of manzanita and chinquapin. In some places the brushy under-story is impinging on the roadway. The forests of the Lake Tahoe Basin were not always like this. The original forests were a mixture of sugar pine, Jeffrey pine, yellow pine and white fir. The insatiable appetite of the Comstock mines in the 1870s and 80s brought in the loggers, who cut everything in sight, with no thought of reforestation. What grew back was a mixture of brush and densely packed fir seedlings. The various pine species had little chance to re-propagate. To make matters worse, the new forest was less resistant to drought, and various species of bark beetles were able to flourish in the weakened trees. The result is an unusually high ratio of dead or dying trees in the Lake Tahoe Basin.

You will soon notice the dusty condition of the roadway. Much of the bedrock surrounding Lake Tahoe is the typical light colored granite found throughout the Sierra Nevada Range. But here the bedrock is a much younger volcanic series, and it is typical of these volcanic rocks to disintegrate to very fine soils that produce flour-like dust. If your car did not need a wash before leaving the highway, it soon will.

The road forks a mile in from the highway. Forest Road 6N76A goes off to the right; swing to the left and continue on. In another mile a road comes in from behind you on the left; continue straight ahead. A mile beyond this second intersection, a third intersection is reached. A Class III road goes downhill to the right. Keep left, going straight ahead. A string of aspen trees line a seasonal watercourse off to the right. They are very picturesque from late September into mid-October. At a point 3.4 miles in from the highway, the road forks again. For Martis Peak, engage your four-wheel drive and double back to the left fork. Until recently, the right fork continued on to a jeep trail leading to a highpoint overlooking Lake Tahoe. In the summer of 2001, the Forest Service blocked the road a quarter of a mile ahead, obliterating access to the jeep trail. To see the fall colors, take the right fork a quarter of a mile to the road closure, before making a left turn at this intersection.

The road now Class III, becomes steep, rocky, and as always, very dusty. Stay on the main road, ignoring the logging spurs going off to the left and right. After 0.7 go to the left, and go left again 0.3 miles beyond. The road now improves to Class II, and remains that way for another 9.4 miles. Then suddenly, a paved road is reached.

This was once a perfectly good Class II road coming in from the north side of Brockway Summit. Having some Lake Tahoe restoration funds to spend, in the summer of 2000 the U.S. Forest Service put a layer of gravel on this road, followed in 2001 by asphalt. The road is now paved over all of its four miles from State route 267 to the Martis Peak Fire Lookout.

In spite of the fact that a high standard road now goes to Martis Peak, the lookout tower is still a worthwhile destination. Turn right and proceed on. In 0.2 miles you will find a very sturdy gate. When the lookout is staffed, the gate is open. Otherwise the gate is closed and locked. During the 2001 Fire Season, the lookout was staffed only three days a week, and even that partial coverage did not begin until mid-August (two months after the nearby Martis Fire had already burned 14,500 acres). So the chances of finding the gate closed are quite good. If this is the case, simply park and walk up the road. The lookout is only 0.4 miles ahead.

The lookout structure is built on an 8,656' rock outcrop on an otherwise forested ridge. It is not actually on 8742' Martis Peak, which is a tenth of a mile to the southeast. Martis Peak Fire Lookout is of the style built in the 1940s, and it is one of three such lookouts in the immediate Lake Tahoe area. This particular lookout is operated by the California Department of Forestry and Fire Protection and is staffed by volunteer spotters. Two other lookouts in the Lake Tahoe Basin, Stateline and Angora Peak, are under control of the U.S. Forest Service. They have been closed by budget cuts, although they may have temporary observers during thunderstorms.

The first two fire lookouts in California were built in 1908, not too long after our system of U.S. National Forests was established. During the 1930s the Civilian Conservation Corps (CCC) built, and rebuilt, over two hundred of these facilities in the mountains of California. Eventually six hundred of these sites were established. Times have changed and, with budgetary limitations, most fire lookouts have closed. By 1986 only 185 were still in active use, and even that number was greatly reduced in the 1990s. Of those lookouts that are still open today, many are staffed by civilian volunteers. Indeed, the author's wife has served as such a lookout in the Sierra National Forest.

Within the Tahoe National Forest, the lookouts on Babbitt Peak, Duncan Peak, Saddleback Peak, Mosquito Ridge, Calpine Mountain, Grouse Ridge, and Verdi Peak are also closed. Other fire lookouts, including the one here on Martis Peak, are staffed only under extreme fire conditions.

Martis Peak Lookout is one of those operated by the California Division of Forestry and Fire Protection. If it is open, visitors are welcome to come inside and visit with the observer on duty. He or she will gladly explain how forest fires are spotted, and then located with the use of an *Osborne Firefinder*. Be sure to sign the lookout's guest book. Outside are a rest room and a picnic table beneath one of three old Sierra Juniper trees on the south side of the lookout. As you might expect, the lookout has a nice view. To the south is the Lake Tahoe Basin and to the north is the upper Truckee River drainage. The Martis Peak Lookout has also become a popular destination for snowmobilers during the winter. The view is just as grand when the land is blanketed by snow.

Martis Peak Lookout

In his book *The Saga of Lake Tahoe, Volume II,* author Edward Scott tells of "Moocher", a domesticated chipmunk that had grown so accustomed to human visitors at the lookout that he would search shirt pockets and lunch boxes for tasty morsels of food. Moocher's descendants still occupy the rocks around the lookout, and they too have become quite bold in their quest for tasty tidbits to munch on.

If you are observant, you will notice more than one kind of little critter scampering around the rocks. The smaller animal, with stripes running on top of its back to the tip of its nose, is a chipmunk (genus *Eutamias)*. There are actually eight different species of chipmunk in the Sierra Nevada, although normally no more than two cohabit the same area.

The larger, and often more bold animal is the ground squirrel (genus *Citellus)*. There are three species of ground squirrel in the Sierra Nevada: the California Ground Squirrel *C. beecheyi,* the Belding Ground Squirrel *C. beldingi*, and here on Martis Peak, the Golden-mantled Ground Squirrel *C. lateralis*. Its stripes are on its flank and they do not extend to the head. This little guy is a whirling dervish of perpetual motion, darting from one rock to another. It thinks nothing of scampering inside the lookout to raid the pantry.

The Golden-mantled Ground Squirrel *Citellus lateralis*

Mono chipmunk *Eutamias nus*

Beyond the lookout, a short Class III extension of the road goes up to the rock outcrop that is actually the top of Martis Peak. A two-minute scramble on foot will take you to the summit. The view from the fire lookout is actually better than the summit of the peak, because trees surround the latter. The name "Martis" seems to come from an early rancher who occupied the valley just to the north. The name has also been given by archaeologists to an early Paleo-Indian culture, which occupied the western end of the Great Basin between 500 and 4,000 years ago.

To return to Highway 267 simply follow the paved road back. It joins the highway a half-mile north of Brockway Summit.

A Word About Tires

The high road clearance, the added traction of four-wheel drive, and the carrying capacity of most SUVs make them a good general-purpose backcountry vehicle. SUVs are a reasonable compromise between the comfort and luxury of a conventional automobile and the spartan raw power of a farm tractor.

Unfortunately the stock tires your SUV came with do not share that compromise. They are probably "city tires" designed for ease of ride and comfort. They will probably be grossly inadequate to stand up to the rigors of rough roads. If you do much backcountry exploring, your first priority should be making sure that your vehicle has proper footwear.

It is not the size of the tire, or the tread design that should be your major concern, but rather the ability of the tire's tread surface, and sidewalls, to stand up to rocks and other road hazards. In 45 years of four-wheeling in this country and abroad, I quickly learned that a 4-ply passenger car tire is going to let you down, and at the worst possible moment. What is needed is a 6, 8, or even 10-ply truck tire. Shop carefully and talk to other four-wheelers before making your selection.

Chapter III
Trails Out of South Lake Tahoe
(Lake Tahoe Basin Management Unit and Humboldt Toiyabe National Forest)

Lake Tahoe is surrounded by small communities whose populations may triple and quadruple on busy weekends. Originally these small villages were temporary homes to loggers, who would move on after they cut the most easily accessible timber. But as word of Lake Tahoe's beauty got out, tourism replaced timber production as the economic basis for the communities around the lake. Since World War II, the scenic attractions of Lake Tahoe have been augmented by the development of several ski areas and, of course, the presence of resort casinos on the Nevada side of the lake.

Until 1973 the forestland surrounding the lake was being administered by three national forests under two different forest service regions. Problems common to the basin as a whole, such as deteriorating water quality in the lake, were sometimes handled differently from one ranger district to the next. The people and resource management problems became so critical that the U.S. Forest Service took portions of the Tahoe, El Dorado, and Toiyabe National Forests and lumped them into a unique Lake Tahoe Management Unit. Now land management decisions are made on a regional basis. Be sure to stop at the U.S. Forest Service's Taylor Creek Visitor Center, just off Highway 89 west of Camp Richardson, for information on the basin's history and natural history. Of course, information about the basin's backroads can also be obtained.

With a permanent population of about 25,000 people, the City of South Lake Tahoe today has the largest year around concentration of people in the basin. While I admit that I am turned off by the crowds, the endless traffic jams, and the gaudy appearance of the businesses and their signs lining Highway 50, South Lake Tahoe, nevertheless, makes a good base of operations from which to explore hundreds of miles of backroads in the nearby mountains. The community offers a variety of markets, shops, restaurants, service stations, and an endless supply of motels. There are also several campgrounds nearby, primarily west of town.

There are three museums in the Lake Tahoe area worthy of the visitor's attention. There is the Lake Tahoe Museum on Lake Tahoe Boulevard in South Lake Tahoe. There is a collection of three opulent and elegant Turn of the 20th Century houses at the Tallac Historic Site, just west of Camp Richardson. The Baldwin, Pope and Heller estates turned them over to the U.S. Forest Service to protect and display. There is also the Gatekeepers Cabin and Museum in Tahoe

City, operated by the North Tahoe Society. All of these museums are open during the summer months.

All backroad excursions in the Lake Tahoe Basin should start here at the Taylor Creek Visitor Center, where current information on road conditions can be obtained.

After checking in at the Visitor Center, be sure to walk over to the Tallac Historic Site next door to visit some of the old homes of the 19th century wealthy familes.

6

Descending Kings Canyon

Primary Attraction:	This little-used backroad is an alternative route to busy U.S. Highway 50 between Lake Tahoe and Carson City. The road has changed little since it was opened in 1863 as a toll road.
Time Required:	With occasional stops to view the scenery, this route can be done in less than two hours.
Miles Involved:	The distance is twelve miles from Spooner Summit on Highway 50 to Highway 395 in downtown Carson City.
Degree of Difficulty:	While 95% of the route is Class I or II, there are at least two short sections of Class III, where the road is washed out and shrubbery is encroaching upon the roadway.

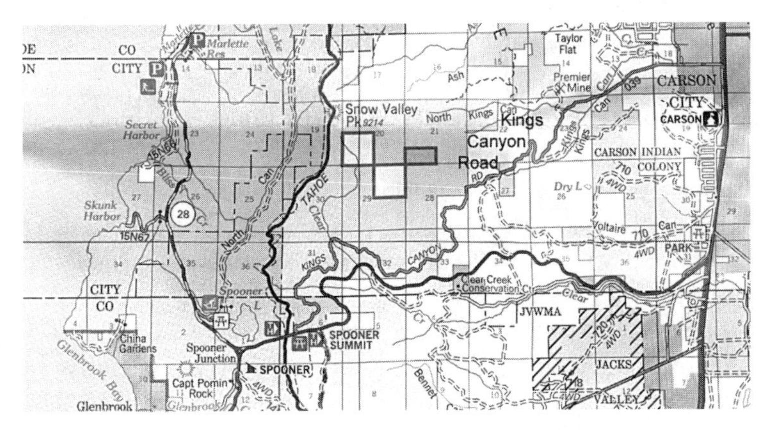

The old "Lake Bigler Toll Road" connecting Lake Tahoe and Carson City was inaugurated on August 6, 1863. Its main customers were the operators of freight wagons hauling timber from Glenbrook on Lake Tahoe to the many mines of Virginia City, but the road saw stagecoach traffic as well. Traffic on the road declined in the 1890s, when Virginia City's mines began to run out of ore and close. Eventually it was no longer economical to maintain a toll taker, and anyone could use the road for nothing, a condition that still exists today.

From South Lake Tahoe, take U.S. Highway 50 eastward into Nevada. Pass through the small communities of Zephyr Cove and Glenbrook, following the highway up to 7,146' Spooner Summit. Just over the summit, the U.S. Forest Service's Spooner Picnic Area can be seen on the right. A tenth of a mile beyond, a dirt road on the left leaves Highway 50. (In recent years there has not been any sign to mark this road.) Turn off the highway here, and note your odometer reading or reset your trip odometer to zero.

A Class I dirt road contours eastward around the mountainside. This south-facing slope supports a forest of Jeffrey pine, with manzanita in the more open areas. But as you curve around the mountain to the north-facing slope, the vegetation makes a subtle change, with fir replacing the pine and chinquapin replacing the manzanita. A mile and a half from Highway 50, a small cluster of aspen trees are passed, and 0.4 miles beyond them are good views eastward into the Carson Valley. Clearly visible across the valley to the east and southeast is the Pine Nut Range. Looking down the range from north to south, you can see 8,343' Rawe Peak, 8,763' Lyon Peak, 8,317' Mineral Peak, and 9,451' Mount Siegel, the high point of the ridge. Just to the south is 9,418' Galena Peak. (See *Western Nevada SUV Trails* for backroad excursions in the Pine Nut Range.)

The road forks at a point two miles from Highway 50; stay left. In a half mile pretty little Clear Creek is crossed. Just beyond, there is a nice campsite off to the right. This is habitat of the Golden-mantled Ground Squirrel, *Citellus lateralis.* This energetic little critter and its cousin, the Allen Chipmunk, *Eutamias townsendi,* are very abundant here. They scamper about, filling the pouches in their cheeks with tasty morsels of seeds, berries, buds, and nuts, and then scurry off to bury them or cache them in their nests, to be eaten later as a mid-hibernation snack. They are very curious creatures, and, if not threatened, can be tempted to come close by pieces of cookies or potato chips.

After about two and a half miles the road passes the site of Swift's Station, a one-time rest stop offering meals and overnight accommodations. Alas however, nothing remains.

At 2.9 miles from the highway, the road is partially washed away by erosion. **The roadway is very narrow. Drive slowly and drive carefully!** In the next quarter of a mile, two more narrow places are encountered in the roadway, this time having mud holes. The route through the first mud hole should be considered Class III. **These short muddy sections should present no real problem, but always check the water depth before attempting to drive through.** By early autumn they may be all dried up.

At 4.3 miles from U.S. Highway 50, the second short Class III section is encountered. Once you are through it, stop for a moment to enjoy the grand views to the east. Soon another badly eroded section of roadway is encountered.

Again, go slowly. If in doubt, send a spotter ahead on foot to guide you through.

At 5.6 miles from Highway 50, there is an abundance of wild currants along the road. There are thirty species of currants and their close cousin, the gooseberry, in California. These bushes produce berries in the late fall. These can be collected and made into homemade jelly, which tastes great and is high in vitamin C. Some Native American tribes dried the berries, and then made a type of pemmican by adding meat and fat and then compressing the mix into loaves or cakes. The resulting product was then easy to carry on hunting trips.

One more narrow place, overgrown with vegetation, is encountered at 5.7 miles, and then the worst is over. At 6.9 miles, a major unmarked side road goes right, down into the valley to rejoin Highway 50. Stay left starting down Kings Canyon. The next couple of miles are all Class I.

The old "Lake Bigler Toll Road" today.

The first houses of Carson City's outskirts are reached at 9.1 miles from Highway 50, and, with them, you are back on the pavement again. This is Kings Canyon Road. To the left a poignant memorial sign reads:

> *In memory of Kenneth Carvin, James Davidson, Jon Ivins, who were fatally injured in a helicopter crash while fighting a fire caused by a careless camper, in Kings Canyon, approximately two miles west of this spot on July 5, 1976.*

Another sign on the right side of the road points out the old Borda Ranch, one of the pioneering cattle ranches out of Carson City. Still another historical marker 1.5 miles beyond, on the left, reminds one of Camp Nye, a military post in the waning days of the Civil War. Unfortunately, civilization has encroached on the site today, so that no trace remains.

Continuing eastward, Kings Canyon Road turns into West King Street in less than a mile, and soon the State Attorney General's office blocks your way to Highway 395. You must jog over one block north to Musser Street, or one block south to Second Street in order to go that last block east to U.S. Highway 395, Carson City's main thoroughfare.

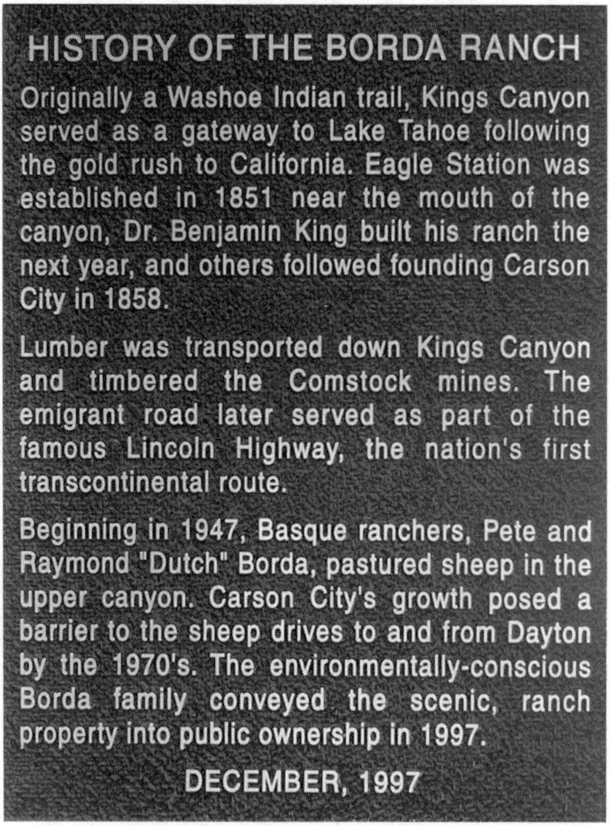

HISTORY OF THE BORDA RANCH

Originally a Washoe Indian trail, Kings Canyon served as a gateway to Lake Tahoe following the gold rush to California. Eagle Station was established in 1851 near the mouth of the canyon, Dr. Benjamin King built his ranch the next year, and others followed founding Carson City in 1858.

Lumber was transported down Kings Canyon and timbered the Comstock mines. The emigrant road later served as part of the famous Lincoln Highway, the nation's first transcontinental route.

Beginning in 1947, Basque ranchers, Pete and Raymond "Dutch" Borda, pastured sheep in the upper canyon. Carson City's growth posed a barrier to the sheep drives to and from Dayton by the 1970's. The environmentally-conscious Borda family conveyed the scenic, ranch property into public ownership in 1997.

DECEMBER, 1997

7

Genoa Peak

Primary Attraction:	A pleasant High Sierra country drive with nice views overlooking the Carson Valley.
Time Required:	Budget at least a half day for this outing.
Miles Involved:	From US Highway 50 near Spooner Summit to the Kingsbury Grade, it is a little more than twelve miles, including a one-mile side-trip to Genoa Peak.
Degree of Difficulty:	While the road is often rough and rocky, it is generally no worse than Class III.

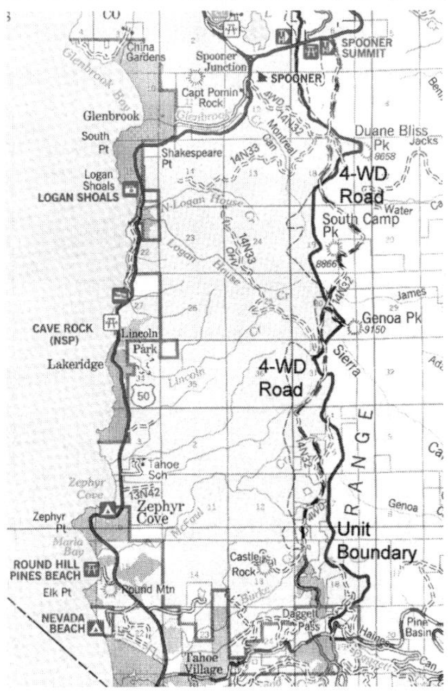

This backcountry route connects U.S. Highway 50 near Spooner Summit with Nevada Route 207, the Kingsbury Grade road connecting Minden with Zephyr Cove. The trail can be taken from south to north, or visa versa. Because the southern end starts in a housing track, where streets suddenly change names causing some confusion, we will follow the road in a north to south direction.

From South Lake Tahoe, take U.S. Highway 50 eastward, crossing into Nevada at Stateline. Continue north along the lake's eastern shore for twelve miles, to a point where State Route 28 goes off to the left. Remain on Highway 50, but note your odometer reading at this intersection.

The trail begins at the Spooner Highway Maintenance Station on Highway 50, just 0.4 miles south of the intersection of Highways 50 and 28. The elevation here is 7,000 feet. Turn east off of Highway 50, setting your trip odometer to zero. Keep to the left just before reaching the facility's main gate. Forest Road 14N32 follows the chain link fence, enters the forest, and soon passes through an area burned in the mid 1990s. The first 3½ miles of this road are Class II.

In just less than a mile from the highway, the road to White Hill takes off to the left. It soon dead-ends; keep right. At a point 1.5 miles from Highway 50, a second fork is reached. The right fork is Forest Road 14N33, a Class III route which goes over to North Logan House Creek, and then eventually rejoins 14N32 south of Genoa Peak. To visit Genoa Peak, however, go left at this intersection, staying on 14N32.

This is a mixed forest of Jeffrey pine and white fir, with an occasional grove of quaking aspen. In the wet areas, often around the aspen groves, midsummer displays of larkspur and columbine are common. In drier areas, Indian paintbrush, Western Mountain Aster, and lupine can be found in abundance. You may also notice the little Golden-mantled Ground Squirrel, *Citellus lateralis,* scampering across the forest floor. This energetic little critter and its cousin, the Allen Chipmunk, *Eutamias townsendi,* are very abundant here. They fill the pouches in their cheeks with tasty morsels of seeds, berries, buds, and nuts, and then scurry off to bury them or cache them in their nests, to be eaten later as a mid-hibernation snack.

At a point 2.5 miles from the highway, one gets glimpses of Lake Tahoe to the west. A few hundred yards more and the Tahoe Rim Trail is crossed. This is a 150-mile long hiking trail that completely encircles Lake Tahoe, which took more than a decade for the volunteers of the Tahoe Rim Trail Association to complete. When the last three miles were completed in September of 2001, the organization justly celebrated their achievement. Most persons wanting to hike the entire trail do it in segments over a period of time. Hardcore backpackers wishing to complete the circuit at one time usually budget ten to fourteen days to do so.

Three miles from the highway we are provided with a glimpse east of the rounded summit of 8,658' Duane Bliss Peak. The peak was named after a prominent banker of the 1870s and one of the principal partners in the Carson and Tahoe Lumber and Fluming Company, which eventually went on to produce all the timbers used in the mines of Virginia City. By the time you pass Bliss Peak, the road, still Class II, has climbed 800 feet since leaving Highway 50.

At a point 3.6 miles in from the pavement, a third fork is reached. We will want to go right. Before doing so, however, take a short walk through the lodgepole pine forest to the left. From the hilltop a quarter of a mile to the east, there are grand views down onto Minden and Gardnerville, some 3,300 feet below. Beyond the valley and off to the southeast is 9,450' Mount Siegel, the highest point in the Pine Nut Range.

Engage your four-wheel drive upon leaving this third intersection, for you will soon need it. Although not particularly difficult, the road ahead is rocky with poor traction. The Class III portion begins here. A couple of switchbacks are encountered, and a ridge is crossed. At a point 5.5 miles from Highway 50, at an elevation of 8,600', a half mile long side road to the left climbs to an electronic site near the summit of 9,160' Genoa Peak. The last tenth of a mile is an easy scramble on foot of 150 vertical feet to the summit. The view in all directions is worth the effort.

The summit of Genoa Peak is festooned with radio antennas.

After soaking in the scenery, and backtracking the half mile to 14N32, we now turn south again. In a quarter of a mile, the previously mentioned Forest Road 14N33 comes in from the right. From here on, logging spurs will go off to the right and the left, but the main road continues south. Two and a half miles beyond, a large flat is encountered amid the red fir and lodgepole pine. Roads seem to go off in every direction. If your four-wheel drive club is looking for an area to camp where there is plenty of space, this is the place. From here it is only 1.3 miles of Class III roads to the pavement at Andria Drive, where civilization begins, and only three miles to State Route 207 just above Zephyr Cove.

Indian Paintbrush Lupine

Larkspur Columbine

Photos by Loris Mitchell

8

The Barker Pass Circuit

Primary Attraction:	An easy to moderate route with nice mountain scenery.
Time Required:	If you rush, this circuit could be done in half a day, but with so many diversions along the way, you should reserve an entire day. This outing can be coupled with the side trip to the summit of Ellis Peak, as described in excursions #9 or #10.
Miles Involved:	From its starting point on Highway 89 and back again, the entire loop is 21 miles.
Degree of Difficulty:	This is a relatively easy Class II and III trail suitable for most bobtail rigs, SUVs, and four-wheel drive pickups.

From South Lake Tahoe, take U.S. Highway 50 west to State Route 89 and go north 23 miles on Highway 89 past Tahoe Pines to the Blackwood Canyon Road, also known as the Barker Pass Road. This is on the west side of Lake Tahoe, roughly half way between Tahoe City and Meeks Bay at the entrance to the U.S. Forest Service's Kaspian Campground. Note your odometer reading as you turn off State Route 89.

The paved road proceeds up Blackwood Canyon through a mixed forest of ponderosa pine, lodgepole pine, white fir, white alder, and aspen. Signs announce that there is a three-day limit on camping in the canyon, and that Blackwood Creek is closed to fishing. After 2.3 miles an improved side road left goes to up to Barker Pass. We will be going there, also, but by a more interesting route.

Proceed straight ahead on Forest Road 38. The pavement ends here, but the next half-mile is rated Class I. There are a number of unimproved campsites along here, where one may camp for a few days with no fee. At a point 2.7 miles west of State Route 89, the Blackwood Middle Fork OHV Trail begins. The North Tahoe Trail Dusters 4WD Club looks after the next three miles. The real four-wheeling does not begin for another half mile. At a point 3.3 miles from Highway 89, a side road right goes up the North Fork of Blackwood Creek and comes to a dead-end. It is the North Fork that is spanned by a culvert a quarter mile further on the Middle Fork Trail.

At a point 4.2 miles in from Highway 89, ford a small stream, and here you should engage your four-wheel drive. The next 0.6 miles are all Class III as you climb up the narrow twisting track. Next the trail levels out on a ridgetop, where there are several acres of mule ears growing on the dry slopes.

A member of the sunflower family, mule ears, *Wyethia mollis*, has yellow flowers.

My wife and I were stopped here on one occasion, trying to identify a yellow composite, when a late model Jeep Grand Cherokee passed containing four middle aged women. They were laughing and seemingly having a great time as they waved to us. We later caught up with them up on Barker Pass, where we learned they had left their husbands watching Sunday afternoon football back at Tahoe City while they went for a drive. None of them had ever been four-wheeling before, and their car had never before been off the pavement. I suspect the Blackwood Trail made at least one convert and that car now has a lot of backcountry miles on it.

The trail begins to climb again, first over metamorphic rocks and, soon thereafter, volcanic rocks. The treeless summit of dome-shaped Barker Peak stands out on the western skyline. Switchbacks take you up the hillside to the south and soon you will be on top of the ash-covered ridge. Barker Pass is reached at a point 5.8 miles in from Highway 89. The graded road you encounter here is the same road that went to the left only 2.3 miles after leaving Highway 89.

Barker Pass is one of the many trailheads for the Pacific Crest Trail, a 2,658-mile hiking trail that runs from the Mexican border to the Canadian border. If you don't have the six months needed for that walk, you might try the easy scramble up 8,166' Barker Peak just to the west. For the next couple of miles, our jeep trail will parallel the route of the Pacific Crest Trail to the south.

Barker Peak

To continue our circuit, leave the trailhead area, again noting your odometer reading. Cross the graded road, and get on a Class II road which starts down the drainage to the south. The road forks after 0.3 miles. The left fork dead ends; stay to the right. A sign announces that this portion of the trail is maintained by the Reno Jeepers.

The Class II road crosses the headwaters of Barker Creek, a tributary of the Rubicon River, (we are actually on the western slope of the Sierra crest here) and makes its way through a forest of white fir and lodgepole pine down the western side of the creek. A meadow is passed to the left, and a mile below Barker Pass the road deteriorates to Class III. Suddenly, 1.8 miles below Barker Pass, a good graded road is encountered. Turn left, crossing the concrete ford. At a point 0.3 miles beyond the creek, a Class III trail on the right leaves the graded road. This route will take you down the creek to join the Rubicon Trail. **Be warned, however; this route has Class IV portions and is suitable only for bobtail rigs with a short wheelbase.**

To more easily join the Rubicon Trail, continue eastward along the Class I graded road. This road was put in as part of a timber sale, the stumps of which are readily apparent. Four miles from Barker Pass, a Class II side road to the right goes the quarter of a mile down to Bear Lake, where there are a number of unimproved campsites.

Slightly more than half a mile beyond the Bear Lake turnoff, the graded road now tops a ridge and encounters a 'T' intersection. To the left is a rough Class IV route up to Ellis Peak (see Excursion #9). This is the first of three roads we will encounter which lead to Ellis Peak. To complete our loop, go right. Ahead are nice views south into the Desolation Wilderness. The area was so named because Plio-Pliestocene glaciers have stripped away all the topsoil, leaving few places where trees can gain a foothold. Our road soon deteriorates to Class II. At a point six miles from Barker Pass, a Class III road comes in from the right. This is the McKinney-Rubicon Trail (see Excursion #11). To return to Highway 89 turn left. The road now is a rough and dusty Class III.

At a point 6.5 miles from Barker Pass the second rough side road to the left climbs to Ellis Peak. Straight ahead is a lake overgrown with pond lilies. The aquatic plants that have taken over the lake are the Indian Pond Lily, *Nymphaea polysepala.* They are thriving here on Miller Creek, and just over the Sierra Crest ahead on McKinney Creek. A half-mile farther is Miller Lake, the only lake in this chain of four that is not covered by these lily pads.

The Sierra Crest is imperceptible here. It occurs somewhere after you pass the second lake, but before reaching the third lake. The elevation here is a mere 7,180 feet. At the third lake, Lily Lake, you are now descending the McKinney Creek drainage, which flows into Lake Tahoe and the Truckee River.

Miller Lake

At a point 2.7 miles from the last road to Ellis Peak, the third route to that mountaintop is encountered. **If you turn to the left, expect a rough Class IV route.** By following the Rubicon Trail straight ahead, the OHV staging area is just 0.3 miles beyond. From here a paved road goes 2.5 miles to State Route 89, and, from there, the Blackwood Canyon Road where you began this excursion is just 3.5 miles to the left.

9

Ellis Peak, The Easy Way

Primary Attraction:	An only slightly challenging route up to one of the mountaintops along the western shore of Lake Tahoe.
Time Required:	If you hurry, this route could be done in half a day out of South Lake Tahoe, but why would anyone want to rush?
Miles Involved:	From State Route 89 to Ellis Peak the distance is seventeen miles.
Degree of Difficulty:	Although this route involves some ten miles of dirt roads, only the last three miles are Class III.

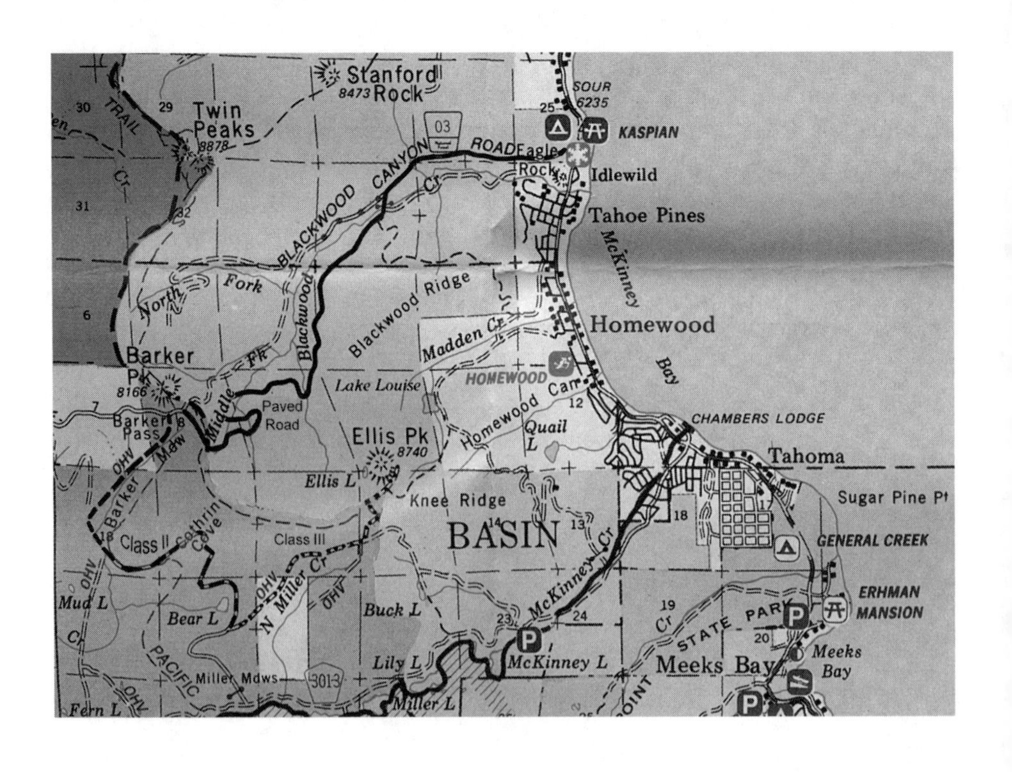

There are half a dozen ways in which vehicles can get to the top of Ellis Peak. I call the three usual routes, "hard, harder, and easiest". This excursion describes the "easiest".

From South Lake Tahoe, take U.S. Highway 50 west to State Route 89. Turn north and drive through Tahoma and Homewood to Tahoe Pines. At a point a little over 23 miles north of the intersection of Highways 50 and 89, look for the U.S. Forest Service's Kaspian Campground on the left. Turn left here onto the Blackwood Canyon Road and note your odometer reading. The paved road passes the campground on the right, and proceeds up Blackwood Canyon through a mixed forest of ponderosa pine, lodgepole pine, white fir, white alder, and aspen. Signs announce that there is a three-day limit on camping in the canyon and that Blackwood Creek is closed to fishing. After 2.3 miles take Forest Road 3, the paved side road to the left. Soon it begins to climb steeply up the mountainside through very old, highly metamorphosed rock. The pavement ends at a point seven miles from Highway 89, but the road, now with a good graded surface, continues on. The Barker Pass trailhead on the Pacific Crest Trail is passed 7.5 miles from Highway 89, but continue heading westward. Finally, at the nine-mile point, leave Forest Road 3 by turning left onto the good graded road that heads south. This Class I road will take a circuitous route, as it winds down the ridge to cross Barker Creek at a point a little over eleven miles from Highway 89. In a little over two miles, Bear Lake can be seen below you to the right. About fifteen miles from Highway 89 look for a Class II road to the left. It is here that the "easiest" route meets the "hard" route.

Turn left, and again note your odometer reading. Our road now deteriorates and gradually gains elevation as it passes through an old timber sale area. You may feel more comfortable with the additional traction provided by engaging your four-wheel drive. A fork in the road is encountered after 0.6 miles; go to the right. After only 0.4 miles another fork is encountered. This time stay to the left. (The right fork is the "hardest" route coming up from Buck Lake.)

A broad ridgetop is reached in a half-mile. The meadow to the left is filled with mule ears, and a variety of wildflowers if you pass this way in June. Beyond the meadow the road climbs more steeply and yet another fork is reached. The left fork soon dead-ends at Ellis Lake at an elevation of about 8,200 feet. For Ellis Peak, go to the right. This branch will climb to an elevation of about 8500 feet, where it too comes to a dead-end. The final ascent of 8,740' Ellis Peak must be on foot, but the distance is less than a half-mile and there is a good hikers' trail. (Stay to the right of the false summit a few hundred yards above you.)

The summit of Ellis Peak.

The view from the top of Ellis Peak is grand. To the northeast the entire north end of Lake Tahoe can be seen. In the opposite direction to the southwest, Loon Lake, the start of the infamous Rubicon Trail, stands out in the distance. Directly to the south, the barren rock surfaces of the heavily glaciated Desolation Wilderness stand out in marked contrast to the thick forest cover elsewhere. And speaking of trees, the fir forest extends nearly up to the top of Ellis Peak. At the windswept summit, however, is the domain of the stunted, but otherwise hardy, whitebark pine.

Whitebark pine, *Pinus albicaulis,* on the summit of Ellis Peak.

Incidentally, Barbara Lekisch, who wrote *Tahoe Place Names,* says that Ellis Peak gets its name from Jock Ellis, who raised cattle and sheep on a ranch between McKinney and Georgetown. This must have been sometime before 1881, because the Wheeler map of that year shows Ellis Peak.

10

Ellis Peak, The Hard Way

Primary Attraction:	A bone jarring, moderately challenging route up to one of the mountain summits along the western shore of Lake Tahoe.
Time Required:	This is a full day's excursion out of South Lake Tahoe.
Miles Involved:	From Highway 50 it is nearly twenty miles via State Route 89 to the McKinney-Rubicon Road, and then another 2½ miles to the OHV staging area where the pavement ends. Next comes eight miles of rough dirt road to the summit.
Degree of Difficulty:	The dirt road portions of this route are a rough Class II and III. At the hands of an experienced four-wheeler, most SUVs should be able to negotiate this route with no body damage. Nevertheless, **the first 3½ miles of this road are not recommended for the novice four-wheeler.**

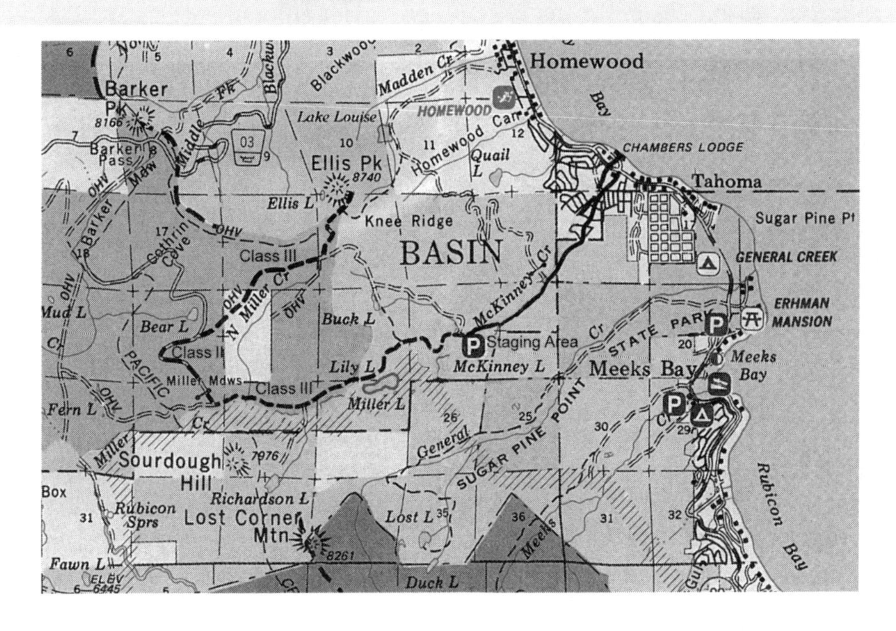

There are many ways to drive up Ellis Peak. I call the three most popular routes, "hard, harder, and easiest". This excursion describes "hard".

From South Lake Tahoe, take U.S. Highway 50 west to State Route 89, turning north to go through Tahoma. The route up Ellis Peak begins off State Route 89, at a point just north of Tahoma. Look for signs to the McKinney-Rubicon Road. This is also Forest Road 14N34. The road enters a housing tract, where signs will guide you through it to the trailhead. At 0.3 miles from Highway 89 turn left onto Bellview, and then at the STOP sign, turn right onto McKinney. After 0.3 miles turn left; soon you will leave the tract behind and you will be on your way.

The pavement ends at a point 2.4 miles from Highway 89. Here is a large OHV staging area where ATVs can sometimes be rented on busy summer weekends. This is the eastern terminus of the infamous Rubicon Trail, which comes over the crest of the Sierra Nevada from Wentworth Springs and Loon Lake. The elevation here at the staging area is 6,665 feet. In the next eight miles to the summit of Ellis Peak you will climb nearly 2,100 feet.

Note your odometer reading, engage your four-wheel drive, and start west up the McKinney-Rubicon Trail. After only 0.3 miles an unmarked road to the right heads northward through the forest towards Knee Ridge, a spur off of Ellis Peak. A sign indicates that the North Tahoe Trailbusters 4WD Club maintains the route. This is the Buck Lake route, the one I call "hardest". If you do not mind some Class IV rock piles to overcome, it is the shortest and steepest way to ascend Ellis Peak.

For our purposes, however, we are going to continue westward on the McKinney-Rubicon Trail. The rough, rocky, and sometimes badly rutted road passes McKinney, Lily, and Miller Lakes. At a point 2.6 miles from the OHV staging area, ignore the road to the right and continue straight ahead. But a mile farther at 3.6 miles from the pavement, there is a second major road intersection, and here we turn right, leaving the McKinney-Rubicon Trail. A sign on the right fork indicates it is nine miles to Barker Pass. Pass through the open gate and the road will suddenly get better. It changes from Class III to Class II.

The road climbs the hillside to the north through a forest of red fir. Once on top of the ridge there are nice views south into the Desolation Wilderness. At a point 1.3 miles above the McKinney-Rubicon Trail (4.8 miles in from the OHV staging area), look for a road to the right. This is where the "easiest" route comes in; now together, they are the way to the summit of Ellis Peak.

Turn left and again note your odometer reading. Our road now deteriorates, passing through an old timber sale area as it gradually gains in elevation. You may feel more comfortable with the additional traction provided by engaging your four-wheel drive. A fork in the road is encountered after 0.6 miles; go to the right. After only 0.4 miles another fork is encountered. This time stay to the left. (The right fork is the "hardest" route coming up from Buck Lake.)

A broad ridgetop is reached in a half-mile. The meadow to the left is filled with mule ears, and a variety of wildflowers if you pass this way in June. Beyond the meadow the road climbs more steeply and yet another fork is reached. The left fork soon dead-ends at Ellis Lake at an elevation of about 8,200 feet. For Ellis Peak, go to the right. This branch will climb to an elevation of about 8500 feet, where it too comes to a dead-end. The final ascent of 8,740' Ellis Peak must be made on foot, but the distance is less than a half-mile and there is a good hikers' trail. (Stay to the right of the false summit a few hundred yards above you.)

As you hike up the last few hundred yards to the summit, look at the rough rocks at your feet. The bedrock to the north of Ellis Peak consists of the very old metamorphic core of the Sierra Nevada Range. These rocks may be 200 million years old. The bedrock to the south of Ellis Peak, in the Desolation Wilderness, is 70-90 million year old granodiorite of Cretaceous Age. Ellis Peak itself, however, is made up of relatively recent volcanic rock, perhaps only ten million years old. At the summit, someone has crafted a bench from these rocks, an excellent place to rest and take in the sights.

I cannot think of a better view of the Lake Tahoe Basin than from 8,740' Ellis Peak. There are higher summits to be sure, but none of them are as close to the lake, and none as intimate as this viewpoint. To the northeast the entire north end of Lake Tahoe can be seen. In the opposite direction to the southwest, Loon Lake, the start of the Rubicon Trail, stands out in the distance. Directly to the south, the barren granite surfaces of the heavily glaciated Desolation Wilderness stand out in marked contrast to the thick forest cover elsewhere. And speaking of trees, the fir forest extends nearly up to the top of Ellis Peak. The windswept summit, however, is the domain of the stunted, but otherwise hardy whitebark pine.

View south into the Desolation Wilderness.

The McKinney-Rubicon Trail

11

The McKinney-Rubicon Trail to the PCT

Primary Attraction:	This excursion is along the relatively easy western end of the infamous Rubicon Jeep Trail. The excursion described below climbs to the indistinguishable crest of the Sierra Nevada Range and a little beyond, where it is crossed by the equally famous Pacific Crest Trail for hikers.
Time Required:	This is an all day outing.
Miles Involved:	The distance from Highway 89 to the PCT is seven miles.
Degree of Difficulty:	The entire 4½ miles of this jeep trail are generally no worse than a rough Class III. At the hands of an experienced four-wheeler, most SUVs should be able to negotiate this route with no body damage. Nevertheless, **this road is not recommended for the novice four-wheeler.**

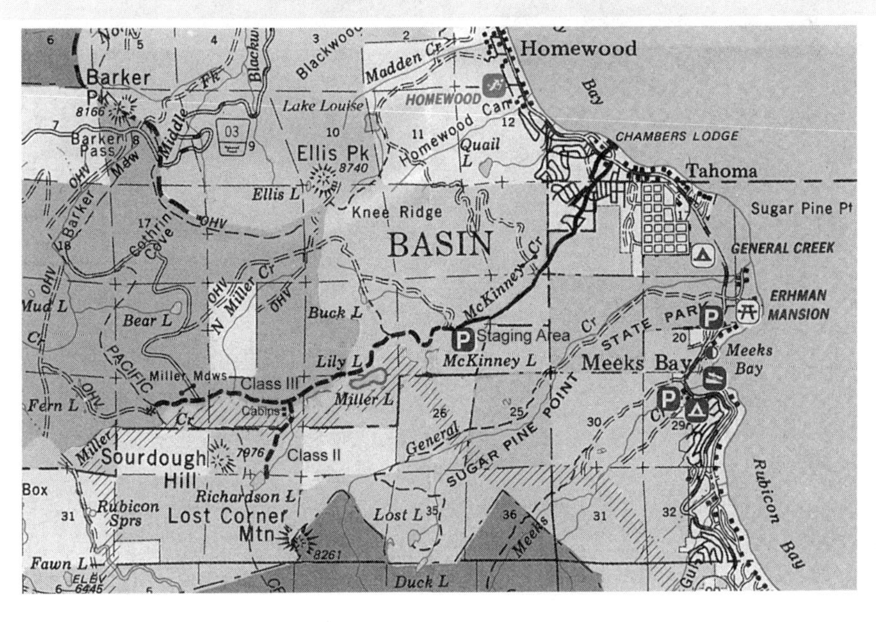

From South Lake Tahoe, take U.S. Highway 50 west to State Route 89, turning north to go through Tahoma. The McKinney-Rubicon Road begins off State Route 89 at a point just north of Tahoma. This is also Forest Road 14N34. The road enters a housing tract, where signs will guide you through it to the trailhead. At 0.3 miles from Highway 89, turn left onto Bellview, and then at the STOP sign, turn right onto McKinney. Turn left after 0.3 miles. Soon you will leave the housing tract behind, and you will be on your way to one of the most challenging four-wheel excursions in the Sierra Nevada.

The pavement ends at a point 2.4 miles from Highway 89. Here is a large OHV staging area where ATVs can sometimes be rented on busy summer weekends. This is the eastern terminus of the infamous Rubicon Trail, which comes over the crest of the Sierra Nevada from Wentworth Springs and Loon Lake. (See *High Sierra SUV Trails, Volume II-The Western Slope* for a description of that complete route.)

As you leave the staging area, note your odometer reading, engage your four-wheel drive, and start west up the Rubicon Trail. After only 0.3 miles, an unmarked road to the right heads northward through the forest towards Ellis Peak. A sign indicates the North Tahoe Trailbusters 4WD Club maintains the route. This Class IV route is one of the more difficult routes to the top of Ellis Peak. To follow the Rubicon Trail continue straight ahead.

Lily Lake

A mile from the staging area, lily pad choked McKinney Lake can be seen below you to the left. This is the first of a series of four lakes to be passed in the next 2½ miles. The second lake in this series is appropriately called Lily Lake. It comes 1.5 miles from the staging area, and it, too, is covered with these so-called lily pads. These hardy aquatic plants, of the genus *Potamogeton,* survive when the lakes freeze over each winter and come back each spring. If you pass this way during the early evening hours, your auditory senses will tell you that there is a substantial frog population in Lily Lake. What you are probably hearing is the Pacific treefrog, *Hyla regilla,* although the Mountain yellow-legged frog, *Rana muscosa*, is present here, too. Unfortunately, the widespread use of pesticides in California's Central Valley, particularly those containing diazinon and chlorpyrifos, seem to be affecting the sensitive frog and toad population way up here in the High Sierra. Some day in the not too distant future, perhaps the mating cry of the treefrog will no longer be heard at Lily Lake.

Miller Lake is just a tenth of a mile beyond Lily Lake. Here the crest of the Sierra Nevada Range is imperceptible. Yet water from Lily Lake feeds McKinney Lake, and then via McKinney Creek feeds Lake Tahoe and the Truckee River, to ultimately end at land-locked Pyramid Lake in Nevada. But Miller Lake, just a few feet away, is the source of Miller Creek, a tributary of the Rubicon River that flows into the Middle Fork of the American River, and ultimately down the delta to San Francisco Bay and the Pacific Ocean. The elevation here at this watershed divide is but 7,150 feet.

The *Potamogeton* has not yet taken over Miller Lake. Anglers have established a number of nice, but unimproved, campsites on its north shore next to the road, but if you stay here, expect a hungry mosquito population early in the summer. Just a few hundred feet beyond Miller Lake, a Class II side road to the left passes several old wooden cabins and climbs southward 0.8 miles to Richardson Lake, lying at the base of 7,976' Sourdough Hill. This lake is also popular with fishing four-wheelers.

Richardson Lake

Continuing westward on the Rubicon Trail past the turnoff to Richardson Lake, the road passes the fourth lake in the broken chain. It has no official name, but some call it Lower Miller Lake. Like McKinney and Lily Lakes, it is choked with *Potamogeton.* At a point 3.1 miles from the staging area, a major fork in the road is encountered. The right fork is one of half a dozen roads that head to the top of Ellis Peak. Keep to the left to follow the Rubicon Trail. After only 0.4 miles a second fork appears. Again, the right fork climbs Ellis Peak. (See Excursion #10 for the route description from here.)

The Rubicon Trail goes to the left, heading down Miller Creek. In slightly less than a mile the Pacific Crest Trail crosses the Rubicon Trail. The PCT is a 2,658-mile long hiking trail that connects Campo, California, on the Mexican border with Manning Provincial Park, British Columbia, on the Canadian border. Even with a start in the south in late April, it is very difficult to complete the portion in the Cascades before the winter snows begin in October. For this reason, most hikers who attempt to walk the entire way do it in segments over a number of years. Nevertheless, the entire PCT has been completed in a single year! This particular segment of the PCT also doubles as part of the 150-mile long route of the Tahoe Rim Trail. Backpackers wishing to hike the TRT need only devote half a month, not half a year!

Just a quarter of a mile beyond the PCT, the Class III road turns to Class IV and V, as it begins to steeply make its way down Cadillac Hill to Rubicon Springs, once the site of a resort hotel. As incredible as it may seem, during the summers of 1901-1906 and 1909-1913, there were enough people coming in here to warrant the seasonal establishment of a post office.

The western portion of the Rubicon Trail is described in *High Sierra SUV Trails Volume II-The Western Slope*, but always keep in mind: **the Rubicon Trail is extreme four-wheeling, and not recommended for stock SUVs!**

Never underestimate the Rubicon Trail!

Chapter IV
Trails Out of Markleeville
(Humboldt-Toiyabe National Forest)

John C. Fremont came through this little valley in February of 1844, during his second expedition west. He almost froze to death. The first permanent resident, however, was Jacob J. Marklee who homesteaded here in 1861. Three years later Markleeville is said to have had a population of 2620 people, which is considerably more than live there today. Serving as their supply point, the town prospered and grew up with the nearby mining camps of Monitor, Mogul and Silver Mountain City, originally called "Konigsberg". When the mines gave out, Markleeville managed to hang on, barely, but survive it did in spite of a devastating fire in 1885.

Markleeville is nestled in a picturesque little valley at the foot of Ebbetts Pass and Monitor Pass, astride State Highways 4 and 89. It has been the seat of Alpine County since 1875, because it is the largest permanently inhabited community in Alpine County (although on a winter holiday weekend, crowds at the popular Kirkwood and Bear Valley ski areas cause the 1100 person population of Alpine County to triple). The present day courthouse replaced the original structure in 1928. It is made from blocks of rhyolite tuff brought in from Silver Mountain City. Some of Silver Mountain's buildings were also moved to Markleeville, including today's Alpine Hotel, known as the Fisk Hotel when it was in Silver Mountain City. The "glory days" of Markleeville are recalled in the old buildings and other exhibits at the Alpine County Historical Complex on the hill above town.

Today Markleeville has a population of only 150 people and, as such, only limited services are available. Nevertheless, if you want to get away from the hoards of people at Lake Tahoe, Markleeville makes a good base of operations. There is a market, a hotel, a motel, and several places where you can eat and get gas. There is a small ten-unit U.S. Forest Service campground just east of town and another USFS campground at Centerville Flat, just a few miles south on Highway 4. The latter has no water, but it is open all year long.

Rush hour in Markleeville.

The Alpine County Museum is a worthwhile stop.

12

Scotts Lake

Primary Attraction:	This trail offers grand views of high mountain scenery in the Carson Pass area.
Time Required:	This half-day outing from Markleeville can be combined with Excursion #14 for a full day of four-wheeling.
Miles Involved:	From Markleeville to the Highway 88 turnoff, the distance is 14½ miles. From there it is another four miles of dirt roads to Scotts Lake.
Degree of Difficulty:	The dirt road portions of this route are generally only Class II, although steep grades and loose traction make many drivers feel more comfortable in four-wheel drive.

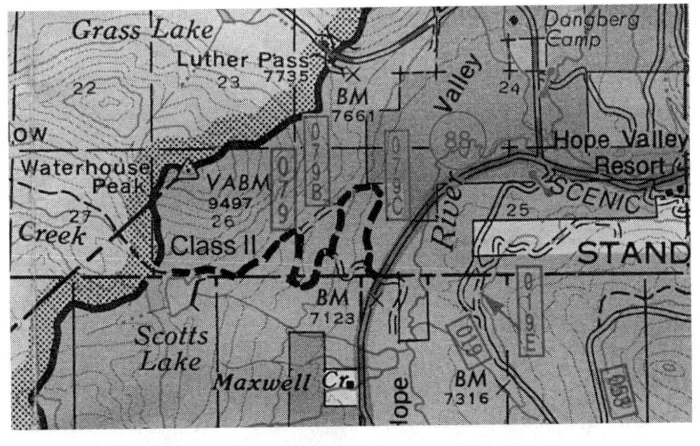

To find the Scotts Lake trail, take State Route 89 north out of Markleeville. After seven miles, turn left onto Highways 88 and 89 at Woodfords. Six more miles from here Highway 89 turns off to the right, as it heads up Luther Pass toward Lake Tahoe. Note your odometer reading at this intersection, but continue straight ahead on Highway 88 in the direction of Carson Pass.

At a point 1.4 miles beyond the intersection of Highways 88 and 89, look for a good dirt road going off through the fence to the right; a sign identifies this as Forest Road 079. Again note your odometer reading as you leave the pavement.

A "T" intersection is reached after 100 yards or so; stay to the right on Road 079. This is a popular, though unofficial, camping place for people fishing the nearby streams and lakes. Within 0.4 miles from Highway 88, Road 079 deteriorates to Class II, as it begins to switchback up the mountainside through a forest of pine and fir and an occasional grove of aspen. At 2.4 miles in from the highway, Road 079B goes off to the right; stay to the left. While Forest Road 079 is essentially a Class II road, the steepness of the grade and the loose traction may cause many drivers to slip their vehicle into four-wheel drive, even though it might not be needed technically.

As the ridgetop is approached, some 2.4 miles from Highway 88, there are some huge Sierra junipers, *Juniperus occidentalis,* on both sides of the road. In the Sierra Nevada, the junipers seem to thrive in the most barren, dry, and windswept places, where other trees cannot survive. While these trees do not grow to be very tall, some of these hardy giants have trunks six to nine feet in diameter.

Once you top the hill, pause a moment and look into the Mokelumne and Carson-Iceberg Wilderness areas to the south. If it is early in the summer, the Dardanelles and Airola Peaks are still likely to have snow hiding on their shaded northern slopes. If it is late in the season, the hills and valleys are likely to display splashes of bright orange from the groves of aspen.

At 4.0 miles in from the highway and continuing for the next quarter mile, little side roads to the left go to various unimproved campsites at the edge of Scotts Lake. The earth-filled dam that created this lake inundated a number of trees as the waters rose. Grotesquely shaped trunks still protrude out of the water. Anglers with the best chances of success seem to be using inflatable rafts to access the deepest portions out in the middle of the lake.

Scotts Lake

13

Crater Lake and the Alpine Mine

Primary Attraction:	This trail has a little of everything: high mountain scenery, a pair of old mines, fishing, and a challenging trail.
Time Required:	This outing makes for a full day of four-wheeling when coupled with a visit to Scotts Lake (Excursion #12).
Miles Involved:	From Markleeville to Crater Lake the distance is about twenty miles.
Degree of Difficulty:	The dirt road portions of this excursion involve 1½ miles of Class II and 3½ miles of steep, and sometimes rough, Class III.

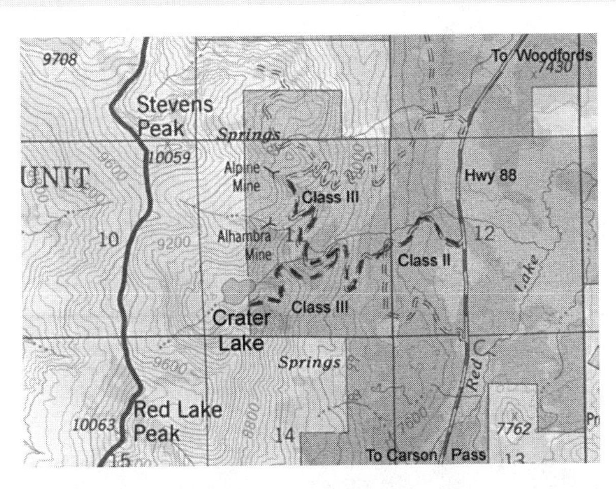

To find this excursion, take State Route 89 north out of Markleeville. After seven miles, turn left onto Highways 88 and 89 at Woodfords. In another six miles Highway 89 turns off to the right, as it heads up Luther Pass toward Lake Tahoe. Continue straight ahead on Highway 88 in the direction of Carson Pass, but do note your odometer reading.

You are now entering Hope Valley, the most northerly in the trio of Faith, Hope and Charity Valleys. Hope Valley was a busy place in the first few decades after the Carson Pass toll road was established in 1850. Ranchers moved their cattle up here each summer. Several dairies were turning out milk, cheese and butter. The *Pacific Coast Business Directory* for 1867 has listings for three hotels and a lumberyard in Hope Valley!

At a point 4.3 miles beyond the intersection of Highways 88 and 89, look for Forest Road 091 going off to the right. This is 1.8 miles past the turnoff to Blue Lakes and just beyond the culvert where Highway 88 crosses a small stream. Turn right off the highway here, noting your odometer reading as you do so. Pass over the cattle guard and stay to the right on 091.

The road forks at a point 0.6 miles from the highway. Follow the main road to the right. It will soon deteriorate to Class II, as it begins to switchback up the hillside. At the 1.3 miles point, there is a campsite and a major road intersection. Whichever direction you choose next, engage your four-wheel drive here, for both roads are steep and have poor traction.

The road to the left climbs steadily, passing the tailings dump of an old mine. Two miles from Highway 88 it ends on a ridgetop overlooking Crater Lake. This lake sits in what was once a tiny glacial cirque. Although the ground is hard and rocky, fishermen have cleared a few campsites.

Crater Lake

Back at the fork, the road to the right crosses the little stream coming out of Crater Lake, and then steeply climbs the hillside. The Alhambra Mine is reached at the second switchback. The hairpin turn here is so sharp that most drivers must go out onto the tailings dump to get turned around. The view from this point is quite nice.

Road to the Alhambra Mine

The origins of the Alhambra Mine are somewhat obscure, but it is known that gold and silver were mined here during the depression years of the early 1930s. With the advent of the Korean War in the early 1950s, the demand for tungsten went through the roof. It was known that scheelite, the principal ore of tungsten, existed here along the contact zone between granodiorite and older metamorphic rocks, primarily mica schist and quartzite. When the granitic rocks were pushed upward from deep within the earth, they intruded into the older existing rocks. Millions of years of erosion have washed away most of the metamorphic rocks, but here and there in the Sierra Nevada, remnants can still be found. These patches of older rocks are called roof pendants, and it is in these places where tungsten, vanadium and molybdenum have been found. Two tunnels each about 100 feet long were bored into the hillside here, but even with the high prices being brought for tungsten, the percentage of the metal was found to be too low to profitably mine. **Warning, these tunnels are partially flooded and the timbers are rotting. They are unsafe. Stay out of them!**

By following the road just around the corner from the Alhambra Mine, one comes to the Alpine Mine. Alpine County has two Alpine Mines. One is on Colorado Hill, high above Monitor Pass in the Monitor-Mogul District (see Excursion #16). The other Alpine Mine is here in the Hope Valley District. Unlike the Alhambra Mine, this mine made money for its owners. It first operated during World War II, and then again from 1948 to 1956. The ore was extracted from two tunnels, each several hundred feet long. **Warning: one of these tunnels has collapsed already and it is only a matter of time before the other one does, too. Stay out of the underground workings. They are unsafe!**

At one time there were several buildings on a man-made terrace above the ore bunker. They have collapsed under the weight of winter snows. When the Alpine Mine was operating, a road containing six switchbacks went down the hillside to connect with Highway 88. The road is still passable; however, the mother of all pine trees has fallen across it below the last switchback. Until someone comes along with a chainsaw having a ten-foot bar, you will have to turn around at the Alpine Mine and return to Highway 88 on the same road you came in on.

Snow has collapsed the buildings at the Alpine Mine.

14

Red Lake to Blue Lakes

Primary Attraction:	This dusty backroad offers some very nice high mountain scenery.
Time Required:	This is a two or three hour outing from Markleeville, but one that could be combined with Excursions #12, #13, and #15 for a full day or a full weekend of four-wheeling adventure.
Miles Involved:	From Red Lake on Highway 88 to Lower Blue Lake is nine miles.
Degree of Difficulty:	Although this road is no more difficult than Class II, it certainly is not recommended for standard passenger cars.

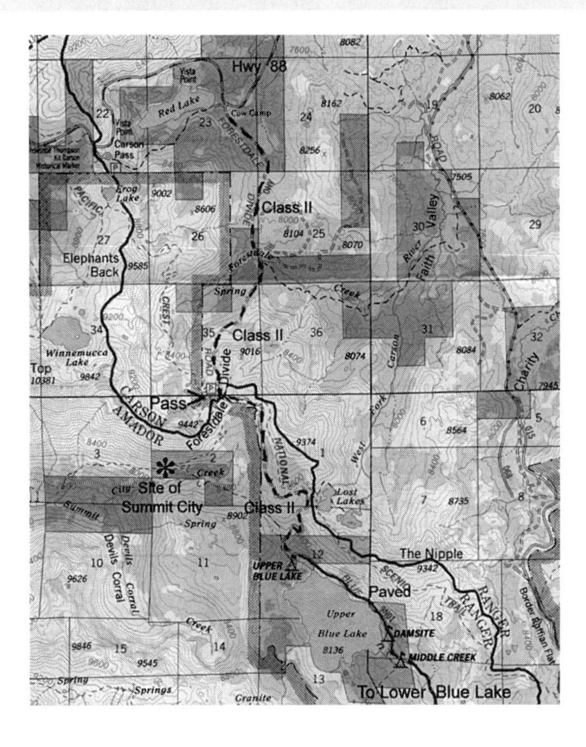

To find this excursion, take State Route 89 north out of Markleeville. After seven miles turn left onto Highways 88 and 89 at Woodfords. After six miles Highway 89 turns off to the right, as it heads up Luther Pass toward Lake Tahoe. Note your odometer reading at this intersection, but continue straight ahead on Highway 88 in the direction of Carson Pass.

At a point seven miles beyond the intersection of Highways 88 and 89, look for a high standard dirt road on the left. There may be no sign at this turnoff. Note your odometer reading as you turn left off of Highway 88. (If you miss the turnoff, continue on to the top of Carson Pass, then note your odometer and come back 2.25 miles.) The dirt road has two branches. The right branch goes a short distance to Red Lake; stay to the left.

It was here in the early 1850s, that 20-year-old John Studebaker set up a shop to repair wagon wheels on the busy Carson Pass emigrant route. He next moved to Placerville to successfully make and sell wheelbarrows for several years. With $8,000 of wheelbarrow money in his pocket, he returned home to South Bend, Indiana, to make wagons and, still later, horseless carriages. That eventually led to the Studebaker Automobile Company. The site of Studebaker's shop can no longer be determined, but it is thought to be a little to the east of the Red Lake dam.

The graded road is pretty good for the first mile, but then a sign warns motorists that the road is not suitable for passenger cars or trailers beyond that point. The sign notwithstanding, the road remains relatively good for another 0.6 miles, where a bridge spans Forestdale Creek. A U.S. Forest Service sign announces that it is three miles to Lost Lakes and four miles to Upper Blue Lakes. There is a small meadow here with several unimproved campsites around it.

Class I up to now, the road deteriorates to Class II as it starts a 1.5-mile long, 800-foot vertical climb to the Sierra crest. The grades are steep and the road surface becomes loose, rocky and rough. Although technically not needed, many drivers will feel more comfortable engaging their four-wheel drive. Called the Forestdale Divide, the top of this barren 8,900-foot ridge is reached. Stop for a moment and look around you; the view is grand. To the east is 9,417' Markleeville Peak. To the west is 10,380' Round Top Peak, a summit easily climbed from this ridge.

Prior to the establishment of the Mokelumne Wilderness in 1984, Forest Road 18E07 turned off to the right at the pass to descend into Summit City Canyon, where there was an old mining camp by the name of Summit City. With the creation of the 110,165-acre Mokelumne Wilderness, this jeep trail has been closed forever. Now if you want to see Summit City, you have to walk a couple of miles, dropping 1400 feet along the way. Should you elect to hike down there, less than a mile from our road at a spot where the canyon narrows, you will come to the site of Upper Summit City. You will have to look close, because there isn't much left of this old mining camp. There are a few stone foundations and other faint evidence of man's presence, hidden among the sagebrush and trees. With a keen eye, you can spot the old mine tailing dumps on the hillsides to the south.

The site of Lower Summit City is another mile down the trail. Like its sister city to the east, little remains here. It is hard to imagine that more than one hundred years ago hundreds of men were living a rough and rowdy life in this now quiet and peaceful canyon. Part of a letter to the *Daily Alta Californian* newspaper of June 15, 1864 reads:

> *We have in Summit City about 600 inhabitants and the town is building up as fast as lumber can be obtained, to furnish which two mills are now in process of erection. The usual amount of stores, blacksmith shop, bakeries, saloons etc. are in full blast and church and school will follow in due time. In the matter of politics we are about a standoff between Union men and rebels.*

In many of the western mining camps, the ore did not turn out to be as rich as the men's hopes and dreams. Such was the case at Summit City, where the cycle between birth, boom and bust was very short. It is easy walking down to Summit City. The hard part is the hike back up to the pass. (You will need a *Wilderness Permit* only if you stay overnight.)

From the top, the road descends the south side of the pass, and in doing so generally goes from Class II to Class I. In 0.6 miles down from the pass the road enters the forest again, and half a mile beyond you get your first views of Upper and Lower Blue Lakes. At a point 1.6 miles from the pass, a side road goes right for a few hundred yards to Lost Lakes. PG&E's Upper Blue Lake Campground is just 0.8 miles beyond on the left. The elevation here is 8,135 feet.

Keep right going away from the paved road leading into the campground. One mile beyond here the dirt road turns to asphalt as it enters PG&E's Middle Creek Campground, and upon leaving, turns to graded dirt again. After another mile and a quarter, PG&E's Lower Blue Lake Campground is reached and once again the road is paved. Finally at a point 5.4 miles from the pass, an information kiosk and a three-way intersection is reached. The left fork goes north through Charity and Hope Valleys to rejoin Highway 88 just 2.4 miles south of its intersection with Highway 89 going over Luther Pass. The right fork, after 0.2 miles, connects with the jeep road going through the Mokelumne Corridor (see Excursion #15).

View north from the Forestdale Divide of the Elephant's Back (left) and Red Lake Peak (right).

Pentstemon grows in rocky places along the road to Blue Lakes.

15

The Mokelumne Corridor

Primary Attraction:	This excursion has a little of everything: high mountain scenery, history, fishing, and a challenging trail. All along the way are nice, but otherwise unimproved, places to camp.
Time Required:	This loop out of Markleeville, starting on Highway 88 and returning via Highway 4, is an all day outing.
Miles Involved:	From Markleeville it is eighteen miles to Lower Blue Lake via Highways 89 and 88, plus another seven miles of jeep trail, followed by another twenty miles back to Markleeville via Highway 4.
Degree of Difficulty:	The jeep trail portion of the route is mostly Class III, with some Class IV and V rocks to overcome. **Skid plates protecting everything vital are strongly recommended. SUVs could suffer a little damage to running boards and other unnecessary appendages. Long wheelbase vehicles, such as full size pickups, are not advised.**

The Clover Valley and Deer Valley route is another of those rare routes that goes in a north-south direction, cutting across the grain of the mountains to join two trans-Sierra highways. Technically the trail lies west of the ill-defined crest near Ebbetts Pass and thus is in the Pacific watershed. I include it here because the trail is nearer to Markleeville than anywhere else. This jeep trail follows the route of an old wagon road that connected Faith, Hope and Charity Valleys in the north with Hermit Valley in the south. This old pioneer route was used mostly in 1856 and 1857.

In order to accommodate access by private property owners when Congress established the 105,165-acre Mokelumne Wilderness Area, a narrow corridor along an existing jeep trail through Clover Valley was intentionally left out of the *Wilderness* classification. While environmentalists objected, and did not like it, off-roaders rejoiced that they could still drive down Blue Creek and over the ridge to Hermit Valley. In that same wilderness legislation, off-roaders had lost the right to drive into the old mining camp of Summit City (see Excursion

#14), but this narrow corridor remaining open helped ease their pain a little. (Sometimes rightly and sometimes wrongly, off-roaders often have a bad public image. They usually get bad press from the national media, and they generally have an ineffective lobby in Washington D.C.)

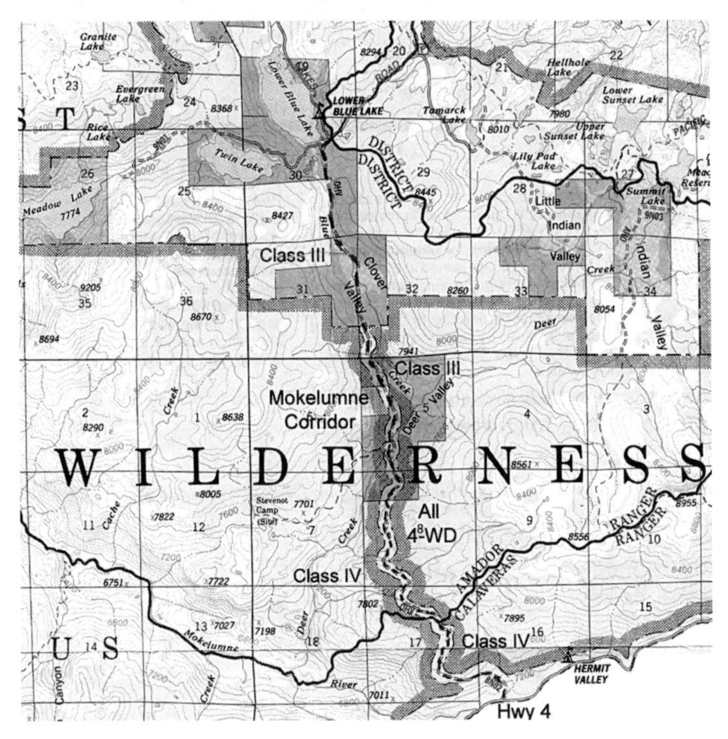

To find this trail, take State Route 89 north out of Markleeville. After seven miles turn left at Woodfords onto Highways 88 and 89. After six miles Highway 89 turns off right as it heads up Luther Pass toward Lake Tahoe. Note your odometer reading at this intersection, but continue straight ahead on Highway 88 in the direction of Carson Pass.

At a point two and a half miles beyond the intersection of Highways 88 and 89 look for the roadside sign pointing left to the Blue Lakes Road. Turn left here. It was near this intersection, 150 years ago, that an informal country fair was held each summer. The highlight of the event was the horse races held on a graded and maintained oval racetrack. The chief contestants were Alpine County's own local ranchers, and ranchers from the west side, who annually brought their cattle up to graze in these meadows. History did not record the winners.

Head south on the paved Blue Lakes road. The small twenty unit Hope Valley Campground is passed 1.8 miles beyond Highway 88. At the six-mile point notice the large Sierra juniper trees on the open slope to the left. There is something about the environment of eastern Alpine County that makes these trees grow bigger than in other parts of the Sierra Nevada.

At a summer ranch, seven miles in, the pavement ends, but the road of good graded dirt continues. Finally the road forks nearly twelve miles south of Highway 88. Pass behind the information kiosk at this three-way intersection, and keep to the left. Follow the signs pointing the way to Twin Lakes. Within 0.2 miles the dirt road to Twin Lakes goes off to the right, while Forest Road 19E01 goes off to the left. A sign announces the distance to Highway 4 as seven miles. Lock in your front hubs and engage your four-wheel drive here. You will need it until you reach State Route 4.

The narrow, but well used jeep trail twists and turns as it winds its way through the forest of lodgepole pine. Large rocks buried in the roadway make the going slow. If you don't like the first half-mile, you had better turn around, for the trail doesn't get any easier. Soon, however, the forest on the right thins to give views of sparkling Blue Creek cascading down the rocks.

At a point 1.5 miles from the Blue Lakes information kiosk, Blue Creek is forded. This ford has a firm sandy bottom, and is not normally a problem. **Before fording any stream, if you have any doubt about the water depth, strength of current, or bottom conditions, get out and check them out before plunging in!**

The Blue Creek ford.

The road re-enters the forest for the next mile and a half, coming out into the sunshine again in the lower end of Deer Valley. In the decades before the creation of the Mokelumne Wilderness, a side road to the right went to Stevenot Camp some two miles to the west. Congress placed that in the wilderness area and closed the road.

Today's jeep trail next fords the stream that is now called Deer Creek. There are several nice unimproved campsites in the area. The site of an old sawmill is a quarter of a mile beyond the ford. The sawmill itself is long-gone, but the remaining piles of cut lumber range from massive timbers to wooden shingles. For some reason this lumber was cut, but abandoned. The round nails found in the debris suggest the sawmill came well after the old wagon road of the 1850s. Nevertheless, there are some large lodgepole pine growing up through the debris.

From Deer Valley at an elevation of 7,400 feet, the jeep trail climbs up the ridge to a high point of 7,750 feet, then steeply descends 650 feet into Hermit Valley, where it connects with State Highway 4 east of the bridge crossing the North Fork of the Mokelumne River. By turning left here, it is about twenty miles back to Markleeville via Ebbetts Pass. If you turn right, it is not far to the very pleasant Lake Alpine Resort and an hour or so beyond that, Angels Camp.

A short Class V section at the Hermit Valley end of the trail.

16

Loope Canyon Loop

Primary Attraction:	Nice scenery, an historic old mining district, and Piñon nut collecting in the fall.
Time Required:	This entire circuit can be done in two to four hours. However, there are lots of side roads to explore, too, so plan on most of the day.
Miles Involved:	It is six and a half miles from Markleeville to the site of Monitor, where you leave the pavement. Then it is nearly eight miles of rough roads up Loope Canyon to the site of Mogul, and beyond to the high standard and graded Leviathan Mine Road.
Degree of Difficulty:	The roads are mostly Class II, with only a couple of miles of Class III.

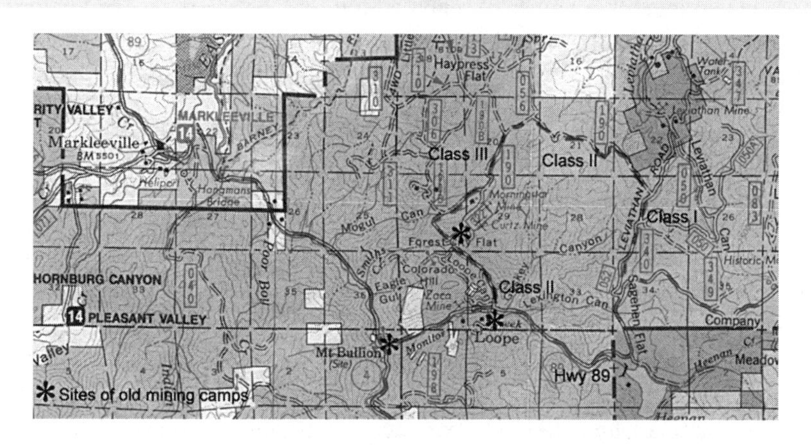

Just east of Markleeville the semi-arid mountains around Forest City Flat and Haypress Flat offer a full day of four-wheeling mixed in with a portion of history and some magnificent scenery. This backroad adventure begins in Markleeville. Take Highway 89 south, across Hangman's Bridge and on to the intersection where Highway 4 begins to make its way up to Ebbetts Pass. This intersection is the site of Mt. Bullion, an old mining camp of which little remains. Turn left here as Highway 89 starts up the western side of Monitor Pass.

After going up the canyon for a mile and a half, you will start to see the tailings dumps of the Zaca Mine on the left, and the mill waste in the canyon bottom to the right. The Zaca Mine was one of the largest mines in the Monitor-Mogul District. Present day Highway 89, just below the Zaca Mine, goes through the site of the old mining camp of Monitor. The camp got its start in 1862 and was named after the ironclad warship used by the Union Navy to turn away a Confederate ironclad in the battle of Hampton Roads. By the following year there was sufficient activity for a telegraph line to be built, which connected Monitor with Genoa, Nevada. It is hard to imagine as you drive along Highway 89 today, but this canyon supported a population of 2,000 people in the 1860s and 70s. Monitor had a post office between 1866 and 1888, and the town was even large enough to support a weekly newspaper, the *Alpine Monitor.* Over a period of twenty years, the entire district produced an estimated three to five million dollars worth of gold, silver, and even some copper. Mining declined after 1888. In an attempt to revive the interest of investors, in 1898 the camp's name was changed to Loope, to woo a wealthy doctor of the same name. He and other eastern investors promised to breathe new life into the mines of Colorado Hill. Money for further mineral exploration was forthcoming, and enough people drifted back to cause the post office to reopen. In spite of the name change, the canyon's glory days were over.

There have been other spurts of renewed interest in the 1930s and again in the early 1960s. Colorado Hill, above the Zaca Mine, may yet hold treasures waiting to be found. As recently as 1997, core drilling was still going on along the upper south face of Colorado Hill.

After climbing 1.8 miles up from the intersection of Highways 89 and 4, a dirt road can be seen on the left. Note your odometer reading and turn left here. This is Forest Road 190, which immediately begins to ascend Loope Canyon. Engage your four-wheel drive here before starting up the narrow canyon. Although the road is a steep Class I, you will feel more comfortable with power to all four wheels.

At a point 0.7 miles above Highway 89, a side road goes sharply off to the left behind you. This leads to the upper workings of the Zaca Mine. These claims remain active and a gate is likely to bar access. Continue on up the canyon. After another 0.7 miles the country opens up and you arrive at 7,000 foot Forest City Flat, the site of Mogul, another mining camp of the 1860s and 70s. There is a crossroads here. To the right, Road 324 is a Class III route that climbs the hill to the north going to the Morningstar Mine. To the left is Road 328, a Class III route that goes steeply up the side of Colorado Hill to the south, where it dead-ends amid a large open pit. Gold and silver were mined here as late as the 1970s. After you have checked out the side roads, continue straight ahead on

Forest Road 190. In less than half a mile, Road 329 goes off to the left passing a primitive campsite with a great view. This Class II side road passes some prospect holes, and then climbs to a small hilltop where the Forest Service once had a fire lookout overlooking Mogul Canyon. Still Class I, Forest Road 190 continues on, dropping down past an aspen grove into a little valley with a small stream. Just after crossing the streambed, Class II Road 190B goes off to the left to Haypress Flat, another side-trip of an hour or so. The main road continues up the valley. The upper end of Forest Road 324 can soon be seen on the right. The remains of the Morningstar Mine are clearly visible on the hillside a quarter of a mile to the right.

You might want to make a side-trip over to this mine. The tunnel has been closed, and it is reasonably safe to look around. This mine was opened in 1863 with the discovery of a large ore body of enargite, an important copper mineral. A tunnel was driven 775 feet back into the hillside, and mining went on periodically until 1904, with renewed activity in the 1920s, 1930s and the 1950s. The ore contained very complex sulfides and the metals were difficult to extract. Some of the unprocessed ore was shipped all the way to Swansea in Wales for smelting. The total production from this mine is estimated at $600,000, mostly in gold and silver, with very little copper produced. The cost to mine it probably exceeded the net return.

The Morningstar Mine

Forest Road 322 can be taken beyond the Morningstar Mine. The Class II road circles around the mountainside for nearly a mile to the Curtz Mine. This ore body, too, was found in 1863 and is located in the same vein as the Morningstar Mine. Indeed, at various times in the past the Curtz Mine, the Morningstar Mine, and the nearby Georgiana Mine were all considered to be part of the same mine.

Disaster Peak as seen from the tailing dump of the Curtz Mine.

Back again on Forest Road 190, the route now deteriorates to Class II as it climbs higher, passing a cool spring in an aspen grove. This water attracts deer and quail, both of which seem plentiful in this area. A quarter of a mile above the spring, an unmarked side road goes left, while Road 190 deteriorates to Class III.

Now crossing rough lava, Forest Road 190 climbs for the next mile before coming to a 'Y' just south of Haypress Flat. The road to the left is Forest Road 056, a Class II route to 8,000' Haypress Flat. Stay right on Forest Road 190, which suddenly improves to Class II as it turns eastward. After 1.4 miles it further improves to Class I. At a point 2.4 miles from Forest Road from the 'Y' with Road 056, Road 190 suddenly comes out on the high standard graded dirt Leviathan Road. By turning right, you will reach Highway 89 in 1.4 miles. By turning left, you will pass the immense workings of the Leviathan Mine (a major producer of sulfur, with production valued at fifteen million dollars) and eventually come to US Highway 395 in Nevada, north of Topaz Lake.

The forest along this part of the East Carson River is largely made up of the single needle Piñon pine, *Pinus monophylla,* whose cones yield a delicious and nutritious nut. October is the time to go "nutting". Select a tree with lots of cones that have opened. Pull the cones from the tree or collect the fresh cones that have recently fallen to the ground. Place your crop of cones in plastic trash bags to take home. There you can remove the individual nuts at your leisure. Many women like to wear heavy plastic kitchen gloves while handling the cones, which are always sticky with pitch. Guys don't often bother, but clean up afterwards using mechanic's waterless hand soap. Anytime you go nutting, it's a good idea to carry some of the mechanic's waterless hand soap, as most brands nicely dissolve the pitch.

For peak flavor, Piñon pine nuts should be slowly roasted in a cast iron skillet on top of a wood stove, in a warm and cozy room at a time when the weather outside is cold, wet, and awful. A football game on TV also enhances the flavor. If that is not available, try a little light classical music played in the background. Once roasted, the nuts can be eaten whole as a snack or in a salad, or be crushed and added to ground coffee. Piñon nuts are also good baked in pastry or incorporated into homemade fudge. (See *Appendix F* for various ways of using Piñon nuts.)

The nuts of the Piñon are very tasty.

17

The 'Lost' Pennsylvania Mine

Primary Attraction:	This easy trail off the Ebbetts Pass Road offers some fine scenery and in the late summer, an opportunity to gather free gifts of nature: wild currants and gooseberries.
Time Required:	This outing can be done in half a day out of Markleeville.
Miles Involved:	From Highway 4 to the end of the road at Pennsylvania Creek, the distance is a little over two miles.
Degree of Difficulty:	This excursion is mostly Class II, but with just enough Class III to keep automobiles out.

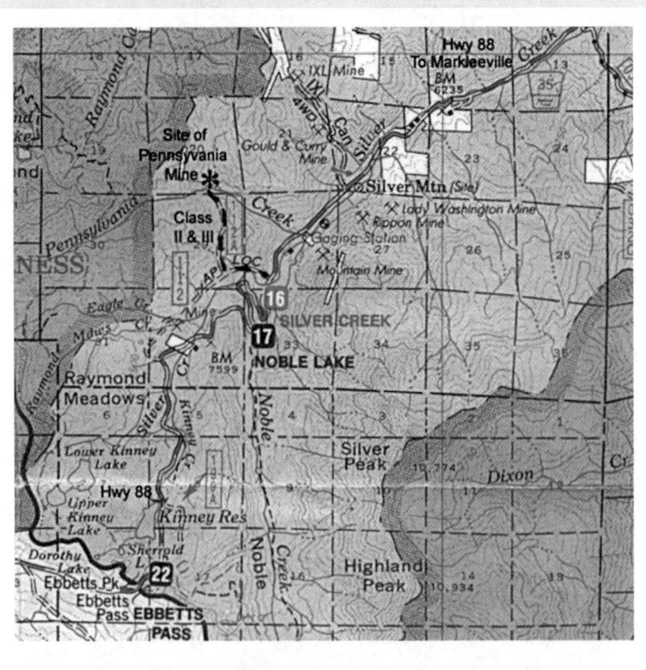

I do not know whether the Pennsylvania Mine is truly lost or not, but I could not find it, so it is lost to me! The mine's location is clearly marked on the 1:24,000 scale U.S.G.S. 1979 Ebbetts Pass topographic map. However, the actual mine has proved to be very illusive.

The Pennsylvania Mine was said to have been located on the eastern side of Ebbetts Pass on Pennsylvania Creek, and so named by prospectors from the "Keystone State". The mine was first located in the 1860s as an outgrowth of the mining boom in the Silver Mountain District. The scant records available indicate the Pennsylvania Mine once consisted of two tunnels and one shaft dug to intercept a three to eight foot vein in a broken and crushed zone of granite rocks. The tunnels were said to be three hundred and nine hundred feet long. They must have left a substantial tailings dump at the tunnels' portals, yet I found no trace of them. If you can manage to find the tunnels or shafts, I would appreciate hearing from you.

You can begin your search for this "lost mine" by taking State Route 89 east out of Markleville. Reset your trip odometer to zero as you pass by the Alpine County Courthouse in downtown Markleeville, and keep a keen eye out for roadside historical markers. For the next eleven miles, the highway will take you past a lot of history. On the eastern side of Ebbetts Pass were the sites of no less than three once-booming mining camps of the early to middle 1860s.

A mile and a half from Markleeville you will cross the East Fork of the Carson River at Hangman's Bridge. The predecessor of the present day bridge was so named in 1874 when a vigilance committee took an accused murderer, by the name of Ernst Reusch, from the custody of deputies and summarily hanged him from the bridge. For some reason, Reusch's attorney did not think Reusch could get a fair trial in Alpine County. He convinced a judge to order that the accused be moved to nearby Mono County for trial, and it was during the transfer that this "quick justice" prevailed.

When I wrote *Eastern Sierra Jeep Trails* in 1971, I described the Barney Riley Trail, a jeep trail that headed north from the east end of Hangman's Bridge. In recent years the US Forest Service has closed that road to vehicle traffic and the access gate is now locked.

Four and a half miles from Markleeville is the intersection of Highways 89 and 4. Today's highway intersection was once the site of our first old mining camp to be found below Ebbetts Pass. The camp was called Mt. Bullion, established in 1860s as a suburb of Monitor just up a side canyon to the east. Nothing remains to note its passing.

Highway 89 turns to the left and starts up Monitor Pass. It is less than two miles up the canyon to the east that the site of the one time mining camp of Monitor can be found. (To learn more about Monitor and its mines of Colorado Hill, follow the route described in Excursion # 16.) To search for the Pennsylvania Mine, however, continue straight ahead at this intersection in the direction of Ebbetts Pass. The highway now becomes State Route 4.

After another two and a half miles, the road passes through Centerville Flat, the site of the second of our old camps in the East Fork Canyon. While a few miners lived here, Centerville was actually more of a crossroads hamlet than a true mining camp. Other than the houses of the people who lived here, the village only consisted of a tavern and a few stores. But, Centerville was on the wagon road that connected booming Bodie with Sacramento and San Francisco. From Centerville, the road to Bodie went to the southeast, past the abandoned mining camp of Silver King, then up Snodgrass Creek to cross a low pass into the West Walker River country. While nothing remains of Centerville's past, the flat today is the site of a forest service campground. It is the only campground in the Carson Ranger District that is open all year long, and one of only two in which no camping fees are charged.

At Centerville Flat, a road goes off to the left up Wolf Creek. Again, in 1971 when I wrote *Eastern Sierra Jeep Trails,* I described a beautiful jeep trail that went up this little valley to pretty Wolf Creek Falls. That jeep trail was lost forever when Congress created the *Carson Iceberg Wilderness Area* in 1984. From the wilderness boundary you can walk the old jeep trail to its end, where the hiking trail goes on to eventually cross Wolf Creek Pass into the Highland Lakes area.

The East Fork of the Carson River is left behind at Centerville Flat, as Highway 4 now starts up Silver Creek. Our next point in history comes nine miles from Markleville when a white house and enormous brick chimney appear on the right. The house is the so-called Chalmers' Mansion. Lewis Chalmers was a Scottish lawyer who, at the age of 39, stumbled into the mining and assaying business in London. His position with the Imperial Silver Quarries Company took him to America in 1867, because his employer had purchased the Michigan Tunnel in Alpine County, California. "Lord Chalmers", as he was called by the locals, built this house in 1868 to be near the mine he was overseeing. Chalmers lived here on British investors' money until 1884, when he returned to England penniless. For a full account of the Chalmers story, read historian Remi Nadeau's excellent book, *The Silver Seekers.*

The chimney standing next to the house is part of the Exchequer smelter, a furnace used to roast the sulfides off Chalmers' silver ore that was extracted from a mine of the same name. Much of the smelter has been reduced to a pile of weathered bricks, but the chimney remains standing as tall and straight as it did 130 years ago.

Beyond the smelter there is a small cemetery on the left. Among those buried here are Chalmers' second wife, Antoinette, and her son by a previous marriage, Harry Laughton, and another son by Chalmers who, at age 7, was accidentally drowned in Silver Creek.

The Chalmers' mansion is just to the left of the Exchequer Furnace.

Eleven miles from Markleville we come to the third and last of our historic sites on the Ebbetts Pass Road. A large wooden sign on the left announces the site. In 1861, high on the steep slopes above Silver Creek, some Norwegian prospectors found quartz veins containing silver. They established their camp on the flat land down by the creek and named it Konigsberg, after a silver mining community near Oslo. The name did not stick, however. By the spring of 1863, as word of the strike got out, newcomers rushed in to stake their claims. The camp was soon renamed Silver Mountain. By summer there were nearly one hundred wooden structures in the town, made with lumber turned out by local sawmills. Wagon roads were being built to the camp from Genoa, Nevada, over Carson Pass from Angels Camp, and over Ebbetts Pass from Sonora. The population was said to be 3,000 people (I suspect that figure was somewhat inflated by town boosters). The following year, when Alpine County was created from eastern Amador County, Silver Mountain became the county seat. The output of the IXL Mine had reached $2,500 per week by the summer of 1865. It was in this heady atmosphere that the Imperial Silver Quarries Company of London, England, bought some promising claims, which brought Lewis Chalmers to America the following year. The boom did not last as long as Chalmers, and by the early 1880s the town was all but abandoned. The only thing that remains of Silver Mountain today are remnants of the stone walls which were once the jail building.

Once you have seen the sights of Silver Mountain, note your odometer reading again and continue driving up Highway 4 towards Ebbetts Pass. At a point 1.4 miles beyond the Silver Mountain sign, and just a few feet before reaching the highway bridge over Raymond Meadows Creek, a Class II dirt road climbs steeply up the hillside to the right. Here we leave the pavement and take Forest Road 112. The road forks after 0.7 miles. At one time the left fork, Road 112, went to a mine higher up on Raymond Meadows Creek. That road has washed out; go to the right on Road 112A. This spur deteriorates to Class III in places, so it is best to engage your four-wheel drive at this intersection.

Both sides of the road are lined with gooseberries and currants for the next mile. In spite of the millions of dollars spent to eradicate them, gooseberries and wild currants are widely distributed throughout the western slope of the Sierra Nevada from 3,500 feet all the way up to timberline. These shrubs are part of the genus *Ribes,* which has many species. Indeed, in the Sierra Nevada there are six different species of gooseberries and three species of currants. In the 1950s the National Forest Service and the National Park Service had programs to destroy these plants, not because they were a nuisance or inherently dangerous, but because they served as the intermittent host to the White Pine Blister Rust, a parasitic fungus which attacks five needled pines, including the very valuable sugar pine. Gooseberries and currants are much less common on the eastern slope of the Sierra Nevada, perhaps because their natural habitat is more restricted. It was along this trail that we found more gooseberries and currants than any other place on the eastern slope of the Sierra Nevada (see Appendix E for wild berry recipes).

Native Americans often made an easily transportable pemmican loaf by pounding dried currants or gooseberries together with meat and animal fat. The Lewis and Clark expedition often collected wild currants along the way to supplement their rations, and gooseberry pie was a favorite among the pioneers and early settlers in the west.

Do not confuse the fruit of *Ribes* with the small red fruit from one of the six species of manzanita found in the Sierra Nevada (genus *Arctostaphylos)*. While many native American tribes utilized the manzanita berry, too, it had to be first crushed and leached thoroughly with hot water to remove the bitter taste of the tannic acid it contains. After this leaching process the moist meal could be made into patties and baked or roasted.

Wild Berries of the Sierra Nevada

wild currants

gooseberries

elderberries

Forest Road 112A climbs a little and then contours around the hillside to abruptly dead end at a small, but pleasant campsite on Pennsylvania Creek at an elevation of 7,300 feet. It is here that the Pennsylvania Mine is supposed to be located, but we found no sign of it.

The bedrock geology here is rather interesting. On the western side of Pennsylvania Creek are the well-weathered and rounded Mesozoic granitic rocks of the Sierra batholith. On the eastern side of the creek, however, is a shear zone containing much younger volcanic rocks of Miocene age. They stand out in shimmering white, in stark contrast to the brown granular granite.

While we never did find the site of our "lost mine", the day was not wasted. It took us only thirty minutes to collect enough gooseberries and currants to return home with sufficient fruit to make two pies and a two-year supply of nutritious jelly that is high in vitamin C. And, on the way out, we were rewarded with impressive views of the precipitous north face of 10,772' Silver Peak, which had been at our backs on the journey coming in.

Silver Peak dominates the view from the east side of Ebbetts Pass.

Chapter V
Trails Out of Bridgeport
(Humboldt-Toiyabe National Forest)

Bridgeport, the county seat of Mono County, is nestled in a valley drained by the East Walker River. To the west of this 6500' basin, the eleven and twelve thousand-foot peaks of Yosemite National Park dominate the skyline. To the north is the Sweetwater Range with 11,673' Mt. Patterson, and to the east are the 9,000' Bodie Hills. In the summer, the weather is very pleasant in Bridgeport, but, in the winter, this enclosed basin tends to be very cold.

On its half mile long Main Street, Bridgeport has half a dozen motels, several places to eat, two markets, an auto parts store, and, of course, gas stations and sporting goods stores. There is even a self-service car wash, and a small hospital. There are seven U.S. Forest Service campgrounds to the east and southeast of town in the Buckeye, Honeymoon Flat, and Twin Lakes areas, plus a number of privately operated resorts that offer camping.

For the first decade after Mono County was created, the seat of local government was in Aurora. But then a funny thing happened in 1863 - a state boundary survey determined that Aurora was in Nevada! Mono County then moved its courthouse to Bridgeport, and it is still there, the second oldest courthouse in California (second only to Mariposa County). Visitors with an interest in history should certainly visit the courthouse and look at the old stone jail building behind it. The Mono County Museum, one block to the west, is also worthy of a visit.

A busy day in downtown Bridgeport.

Bridgeport in the 1880s
(Photo courtesy Laws Railroad Museum)

The Mono County Museum is worth a visit.

18

A Backroad to Sonora Pass

Primary Attraction:	This backroad off the beaten tourist path offers some grand scenery in the Sonora Pass area.
Time Required:	From its lower end on Highway 108 at the Marine Corps base to its upper end below Sonora Pass, the road requires only an hour to drive, providing you don't stop along the way to fish or picnic (both worthwhile endeavors).
Miles Involved:	The dirt road portion is a little over eleven miles in length.
Degree of Difficulty:	The road is generally no worse than Class II, meaning four-wheel drive is not essential. It can usually be negotiated by standard automobiles, if sufficient care is taken.

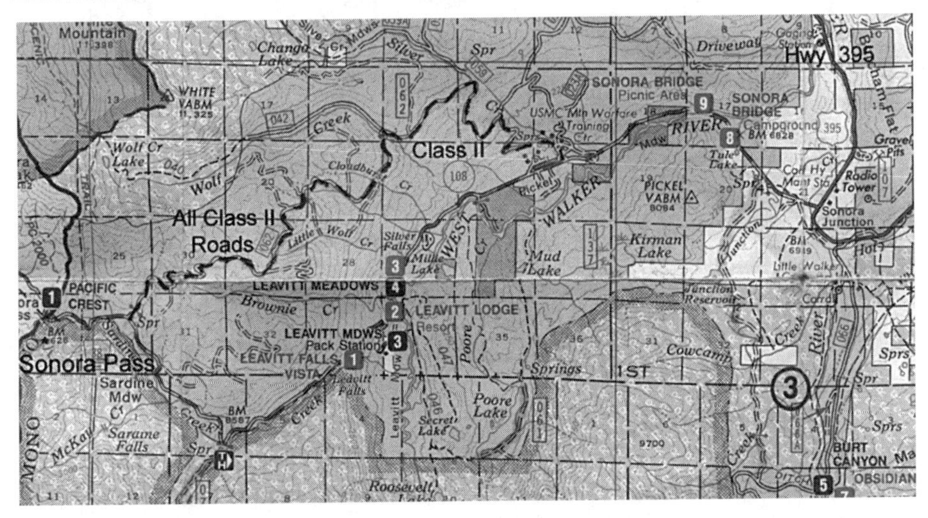

This backroad offers no particular challenge to the serious off-roader. I have included it in this guide, because it is well off the beaten tourist path, and because it offers spectacular views into the Tower Range south of Sonora Pass. You might not want to drive several hundred miles just to take this road, but if your route takes you east to west over Sonora Pass, you may wish to choose this route over that of the paved highway.

Two roads diverged in the wood, and I-
I took the one less traveled by,
And that has made all the difference.
Robert Frost

This dirt road adventure starts at the U.S. Marine Corps Mountain Warfare Training Center, just 6.5 miles west of US Highway 395 on State Route 108. Do not enter the base by the first gate; that goes up to the permanent staff area. Take the second road a quarter of a mile beyond, at the Marine Monument. Look for a U.S. Forest Service sign reading "Silver Creek Access". The dirt road, Forest Road 059, goes to the northwest between the airfield and the modern base building complex, passing the sewage treatment plant on the left.

Most of the Marine Corps base is open to public use.

The Marine Corps base has been here since the end of the Korean War. For many years it was primarily a winter training facility, but in recent years its training mission has expanded to a year round program. The Marines have a cooperative agreement with the U.S. Forest Service that permits both public and military use of the mountains behind the facility. Do not be shocked if you come around a curve in the road to find a Humvee coming in your direction. I have watched a giant Sea Stallion helicopter hovering over my favorite fishing hole, with a squad of fully armed Marines decked out in camouflage battle gear rappelling down to join me at the water's edge.

Road 059 climbs steeply up the hillside above the base, and after 1.7 miles comes to a fork. The right fork, Road 023, works its way north to end at Grouse Meadows; stay to the left on Road 059. At a point 3.1 miles above Highway 108, the road forks again. Again go left, although this time you are on Road 062. The right fork is a continuation of Road 059 that ends at Summit Meadows.

Road 062 leaves the Silver Creek drainage, heading southwest to the Wolf Creek drainage. Along the way are great views south of the Hoover Wilderness. Yosemite National Park starts on the far side of these peaks. At a point one half mile beyond the 059/062 fork, a Class III side road right goes up to tiny Chango Lake. After another 0.4 miles, Road 042 goes off to the right following the north bank of Wolf Creek until it dead-ends.

Our route, Road 062, crosses a bridge over Wolf Creek, and continues on to cross Little Wolf Creek and the lower ends of two meadows. Along the way, there are several Class III trails going off to the left and right, all worth exploring. At a point 9.5 miles from Highway 108 you suddenly find yourself on top of a ridge with terrific views in all directions. To the east, the barren rounded summits of the Sweetwater Range remind one of a lunar landscape. To the south from right to left are the reddish brown spires of 11,180' Forsyth Peak, 11,755' Tower Peak, and 11,240' Ehrnbeck Peak. To the north are curiously eroded pinnacles in the volcanic rock. Just to the west is Sonora Pass, with 11,570' Leavitt Peak on the south side and 11,462' Sonora Peak on the north side. Everywhere you look the mountains are magnificent!

Peaks of layered volcanic rocks just south of Sonora Pass.

Road 062 continues on for another 2.8 miles before dropping down onto Highway 108 once again. The 9,624' summit of Sonora Pass is just 1.4 miles up the 15% grade to the right.

Sonora Pass in the 1940s
(Photo coutesy County of Inyo, Eastern California Museum)

19

Searching For Fremont's Lost Cannon

Primary Attraction:	A needle in a haystack search for a cannon abandoned in 1844 by Lt. John C. Fremont's Second Expedition west to California.
Time Required:	This search can take but a few hours or a lifetime, depending on what you are willing to give it.
Miles Involved:	The miles will vary depending on your persistence and determination.
Degree of Difficulty:	Most of the roads in the search area are generally Class I or II.

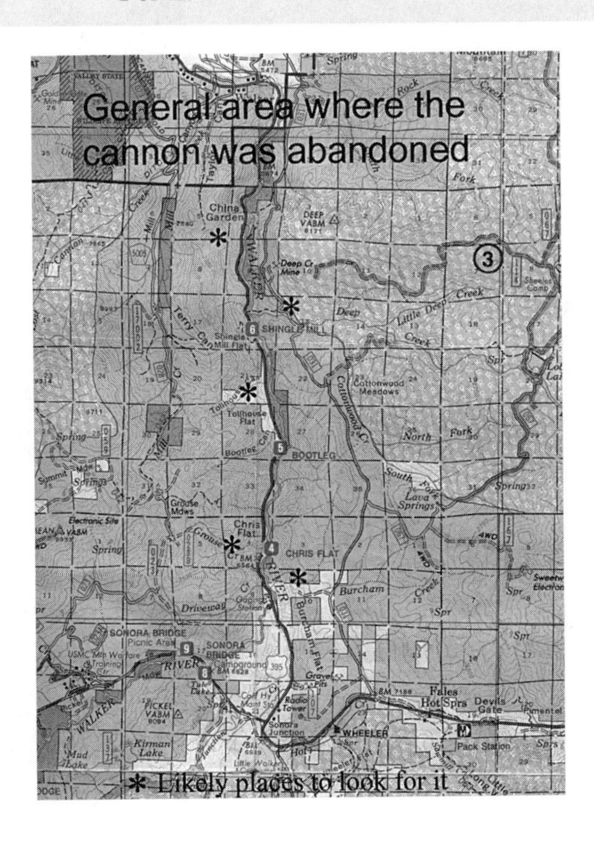

It was a bitter cold January in 1844 that found John C. Fremont and his party of forty men, including the famous scout, Kit Carson, wallowing in crotch-deep snows on the West Walker River near Fales Hot Springs. An Army officer, Fremont was married to the daughter of influential Senator Thomas Hart Benson of Missouri. He was given the responsibility to take a detachment from the Army's Corps of Topographical Engineers to scout possible railroad routes west across the continent. (Never mind that much of the territory he was going into already belonged to Mexico. He was, in essence, on a spy mission to northwest Mexico, laying the geographical foundation for the United States' expansion westward to the Pacific Ocean.) Fremont had already made one scouting trip west in 1842. He was only a Second Lieutenant, but, thanks to his father-in-law, Fremont was given broad latitude in his mission.

Major-General John C. Fremont during the Civil War

Fremont's second expedition west left St. Louis in May of 1843. Because of the threat posed by grizzly bears and the possibility of hostile Indians along the way, Fremont thought that the 33 Hall's rifles his party was carrying needed to be supplemented with a small, inconspicuous cannon. Obviously, one does not use a cannon against a grizzly bear, but one might use a cannon against Mexican troops defending their country.

Over the objections of the quartermaster at the Jefferson Barracks in St. Louis, Senator Benson cleared the way for his son-in-law to pick up a mountain howitzer. It was a 12-pounder of French design. The U.S. Army had purchased several from the French, and then several dozen more look-alikes were purchased from a Boston company between 1836 and 1841. The cannon was normally pulled on its carriage by two mules, but it could easily be broken down and packed by the animals if the country became too rough. The cannon and carriage had a combined weight of 525 pounds and had an overall length of about six feet. The powder and shot weighed twelve pounds per shot fired, and it is thought that they took enough powder and shot to fire the weapon about fifty times. Thus the cannon and its ammunition added another 1000 pounds to the expedition's already heavy load.

Fremont's route to the west took him across the Oregon Trail, which he mapped, to the Pacific Ocean, and then south down Western Nevada. During this incredible journey of well over 1,000 miles, Fremont's diary never once mentions the need to use the cannon to fight off a grizzly bear attack. He was once prepared to repel an attack of Sioux Indians, but the cannon was never needed. Later, however, it was fired once to impress some potentially troublesome Paiutes in Northern Nevada. A few practice rounds were also fired. The expedition's gunner, Louis Zindel, proved he could hit a four-foot high post at a distance of a quarter of a mile away! His skill arose from the fact that he had once served in the Prussian army as a sergeant of artillery.

The soldiers and mountain men in Fremont's party wanted to abandon the cumbersome field piece months before back at South Pass, Wyoming, but Fremont insisted it be brought along. After encountering deep snows in the Bridgeport Valley on January 25th, 1844, the cry once again went out to leave the cannon behind. Fremont knew he was rapidly approaching California with its Mexican garrisons at Monterey and Benicia, and once again he insisted it be brought along. The main party, weary and short of rations, camped just north of what is now Bridgeport on January 25th and 26th. On the 27th, Fremont and an old mountain-man named Thomas "Broken Hand" Fitzpatrick moved up the Huntoon Valley to reconnoiter the route ahead. They passed through Devil's Gate, keeping Fales Hot Springs on their left. They tied their horses somewhere along Hot Creek and walked north up onto Burcham Flat, where they could look down upon the West Walker River. That river canyon to the north must have been a discouraging sight. Fremont and Fitzpatrick returned well after dark to find the main party now encamped near Devil's Gate. The expedition diaries are very good up to this point. Unfortunately, the route descriptions for the next two days are confusing and ambiguous.

View looking west towards Fales Hot Springs. We know Fremont's expedition passed this way on January 28, 1844, but from there the route taken is not clear.

Charles Preuss, the expedition's cartographer, brought the main party up the Huntoon Valley. His map shows their campsite on the 28th at what is now Tollhouse Flat on the west side of the West Walker River, about halfway through its canyon. This infers that the party forded the river at some point during the day of the 28th. The Preuss map shows their position on the night of the 29th to be in what is now the Antelope Valley. Fremont's diary, however, suggests the group did not cross the West Walker River after passing Fales Hot Springs, but rather turned north to camp somewhere north of Burcham Flat on the night of the 28th. Why the two accounts differ remains a mystery. Still others think that the expedition spent the night of January 28th near Grouse Meadows, on the west side high above the river.

Ferol Egan, a noted historian and Fremont biographer, has been out looking for the cannon without success. Based on the Preuss map, he thinks the expedition camped at Tollhouse Flat on the night of January 28th, and from there they tried to climb a 1500 foot ridge to the west, where the cannon was abandoned somewhere between the West Walker River and Mill Creek. That does not make sense to me, because if the party did reach Tollhouse Flat, the logical route would be to continue down the river.

Whatever the route taken, the deep snow drifts finally broke Fremont's will to struggle on with the cannon. Everyone agrees it was abandoned somewhere along the West Walker River country in what is now northwestern Mono County. Has the "lost" cannon ever been found? This aspect of the story is just as controversial as where it was abandoned.

Some say that the cannon was found during the Civil War by a Virginia City newsman, who then took it back home. This cannon later went to Lake Tahoe for guest appearances, and ultimately, in 1941, ended up at the Nevada State Museum where it is still on display today. The museum records are vague and ambiguous as to the origin of their acquisition, and there are interesting technical arguments whether the museum cannon could be the same one carried by Fremont's party.

A second story told is that the cannon was found by two prospectors in the early 1860s, with it eventually being recovered and moved to Virginia City as discouragement to local Southern sympathizers, of which there were many. After the Civil War, the cannon disappeared and reappeared a number of times, and as suggested in Irving Stone's book, *Men To Match My Mountains,* was finally sold for scrap during World War I and melted down. There are credible arguments against this scenario, too.

Still a third theory is that the cannon still lies out there, hidden in a willow thicket or aspen grove, just waiting to be found. I subscribe to this possibility, and with all due respect to Mr. Egan, my bet is that the Fremont party did not cross the river to camp at Chris Flat, Tollhouse Flat, Shingle Mill Flat or anywhere else. No mention is made in any of the writings of crossing the West Walker River. Further, I don't think they would have climbed 2000 feet to camp at Grouse Meadows on the night of the 28th. My guess is that Fremont moved north from Burcham Flat, onto the high wide shelf above the east bank of the river. Travel here in deep snows would be easier than down in the river canyon below. However, reaching the defile of Deep Creek that stretched across their path was the final straw. The cannon might well have been abandoned there.

This is an interesting story you say, but what does all this have to do with High Sierra SUV Trails? Well, dear reader, that cannon may still be out there somewhere just waiting for some enterprising four-wheeler to find it. If it lay out in the open on some sage-covered flat, it would have been found years ago, even though the wooden gun carriage would have likely rotted away. But if it had been abandoned while trying to cross Deep Creek ravine, for example, it could lie in the stream bottom and be quickly overgrown with aspen and willows and thus hidden forever. The barrel was made of brass, or bronze if a Boston-made copy, was 37 inches long, and weighed 225 pounds. It should survive the 150+ years since its abandonment, although months of tedious exploration with a metal detector might be required to find it. But where should you start looking?

View of Lost Cannon Peak from the West Walker River.

If you agree with my theory and want to look for yourself, go north out of Bridgeport on Highway 395 through Huntoon Valley, through Devil's Gate and past Fales Hot Springs. Just before reaching the U.S. Forest Service's Wheeler Guard Station, a good graded road turns north off the highway, double backs to the east on the north side of the creek and then turns north again. This is Forest Road 031. It eventually rejoins Highway 395 in the Antelope Valley. The expedition had already abandoned the cannon before reaching Antelope Valley, so if it was abandoned on the east side of the river, the location would be somewhere near Forest Road 031.

Proceed north across the vast expanse of Burcham Flat. Burcham Creek is crossed and this is one place where Fremont's cannon could lie. There is a Class II road off to the left going down the creek a ways. This is the first area that should be carefully checked. Search Burcham Creek for a mile on either side of Forest Road 031. Keep in mind that this is sheep country, where thousands of animals are sheared each spring. Basque shepherds have wandered these hills for more than a century. If Fremont's cannon were easy to find, it would have been found already.

Once the Burcham Creek drainage is checked to your satisfaction, continue north up the graded road. At a point 4.1 miles from Highway 395, an 8066-foot high point is reached. Here a Class II road goes east to Lava Springs and on to Lobdell Lake and points north. Don't take this side road, but carefully search the country on the east side of the graded road as it descends into the Deep

Creek Drainage. At a point 2.4 miles beyond the summit, a side road goes east to Cottonwood Meadows at an elevation of 7,200 feet. This side road provides access to Deep Creek. It is in the two or three miles above or below Cottonwood Meadows that Fremont's Cannon could lie buried or hidden, just waiting to be discovered.

In the unlikely event that you do find the old fieldpiece, your troubles could be just beginning if you try to take it home. Just the act of attempting to recover the cannon will run you afoul of the law. The find should be reported at the Bridgeport Ranger Station. Otherwise some United States Attorney may choose to prosecute you under the Code of Federal Regulations for violation of *National Antiquities Act of 1906* and the *Archaeological Resources Act of 1979.*

So is the search worth the effort if you can't keep the gun? It certainly is! The finding of that old cannon would answer a lot of questions that have been puzzling historians for over 150 years. Good luck!

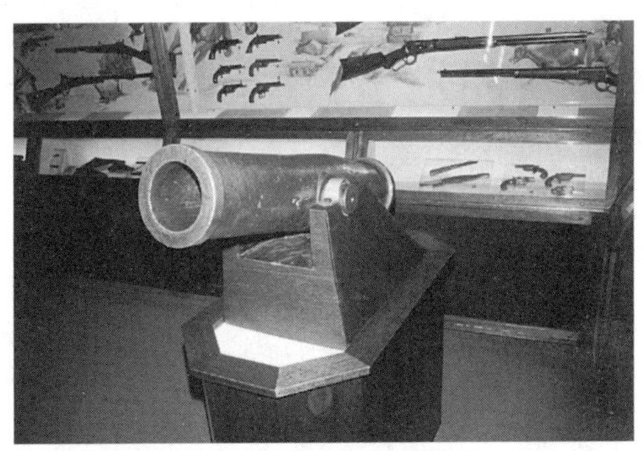

Fremont's mountain howitzer is believed to look very similar to this one on display at the Nevada State Museum in Carson City.

Fremont's cannon might also look like this one on display at the Ordnance Museum at the Army's Aberdeen Proving Ground in Maryland.

20

The Tamarack Trail

Primary Attraction:	This backroad provides easy access to remote Tamarack and Hunewell Lakes with great views of the Bridgeport Valley.
Time Required:	This is a half-day driving excursion out of Bridgeport (add another half day to hike into Tamarack Lake).
Miles Involved:	It is fifteen miles from Bridgeport to the end of the jeep trail.
Degree of Difficulty:	The way is over mostly good roads, except the last 1.5 miles, which are Class III.

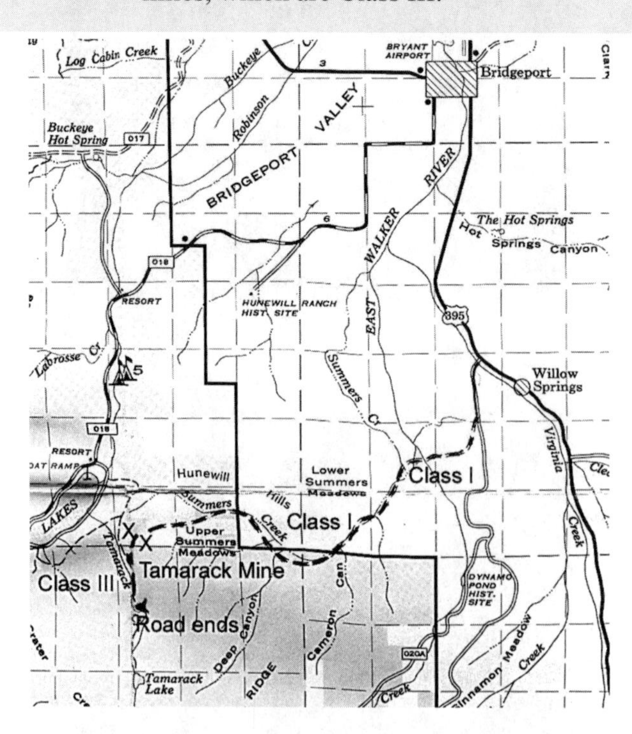

The significant feature of the Tamarack Trail is that it provides relatively easy hiking trail access to two of the Sierra Nevada's most forgotten, and little-fished lakes. With the publication of this guide, that secret is now out of the bag.

To find the Tamarack Lake trailhead, take U.S. Highway 395 to a point 4.4 miles south of Bridgeport. Turn right onto the high standard Green Creek Road, which is also known as Forest Road 142. An intersection is reached after a mile; take the right fork. (The left fork goes on to the site of old Munckton and the Dunderberg Mill, described in Excursion #21.) By turning right, our wide graded dirt road heads off to the southwest, soon crossing Green Creek and passing Lower Summers Meadow. Before long Toiyabe National Forest is entered as the road circles south around a volcanic crater, one of several in the Hunewill Hills.

At a point nearly eight miles off Highway 395, the road deteriorates a little, from graded dirt to Class I. After another quarter mile there are two side roads to the left. These enter private property, the site of the old Tamarack mine camp. Ore from the workings higher up on the hillside was hauled down to here, where it was crushed in a five-stamp mill and processed. The history of the mine remains forgotten by all but a few, but the inscription on the stamp mill housing reads "Prescott Scott & Co., Union Foundry, San Francisco, 1879." **Please respect the private property and obey any *No Trespassing* signs that may be posted.**

The five stamp mill of the Tamarack Mine.

Keep to the right on public lands. The road has now greatly deteriorated to an easy Class III. A tin shack on the right soon marks one of the many Tamarack Mine workings. Two tunnels here have collapsed, but several small piles of ore remain on the tailings dump. From the dump, there is a fine view north, down into Summers Meadow and into the Bridgeport Valley beyond.

The Class III road climbs through patches of aspen to briefly enter the lodgepole pine forest. Once out on the other side of the forest, it climbs steeply up the sage-covered hillside to end on an open knoll with great vistas of the Sierra crest to the west and the Bridgeport Valley to the north. The elevation here is about 8,600 feet. Nice, but waterless, campsites can be found in the lodgepole forest adjoining the viewpoint.

The lower road

The upper road

While the jeep trail ends here, it is a relatively easy walk of a couple of miles, following Tamarack Creek upstream to 9600' Tamarack Lake. Fishing here can be quite good. There are three lakes in this glacial cirque, of which Tamarack is the lowest and the largest. The hiking trail continues for another mile to climb 500 feet higher to Hunewill Lake. The glacial moraines creating these lakes were left in the Tioga phase of the Wisconsin glaciation, some 18,000 to 20,000 years ago. Snow banks in the shady headwall of the cirque tend to last the entire summer.

21

Munckton Memories

Primary Attraction:	This excursion visits the site of a forgotten mining camp of yesteryear. If you visit the site in the fall, you will see some spectacular autumn colors.
Time Required:	This is a half-day outing from Bridgeport.
Miles Involved:	From downtown Bridgeport to downtown Munckton is only 14 miles.
Degree of Difficulty:	Most of the route is Class II or better, although there may be a few Class III moments near the end of the trail.

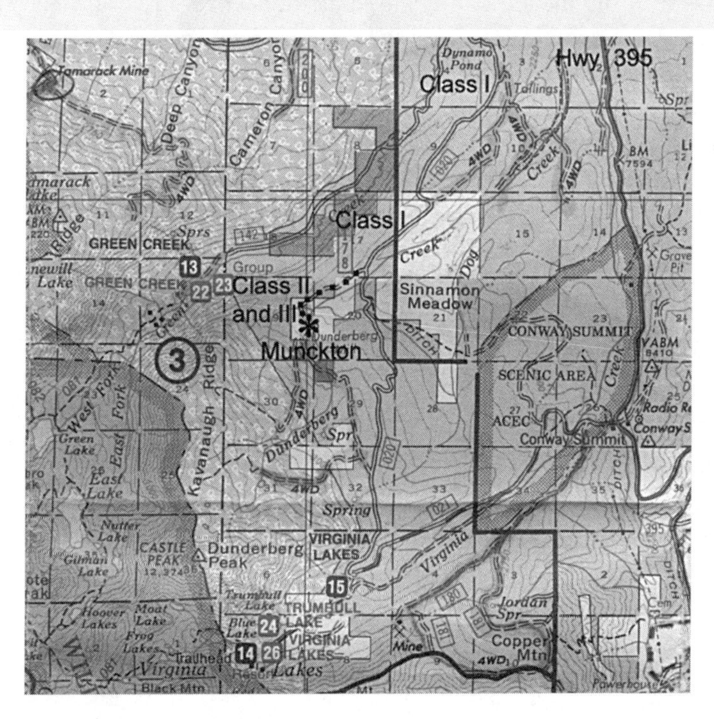

Included in a list of the more famous ghost towns of Mono County are Bodie, Benton, and Masonic; Munckton isn't. Indeed, even such chroniclers of old mining camps as Remi Nadeau and Nell Murbarger fail to mention the site. Ella

Cain, a writer of early Mono County, didn't mention it either. Another local historian, Emil Billeb, mentions Munckton's principal business, the Dunderberg Mill, but not the town. To many, Munckton isn't even a memory. If you have a couple of hours to spare, and want to put Munckton in your memory bank, fire up your Tin Lizzie and head south from Bridgeport.

Four and a half miles south of Bridgeport on Highway 395, the Green Creek Road turns off to the right. Your journey to Munckton begins here. After a mile, keep left at the fork in the road. (The right fork goes to the Tamarack Trail described previously in Excursion #20.) This wide graded dirt road tends to have a washboard surface, so try to find the speed that minimizes the vibrations. A second major intersection is reached after another 2.6 miles; again keep left. The right fork goes to Green Creek.

Continue on for 4.2 miles more to yet a third intersection. The main road, Forest Road 020, goes to the left. This time turn right onto Forest Road 178. Upper Sinnamon Meadow will be to your left. In slightly more than half a mile, the Class I road deteriorates to Class II or worse, as it encounters a mud hole at the upper end of the meadow. Engage your four-wheel drive, if necessary, and continue on. The road circles the meadow, passing a grove of aspen trees with the largest diameter trunks that I can recall ever seeing. Dunderberg Creek is soon forded and the site of Munckton is but a half mile ahead.

Watch the sage carefully for a set of wheel tracks crossing the road. To your left is a low pile of badly deteriorating brick, rusting metal, and other debris. This is the site of the second Dunderberg Mill. One hundred and thirty years ago, the streets of downtown Munckton were a hundred yards ahead and to the right.

The year was 1867 when Charles Snyder followed the gold-bearing placer gravels of Dogtown Creek up onto the eastern slope of Kavanaugh Ridge. Here he found quartz veins that were the source of the yellow treasure. Eventually, Snyder's find would be known as the Dunderberg Mine. Snyder dug a forty foot shaft from which he hauled three tons of ore by wagon to distant Aurora for milling. He was rewarded $150 for his efforts. That was nothing great, but enough to warrant further exploration. Wishing to protect his claims, Snyder and others formed the Castle Peak Mining District in July of 1867. The District was named after a nearby 12,374' peak. (The name Castle Peak was changed to "Dunderberg Peak" in 1878 by the Wheeler Survey team, because the name Castle Peak was in use elsewhere.) As the word got out, others were attracted to the area, and more mines were developed. Eventually a small mining camp grew above Upper Sinnamon Meadow.

Dr. George Munckton, a successful druggist and mining investor from Carson City, noticed the activity. Munckton had made a fortune in a strike at Aurora and was looking for another rich mine. He formed a syndicate, the Munckton Gold

& Silver Mining Company, and bought the Dunderberg Mine. Stock was sold and the money was put into the mine, which was in full swing by 1870. The fledgling mining camp that developed nearby carried Munckton's name. Streets were laid out, buildings were erected, and by 1871 there were sufficient people in town to justify a post office. The camp had the usual amenities of western mining camps: competing saloons, a general store, an assay office, a feed store and livery stable, and of course, a drug store. The largest structure in town was a two-story wooden boarding house.

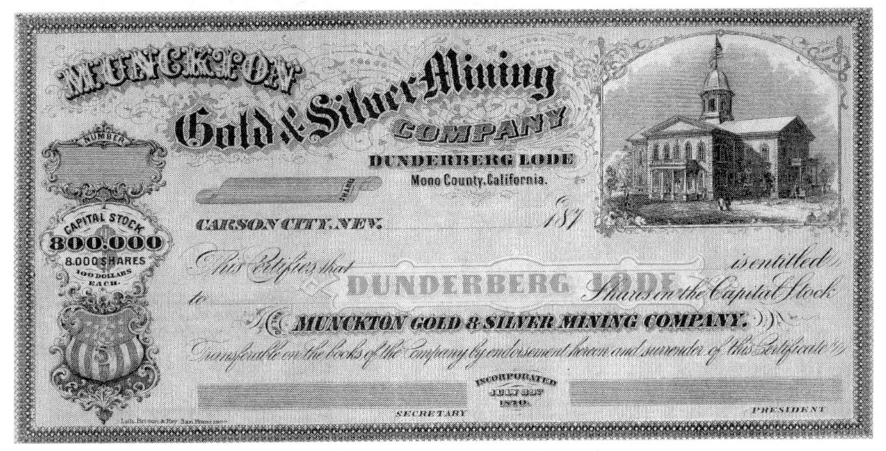

George Munckton sold shares in his new company for $100 per share, a tidy sum in 1870.

By 1872, the Munckton Mine's main tunnel was over six hundred feet long, and crosscuts to either side tapped into the vein. A large ten-stamp mill had been erected nearby to handle the ore, but the high sulfide content of the rock made processing difficult. The cycle of birth to boom to bust at Munckton was a short one. People began to drift away, and the post office closed later in 1872.

In 1878 after being idle for six years, new operators re-opened the Dunderberg Mine, and once again the continuous pounding of the stamp mill resonated across Sinnamon Meadow. The revival lasted barely two years before the stamps ceased their dropping once again. This time, the mill was sold, dismantled, and carried off for use in Bodie.

In 1891 a British syndicate bought the Dunderberg Mine and refurbished its aging timbers. In 1896, a mill was brought in from Silver Mountain near Markleeville. A cyanide and chlorination plant was added to the Dunderberg Mill to enhance the gold recovery. It would be three years before the mill processed its first ton of ore. Litigation stopped further production until 1899.

The operators wanted to operate the mine on a year-around basis to make up for lost time. But deep winter snows caused problems in getting the ore from the tunnel portal down to the mill some five hundred feet away. The response to this problem was to build an elevated trestle with a covered roof, so that ore cars could be moved on rail from the working face right down to the mill. The idea worked, but other factors still closed the mine during the winter months.

By 1900 fifty men were employed. Working conditions in the Dunderberg Mine were tough. Work was conducted by candlelight. At an elevation of 8500 feet the air was rare and the miners tired easily over the course of their twelve hour shift. Water was another serious problem in the underground workings. Streams of cold water constantly poured out of cracks in the rock onto the miners, who had to be clothed in thick rubber suits. If all this was not enough, paydays were sometimes missed. It was not the ideal working environment!

The mine closed in December of 1903, with plans to dig another tunnel from the Green Creek side in the spring. This would hopefully drain the excess water. The expense was great, however, and those plans never materialized. The deathblow occurred a year later when the second mill burned to the ground.

Barely any trace of Munckton remains today. The buildings are long gone, and even the streets have been reclaimed by sage and aspen. The once great Dunderberg Mill has been reduced to a low pile of crumbling orange bricks where the boiler once stood. Elsewhere a few burned timbers protrude from their foundations. The sole wooden building that survived the fire has collapsed under the weight of winter snows.

Only well-weathered wood and brick mark the spot of the Dunderberg Mill.

The portal to the Dunderberg Mine can be found by following the faint roadway from the millsite, west into the aspen grove a few hundred yards, and then by taking a side road left. The tunnel portal has collapsed and only traces of the timbers supporting the elevated tramway remain embedded in the tailings dump. Beyond the mine, a Class III road climbs the relatively gentle east side of Kavanaugh Ridge to some smaller mine sites well above 10,000 feet. If you return to the mill site, you can turn right and follow the Class III road to the south, where it climbs five hundred feet to cross a low ridge, eventually rejoining Forest Road 020 at a point 1.3 miles south of the paved Virginia Lakes Road.

The Dunderberg Mine in the early 1930s
(Photo courtesy Laws Railroad Museum)

Mono Basin Visitor Center

The Mono Lake Historical Society has restored an old school house and turned it into a museum.

Chapter VI
Trails Out of Lee Vining
(Inyo National Forest)

It is said that Leroy Vining took the old Indian trail over Mono Pass in 1853, searching for riches on the eastern side of the Sierra. While history doesn't record what he did for the next decade, we do know that in 1863 he was operating a small sawmill in a canyon west of Mono Lake, which became known as Vining's Gulch. His timber went by wagon to the mines of Aurora, many miles to the north. The present day community of Lee Vining gets its name from this pioneer lumberman.

Today's Lee Vining has a population of only a few hundred people, who largely depend on tourist traffic along U.S. Highway 395 and Highway 120, Yosemite's Tioga Pass Road. The town offers half a dozen motels, several places to eat, a general store and sporting goods shop, and several service stations. Nearby in lower Lee Vining Canyon, Mono County operates several campgrounds where a modest fee is charged.

Lee Vining has been synonymous with the fight to prevent Mono Lake from drying up as the City of Los Angeles diverted the streams flowing into it. Thanks largely to the untiring efforts of one local resident, David Gaines, together with his supporters from all over the world, an agreement to curb water diversions was eventually reached with the city. Once again the lake level is slowly rising. Anyone going through Lee Vining should certainly stop at the U.S. Forest Service's Mono Lake Visitor Center just north of town, to see and hear the story of the Mono Lake country. The films and displays are excellent. Here, too, you can obtain current information about local jeep trails and other forest information. It will be an hour well spent.

Downtown Lee Vining

22

High on Copper Mountain

Primary Attraction:	This road has spectacular views down on the Mono Lake basin, as well as a unique perspective on Lundy Lake and the high country behind it.
Time Required:	This excursion can be done in two or three hours from Lee Vining.
Miles Involved:	The entire loop from Conway Summit and return is less than ten miles, 25 miles round trip from Lee Vining.
Degree of Difficulty:	The dirt road portions of the route are generally Class II and III.

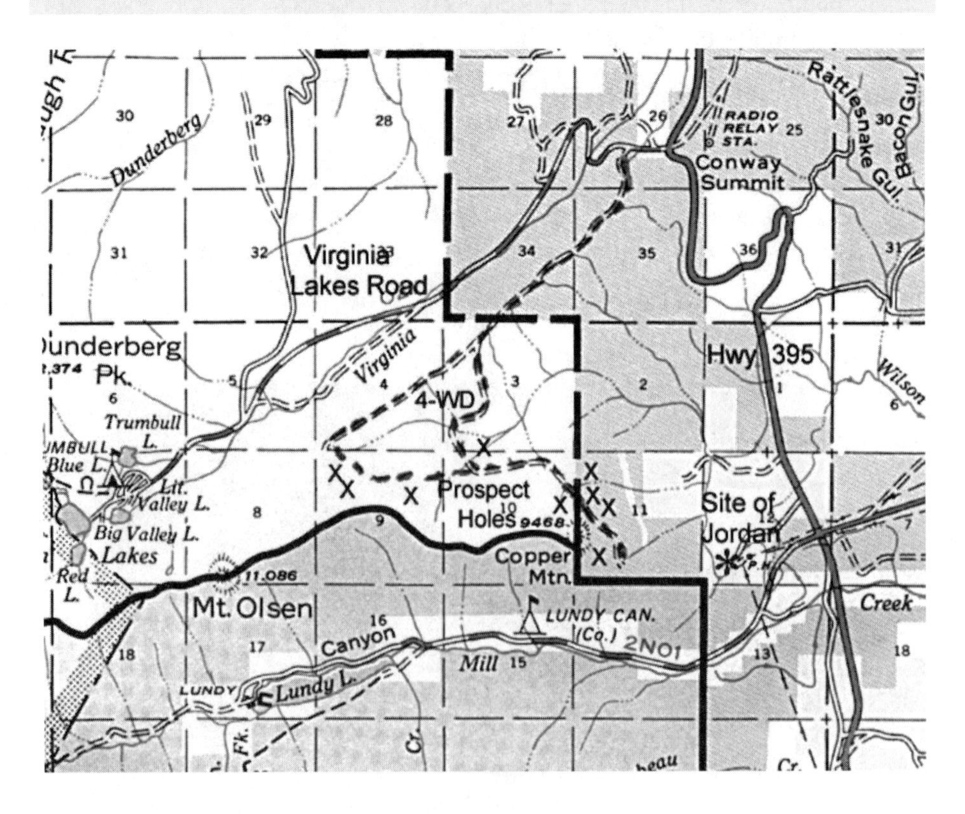

For years mining men have looked up at the heavily mineralized rocks of Copper Mountain, wondering if perhaps their fortunes might be waiting for them there. Many holes have penetrated the barren hillsides, but if great wealth is ever to be made on Copper Mountain, it has yet to happen. The Jordan Mining District, of which Copper Mountain is a part, was established in 1879. The District is said to have produced a million dollars from its placer mines at Dogtown and Monoville, but relatively little from its lode mines. Mono County pioneer, Emil Billib, says that in 1896 the Goleta Consolidated Mining Company built an enormous forty-stamp mill at the base of Copper Mountain, and operated it with water brought in by a three-mile long ditch from Mill Creek. A smelter was also built at the site, marked today by a pile of jet-black slag. Another pioneer of the area, Margaret Calhoun, said the small community which sprang up around the mill was originally called “Copper Mountain”, but the name later changed to “Jordan” after a post office was established. She says in its heyday Jordan had two saloons, two general stores, and a blacksmith’s workshop. The mining venture failed and by 1900 people began to relocate elsewhere. Fortunately, minerals are not the only riches the mountain has to offer. For those who like to get out and explore backroads, the mountain offers great scenery and magnificent views.

The mines of Copper Mountain are easily reached from Conway Summit off U.S. Highway 395 approximately half way between Lee Vining and Bridgeport. Turn west on the Virginia Lakes Road, then immediately after passing the café and two houses, look for a dirt road going off to the left. This is a mere 0.1-mile from Highway 395; turn left here. The Class III road gradually climbs a brush-covered hillside passing several side roads. Continue on the main road 1.8 miles to where the road forks; keep to the left. The road crosses a small stream and after another 1.9 miles forks again. You will want to take the right fork this time, but stop a minute. From your vantage point on this windswept ridge, there is a great view of Mono Lake, some 2,700 feet below.

During the Plio-Pleistocene Ice Age, melt water from the mighty glaciers coming out of Lundy, Lee Vining, and Parker Canyons filled the Mono Basin with water, creating ancient Lake Russell. At its peak, the lake was up 750 feet deep and covered some 267 square miles. It extended to the northeast into what is Nevada today. The overflow from Lake Russell went south into Adobe Valley, where it created a smaller lake covering only twenty square miles to a depth of 75 feet. The overflow from Adobe Lake went down into the Owens River and points south, and then to the east, ultimately reaching ancient Lake Manly in Death Valley.

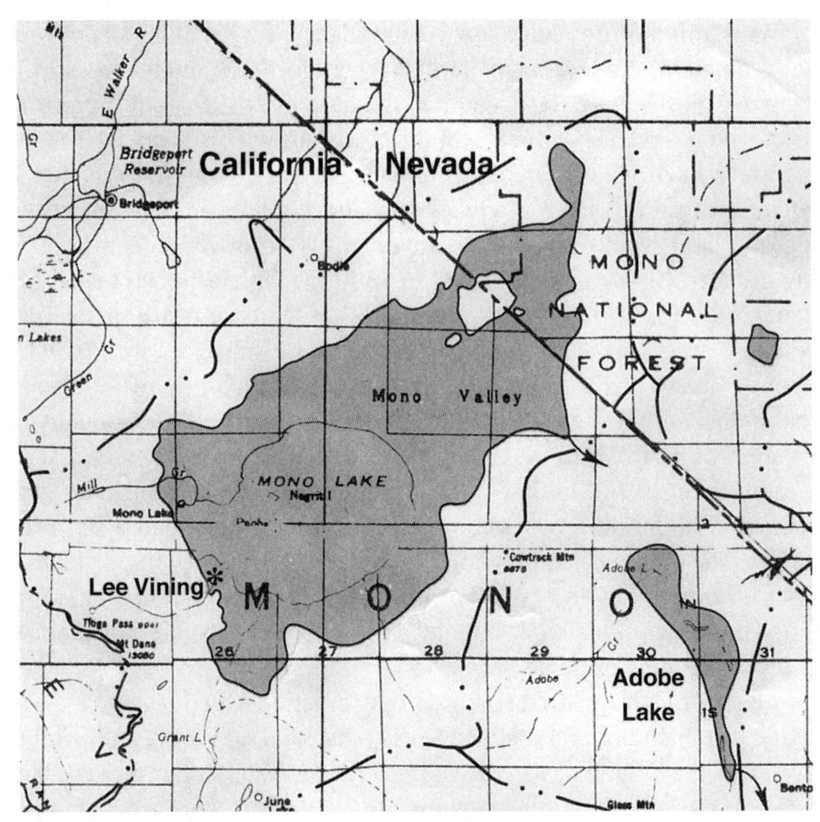

During peak periods of the Plio-Pleistocene Ice Age, Mono Lake was several times larger than it is today. There were also smaller lakes in Adobe Valley east of Lee Vining and in the basin occupied by Lake Crowley. (Map after Snyder, Hardman and Zdenek, 1964)

Today Mono Lake is just a fraction of its original size. Since the time when the last of the glaciers melted, about 15,000 years ago, Mono Lake has had no outlet. As a result of thousands of years of evaporation, the minerals in the water have become more and more concentrated, to the point where the water today is four times saltier than the oceans. Now the lake is so salty that only brine shrimp survive in the tepid water. The concentric rings surrounding the lake clearly indicate the ancient shoreline. Off in the distance, two islands rise from the water's placid surface. The nearest one, black in color, is Negit Island. Negit is a Paiute Indian word meaning "blue-winged goose" (possibly referring to the great quantity of California gulls which occupy the island every summer). The other island is Paoha Island, an obvious volcanic cinder cone. Paoha is the Indian name for "spirits with long wavy hair" (as might be seen rising over hot springs).

In his marvelous book *Roughing It*, author Mark Twain (whose real name was Samuel Clements) tells the story of how early one fine summer day in 1862 he and his friend Cal Higbie rowed a boat twelve miles out to Paoha Island. The lake was smooth as glass that morning. Their series of misadventures began, however, when they ran out of drinking water and could find none on the island. While they were off searching for water, the wind came up and blew their boat out into the lake. With great difficulty they retrieved it, and then barely made it back to the mainland, with the wind driven waves threatening to capsize and sink their tiny rowboat. Clements was prone to exaggeration and never let the truth get in the way of a good story; however, there could be an element of truth to this tale. Many times I have seen Mono Lake look calm and peaceful in the morning and turn into an ugly, churning sea of whitecaps by mid-afternoon. Clements wrote:

There are only two seasons in the region around Mono Lake-and they are, the breaking up of one winter and the beginning of the next!

For more information about the Mono Lake and its basin, be sure and stop at the Forest Service Visitor Center in Lee Vining. There are short films shown regularly and occasional ranger-led nature walks in the summertime.

From this lofty perch on Copper Mountain, if you look carefully at the flat below, north of the road to Lundy Lake and just west of the new powerhouse, you might see some concrete foundations and huge steel pipes hidden among the sage. This was the site of Jordan and the old Mill Creek Power Plant. At 12:01 a.m. on March 7th, 1911, suddenly and without warning, the deep snow on the eastern face of Copper Mountain gave way, sliding down the mountainside at tremendous speed. There were eight people asleep in that power plant when the avalanche struck. Seven would never know what hit them. A woman and her dog would miraculously survive. The avalanche left a path of destruction a mile long and a half-mile wide. Generators and other machinery were torn from their foundations and moved five hundred feet down-slope. If you have the time after you descend from Copper Mountain, take the dirt road west, which leaves U.S. Highway 395 at a point 0.7 miles north of State Route 167 to Hawthorne. It will take you to the seven victims' graves on the site of the old Mattley Ranch; then the Class II road swings south to the ruins where the disaster occurred (see Excursion #23).

Standing on this ridge, you will see two roads going left down the eastern face of the mountain. These roads descend to numerous prospect holes and drilling sites, where mining companies have been exploring for ore bodies. The copper minerals malachite, azurite, chrysocolla, and cuprite are found here along a contact zone between limestone and a granite-porphyry. In order for it to be economically feasible to mine copper, however, the metal must be highly concentrated and there must be lots of it. Alas, the deposits of Copper Mountain did not meet either criterion. Little actual mineral production has ever been taken place here.

Keep right on the third branch, which climbs the backside of Copper Mountain. The Class II route goes almost over the mountain's 9,468' summit. Within a half-mile is yet another fork. The left fork dead-ends after 0.4 miles, but from here there is a grand view of the Sierra crest. You can look up Lundy Canyon for a seldom seen perspective of Lundy Lake. Between 1879 and 1898 the rowdy mining camp of Lundy was situated at the upper end of the lake. Notice, too, the "U" shape of the canyon, so typical of glaciated valleys.

For a unique view of Lundy Lake drive up onto Copper Mountain.

By turning right at the last fork, you can continue up the ridge. The road deteriorates to Class III in places. The jeep trail briefly enters the limber pine forest and then crosses a bump on the ridge at an elevation of 9,738 feet. Another fork is reached. Keep right and drop to the flat; the road suddenly gets better. Here you can turn left and explore an old mining prospect some 0.3 miles beyond, or turn right and return to Conway Summit which is only three miles away.

23

The Disaster at Jordan

Primary Attraction:	This backroad excursion takes us back into history to a little known and long-forgotten natural disaster.
Time Required:	This entire loop can be done in one hour.
Miles Involved:	The dirt road portion of the route begins seven miles north of Lee Vining and is only three miles long.
Degree of Difficulty:	The road is generally no worse than Class II.

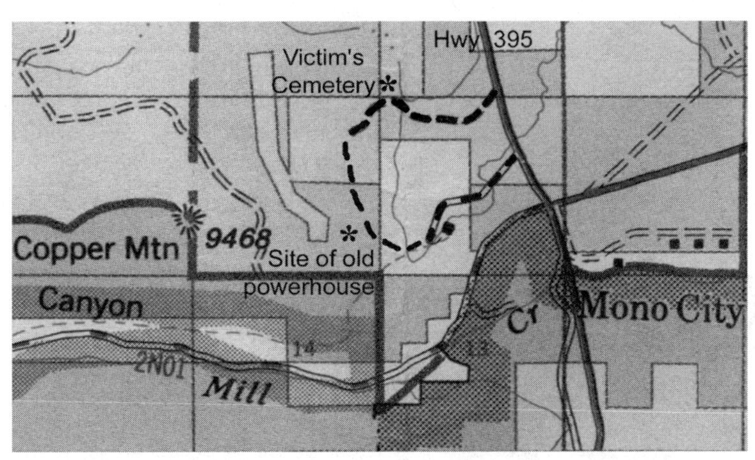

Any mention of Copper Mountain would be incomplete without retelling the story of the great avalanche of March 7, 1911. For the most part the site of the tragedy is forgotten, even by locals, and very few visit the spot today. Yet only a mile away lies busy U.S. Highway 395, traveled by hundreds of thousands of motorists each year. Perhaps more would stop if they knew, but the story of the Copper Mountain avalanche remains one of those brief moments in the history of the west that historians think is too insignificant to mention. For the dedicated off-road explorer, however, such a place is worthy of our attention.

It had been a bad winter, that winter of 1910-11. Record amounts of snow had been falling in the Sierra since December. On March 7th, an avalanche in Silverado Canyon crushed stables and a boarding house that fortunately had been vacated for the winter. In the town of Lundy, two avalanches struck, but again nobody happened to be in the buildings that were hit. A miner named Smith, in the camp of Masonic, was not so lucky; he was killed in a snow slide.

It was a dark and stormy night on a flat below 9468' Copper Mountain. It was well below freezing outside, but it was warm and cozy inside the Mill Creek Power Plant, where the turbines and generators hummed a steady tune. The man standing the night watch over the dials and gauges of the plant's main switchboard may have thrown another log in the stove, as he contemplated the raging blizzard outside. In other nearby structures, seven others slumbered in their beds, unaware of the terrible event about to happen.

Thus it was at 12:01 a.m. on March 7, 1911, when suddenly and without warning an estimated four million tons of snow, perched high on the eastern face of Copper Mountain, gave way under its own weight. An avalanche nearly a quarter of a mile wide came rushing down the steep mountainside and onto the flat below. The Mill Creek Power Plant and the small community of Jordan, with their sleeping inhabitants, were right in the path. There would be seven who never knew what hit them, but miraculously one woman would survive along with her dog.

The outside world did not immediately realize the enormity of the disaster. True, the electric lights in Bodie, Aurora, and Lucky Boy suddenly went out at 12:01 a.m., but that could simply be a line down anywhere in that lonely California-Nevada border country. The telephone lines had already broken under the weight of snow and ice, so it was reasonable to conclude that the power lines were down as well. As dawn tried to break through the wintry storm clouds, the snow continued to fall. Visibility was poor and the disaster would not be discovered for some hours to come. It was not until the storm abated and a nearby rancher walked over to Jordan on snowshoes that the disaster was discovered. Where there once had been four cottages and a power plant, nothing remained but chaos, a trail of debris enclosed in a jumbled mass of snow. The avalanche left a path of destruction a mile long and a half-mile wide. Generators and other powerhouse machinery, weighing tons, were torn from their concrete foundations and shoved five hundred feet down-slope.

Upon discovery, the word for help went out and soon rescue teams arrived on skis and snowshoes. The Conway and Mattley Ranches served as headquarters for the search operations, keeping the men supplied with plenty of food and hot coffee as they probed the snow in sub-freezing temperatures. One frozen body was found, and then another. Before long, the worst was feared, as hope faded.

It was a dog's whimper that gave rescue crews renewed hope. Digging frantically through the splintered wood which had once been cabin #1, they found a large steamer trunk was partially supporting a section of wall which had fallen over on a bed. Beneath the wall, in the bed, was the body of R.H. Mason.

Next to him were his wife Agnes and their dog, both miraculously alive thanks to that steamer trunk. After being extricated from the wreckage, Mrs. Mason was quickly transported by toboggan to nearby Conway Ranch, and from there to the hospital in Bodie. She eventually lost a leg due to gangrene, but otherwise made a full recovery.

When all were located, the remains of the seven victims were transported to the Mattley Ranch, where they were stored in an unheated shed for a few weeks until the roads reopened and coffins could be brought in. The task of digging the graves was a slow process, because the ground was frozen solid. Finally, a priest came and the seven were given a proper burial, with people from all over Mono County attending. The Mattley Ranch is long gone, its site marked only by the bleached skeletons of cottonwood trees. The seven graves remain, however, on a lonely hillside overlooking the scene of the disaster.

To find the site of Jordan and the old Mill Creek Powerhouse, take Highway 395 north out of Lee Vining. At a point 6.6 miles north of Lee Vining (just 0.3 miles beyond the road to Lundy Canyon), turn left at the sign pointing to the Mill Creek Powerhouse. Follow this road 0.7 miles west to the "new powerhouse", rebuilt on higher ground and now operated by the Southern California Edison Company. Just before reaching the gate in the fenced enclosure, keep right on a Class II road that takes you past the modern facility. After only 0.3 miles this road will swing to the north. Within a tenth of a mile you will see concrete building foundations on either side of the road. These and a rusty section of penstock are all that remain from that tragic midnight so many years ago.

Only concrete foundations and rusting pipe mark the site of the old Mill Creek Powerhouse.

The Class II road continues north, following the remains of the old "Mono Ditch" which diverted water from Mill Creek over to the placer mines of Monoville. The road forks after only 0.8 miles. The left fork is a Class III road up to a mine in the canyon a half-mile away. Keep right, making a sharp turn to the east. From here, these two tracks through the sage take you back to Highway 395 in less than a mile. Before returning to the present, however, stop at the small cemetery surrounded by a low wire fence. Here the avalanche victims rest in peace.

Jordan's victims rest here.

24

Beartrack Canyon

Primary Attraction:	Spectacular views of the Mono Lake country, with a good illustration of forest transition zones.
Time Required:	This loop can be done in two or three hours out of Lee Vining.
Miles Involved:	It is less than seven miles from downtown Lee Vining to the end of the road at the Log Cabin Mine gate.
Degree of Difficulty:	While the roads are steep, they are generally no worse than Class II.

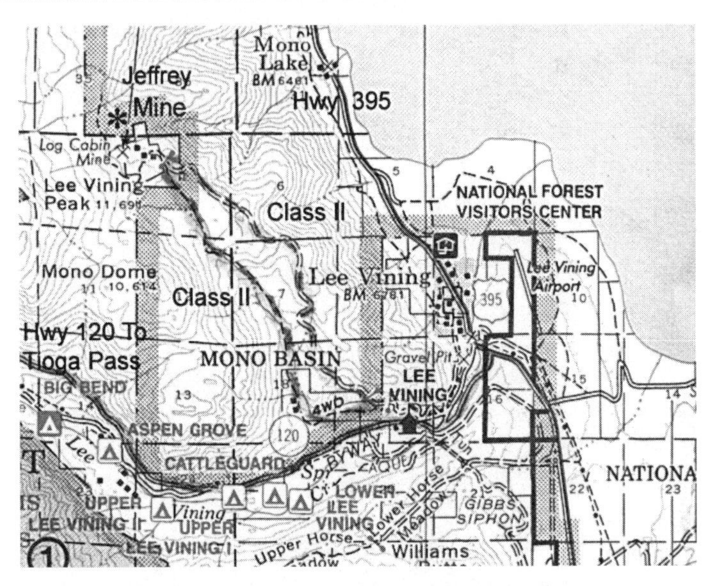

Like the backroad to Sonora Pass, Beartrack Canyon is one of those little known side roads in the High Sierra that cannot technically be considered a jeep trail. In spite of the steep grades and sometimes-poor traction, it is generally no worse than Class II. Four-wheel drive should not be absolutely necessary, although high clearance vehicles are certainly recommended. I have included the route description in this guide because the scenery is outstanding, and I would hate for any dedicated backroad explorer to miss it. The entire round trip loop of twelve miles out of Lee Vining can be easily done in half a day. This outing can be combined with the Copper Mountain trip for a full day of high altitude touring.

The road begins at the mouth of Lee Vining Canyon off the Tioga Pass Road. From downtown Lee Vining, go south on U.S. Highway 395 for 0.8 miles. Here you will want to turn right onto Highway 120. Go up the Tioga Pass Road 1.3 miles, where a sign points to the road on the right. This is across from the complex of buildings that make up the Lee Vining Ranger Station.

The wide graded road begins to climb the canyon wall to the north. In a half-mile, look for Forest Road 1N03 going off to the right; turn here on this narrow Class I road. In a tenth of a mile it will circle around the lower end of the lateral moraine and soon will climb above the moraine.

At the peak of the Plio-Pleistocene Ice Age, the glacier in Lee Vining Canyon was more than fourteen miles long. The sand and boulders pushed outward from the glacier's side left a long pile of gravel four hundred feet high above the ranger station. Curiously the lateral moraine on the south side of Lee Vining Canyon extends nearly a half-mile out from the canyon's mouth, but here on the north side of the canyon, the moraine comes to an abrupt stop just below the ranger station. Why aren't they the same length?

At a point a mile above Highway 120, the Piñon forest is left behind and soon you will enter a forest of pure Jeffrey pine. Stop for a moment and look around. From this vantage point, one gets a good view of those lateral moraines on both sides of the canyon. As you enter the tall trees, you have already climbed six hundred feet since leaving the highway.

The Jeffrey pine is a three-needle pine, just like its close cousin, the ponderosa or yellow pine. Indeed, many plant taxonomists have argued for years as to whether there was any real difference between the two, with the ultimate conclusion that the yellow pine, *Pinus ponderosa,* should be one species and the *Pinus jeffreyi* should be another. If you choose to do so, stop for a moment and stick your nose in the bark of the Jeffrey pine. You should get the faint odor of vanilla. You will be in this forest of Jeffrey pine for the next mile and a half.

If you stop and wander over to the ridge on the right, keep your eyes open where you are walking. It is not likely, but not impossible either, that you might come upon a piece of unexploded military ordnance. Because of the avalanche danger on the slopes above Lee Vining, bazooka-like, recoilless rifles are used to fire explosive charges into the snow above the town. **Not all of the projectiles exploded upon impact with the soft snow. If you should come upon such a shell, leave it alone, even if it is bent or distorted. Under no circumstances should you touch it.** Build a rock cairn ten or twenty feet away, note its location, and call 911 to report it when you get off the mountain. **It cannot be**

emphasized too strongly that these shells are nothing to fool around with.

As suddenly as you entered the Jeffrey pine forest you are out of it, and the scenery suddenly becomes noticeably drier and more austere. Desert mahogany, *Cercocarpus ledifolius*, a large shrub or a very short and stunted tree, replaces the tall timber. Three miles from the highway a short side road goes right to a communications site. This is the first of many spectacular viewpoints of the Mono Lake country to the east.

The road deteriorates to Class II as it begins to wind its way up a series of steep switchbacks where traction may not be the best. You may feel more comfortable engaging your front axle here and dropping into low range. At a point four miles from the highway, there are more great views to the east. Off on the distant horizon is the Excelsior Range on the California-Nevada Border. A little farther to the right and more distant are the mighty Boundary and Montgomery Peaks in the White Mountains. And at your feet, you can look down onto Mono Lake, where the receding shorelines of the last 12,000 years can clearly be seen. To the right a little is the chain of Mono Craters. Notice the one that looks like a castle with a moat around it. This small volcano collapsed in upon itself, and then a volcanic plug pushed up from the center. This is Panum or North Crater, the farthest north crater in this chain and one of the youngest. Turning to the south you can see the twin summits of Mounts Ritter and Banner and, to their left, Mammoth Mountain. If you needed a reason to come up here, this spectacular view is it.

High above Beartrack Canyon

The road continues upward, although not as steeply. Soon you will top out at the head of Beartrack Canyon onto a treeless flat area that is pockmarked with dozer trenches. Ahead at the edge of the limber pine forest is a solitary metal building, part of the Simpson or Log Cabin Mine complex. The road forks into three branches just before reaching this building. You have come only 5.1 miles since leaving Highway 120 far below, but you have climbed 2,500 feet. The elevation here is 9700 feet. The fork to the right goes 0.2 miles down through the trees to a locked gate. The Log Cabin Mine complex is another 0.2 miles beyond the gate. The Log Cabin Mine was said to have been first located in 1890, but it was Jim Simpson who acquired the mineral rights in 1910 and it has been known as the Simpson Mine ever since. In the 1930s a company in the State of Washington purchased the mine, and one summer they had some forty people working there. In 1939 the mine changed hands once again, but with the advent of World War II, President Roosevelt closed all of the nation's gold mines by Presidential Order. After the war more development work was done but little ore was produced. In her book *Pioneers of the Mono Basin,* author Margaret Calhoun repeats the speculation that more than a million dollars worth of gold has been produced here. I suspect the true production is something less. In a complicated three-way land swap, the U.S. Forest Service has recently acquired the mine, but they are not yet prepared for visitors. Please respect any *Keep Out* signs that may be posted.

The Simpson Mine

The middle fork goes a short distance to a Boy Scout Camp. This is private property; please respect it as such. A wide graded, but equally steep road, the left fork is an alternate route back down to Highway 120. It is the main road that you left just above the highway. This route stays in the canyon bottom and does not offer the vistas that you had coming up. The total round trip distance from Highway 120 utilizing both roads is only ten miles. But what a ten miles that is!

Chapter VII
Trails Out of Mammoth Lakes
(Inyo National Forest)

Mammoth Lakes is a popular resort area perhaps best known for its fine winter skiing. The community also attracts a lot of summer vacationers with its five lakes, miles of mountain trails, and other natural attractions.

Mammoth City began in 1877 when prospectors looking for the "Lost Cement Mine" found gold on what would become Mammoth Creek. In the following year the Mammoth Mine opened, as did a twenty stamp mill just down the road in nearby Mill City. In 1879 there were 1500 people in the triple camps of Mammoth City, Mill City, and Pine City, enough to justify the opening of a post office. In that year a second bank of twenty more stamps was added to the mill, as it processed ores from the Mammoth, Headlight, Monte Cristo, and Lisbon Mines. The future seemed rosy, but it was not to be. By 1881 the Mammoth Mine had produced some $200,000 in gold; however, the expenses to obtain and process the ore were greater than the net return. It closed, as did the other mines. By 1888 there were only a handful of people left in Mammoth City. Mill City and Pine City were completely abandoned and ceased to exist. The gold mined by today's citizenry in Mammoth Lakes comes from the tourists' pockets.

Summer visitors to Mammoth Lakes should certainly make their first stop at the Forest Service Visitor Center on Highway 203 as you enter town. There are not only attractive displays, but information can be obtained on what to see and do. The author recommends that any first time visitor walk through the earthquake fault, and visit Devil's Postpile National Monument. For the anglers, the possibilities are unlimited, not only in the five Mammoth Lakes, but also anywhere along the June Lake Loop just to the north, or in the creeks, rivers, and lakes just to the east along U.S. Highway 395. The outdoorsman can easily spend two weeks in the Mammoth area, doing something different each day.

Mammoth Lakes and the nearby communities offer a full range of basic services. Room accommodations are generally plentiful in the summer, and the U.S. Forest Service has nine campgrounds in the Mammoth Lakes area and a dozen more in nearby areas.

Mammoth Lakes got its start in the 1870s as a mining camp.

In the 1920s and 30s, Mammoth Lakes became a summer resort.
(Photo courtesy Laws Railroad Museum)

The Mammoth Lakes of today is a world class all-seasons resort.

25

Inyo Crater Lakes and Crater Flat

Primary Attraction:	This short outing includes an easy walk to Inyo Crater Lakes and a scenic drive across Crater Flat to see the interesting volcanic features along Deadman Creek.
Time Required:	This is a three hour round trip from downtown Mammoth Lakes, including the ¾ mile hike to Inyo Crater Lakes.
Miles Involved:	The complete loop, from downtown Mammoth Lakes and back again, is less than eighteen miles.
Degree of Difficulty:	The roads are generally no worse than Class II, and should be readily negotiable by any driver in a high clearance vehicle.

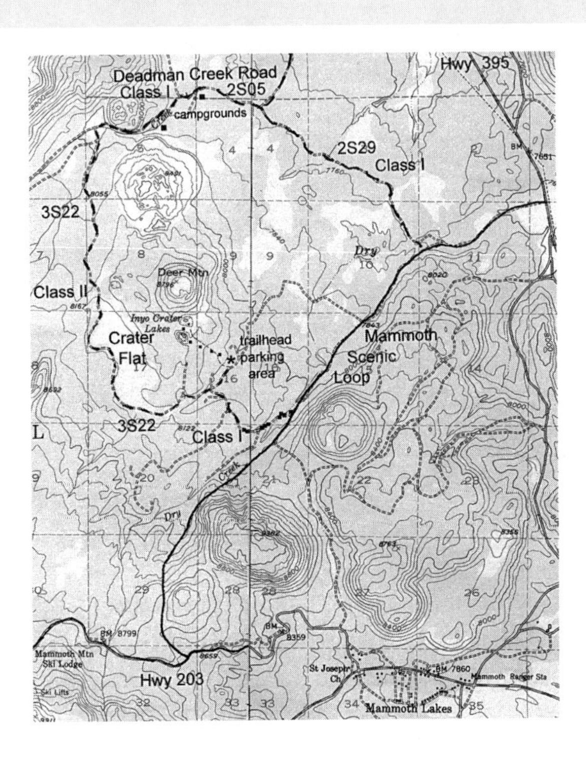

Hidden in the forest just north of the town of Mammoth Lakes are a number of interesting volcanic features accessible only by back roads. This excursion will introduce the reader to a few of those geologic wonders.

From the intersection of Main Street and Old Mammoth Road, go up Main Street (State Route 203) a mile to the traffic signal. Turn right here following Highway 203 in the direction of the ski lifts. After nearly another mile, turn right again onto a paved road euphemistically identified as "Mammoth Scenic Loop". (As scenic as the road may be, it was actually built as an alternative emergency escape route from the town of Mammoth Lakes, should volcanic or seismic activity ever close Highway 203. The village sits at the edge of a not so dormant volcano, with local earthquakes regularly reminding the residents of that fact.)

Proceed along the Scenic Loop for 2.7 miles to where a sign points left to the Inyo Craters. Note your odometer reading and turn left here onto the graded dirt road. The road forks after a quarter of a mile; stay to the right. The road forks again after another 0.4 miles; again stay right. Yet a third fork is encountered 0.3 miles beyond. For Crater Flat you will want to turn left here, but first a side trip right 0.7 mile takes you to the Inyo Crater Lakes trailhead. This is an easy and pleasant round trip walk of less than a mile through the forest. It is an hour well spent.

The Inyo Craters are a series of north-south trending volcanoes running from just north of the town of Mammoth Lakes northward to Wilson Butte just west of Highway 395. (The Mono Craters is an extension of that same line of volcanoes on the east side of Highway 395. This chain extends northward to Panum Crater on the south shore of Mono Lake.) Rhyolite began to ooze out along an eighteen-mile long crack in the earth's surface about 40,000 years ago, and has not stopped since then. In the last 2,000 years, at least thirty new vents have opened along the chain, spewing ash and cinders. About six hundred years ago, magma from a depth of five or six miles rose to only seven hundred feet below the surface before erupting. Ash was thrown high into the air, blanketing the surrounding countryside. Scientists, who have uncovered the remains of trees killed by this ash, can count the tree rings and accurately date the eruptions to about 1400 A.D.

At the southern end of the Inyo Craters chain are three explosion features, large holes blown out when the rising hot magma came in contact with ground water which flashed to steam, expanded rapidly and blew upwards, creating a crater. This event occurred around 1470 A.D. The resulting holes are still there today. While the crater on top of Deer Mountain takes a bit of a hike to see, two others are much more easily accessed by an easy quarter mile long trail. Both craters are about six hundred feet across. The northern most crater of the pair is one hundred feet deep, the southern crater about two hundred feet deep. Since the great steam explosions, the bottoms of the craters have filled with water; thus they are called the Inyo Crater Lakes. You anglers need not make the treacherous way to the bottom; they contain no fish.

South Inyo Crater Lake

North Inyo Crater Lake

Once you have had your fill of the lakes, return to the parking area and back-track the 0.7 miles to the intersection a mile in from the Scenic Loop Road. Turn right here onto Forest Road 3S22. This roadway is not nearly as good as the road to Inyo Crater Lakes, but it is no worse than Class II, and four-wheel drive should not be needed.

In a half-mile the road makes a sharp turn to the right and enters the vast expanse of Crater Flat. The soil here, such as it is, is largely Rhyolite ash and pumice that was thrown out of the various Inyo Craters during the late Pleistocene and into the Holocene. The U.S. Forest Service has posted signs requiring drivers to stay on the established roadway, but, of course, some irresponsible four-wheelers think those instructions are for other people, and they can spin donuts in the soft soil of the meadow. It is rogues like that who cause public land managers to close areas to all vehicle use. If you enjoy four-wheeling, follow the rules!

It is mindless acts of vandalism like this that cause areas to be completely closed to vehicle use. Follow the rules!

The Crater Flat is nearly a mile long. On the other side of the flat, the road enters the forest of lodgepole pine and continues to make its way north. Short side roads go off to the left and right occasionally, but simply continue north on 3S22. A mile and a quarter north of Crater Flat, a small stream is forded. This is a minor tributary to Deadman Creek, and is likely to be dry from mid-summer on. The ford should cause no problems.

Deadman Creek is reached 0.7 miles beyond the ford. This stream crossing should cause no problems either because the Forest Service has installed a sturdy concrete bridge. On the other side of the bridge Forest Road 3S22 comes to an end, as the Deadman Creek Road (Forest Road 3S26) is reached. This is a Class I road. If you turn left, the road will ascend Deadman Creek for a couple of miles, where it dead-ends. For our purposes, you will want to turn right.

The Deadman Creek Road soon passes through a narrow gap in the long chain of volcanoes that make up the Inyo Crater group. The volcanic mountain on the left is a type of rhyolite rock that came up from the bowels of the earth in Holocene times, only 6,000 years ago. In the ensuing years since its eruption, sufficient rock has broken down into soil to support tree growth.

The mountain to the right is known as the Deadman Dome. Its jagged rock outcrops have weathered very little and look much more fresh. Your perception is correct. Tree ring studies indicate this eruption occurred in the year 1433 A.D.

That is a mere nanosecond in geologic terms. At least two large exposures of shiny black obsidian can be seen among the jagged spires.

These volcanic eruptions must have terrified the indigenous Paiute Indians who spent their summers in this area. Nevertheless, when the earth belched, it provided a great resource for Native Americans. They harvested a bounty of volcanic glass, obsidian, which they fashioned into very effective arrowheads and scrapers. Not only was this mineral immediately useful, it was also a commodity which was easily transportable and thus used for trade goods with other tribes on the western side of the Sierra Nevada. In the 1950s archaeologist Margaret Hindes made a study of archaeological sites in the greater Huntington Lake area. She identified nearly three hundred sites in the region, most of which contained obsidian flakes and artifacts that came from the Mono Lake, Inyo Craters, and Glass Mountain areas. Indians from both sides of the Sierra Nevada would cross the crest via Mammoth Pass, Mono Pass, and Paiute Pass to trade with tribes from the other side. Those on the east side had obsidian, Piñon nuts, rabbit skin blankets, and rock salt to trade. Those on the western slope had acorn flour, seashells, manzanita berries and buckskin.

Continuing east on the Deadman Creek Road, two Forest Service campgrounds are soon reached. On the left is the Obsidian Flat Group Camp, and on the right side, on both sides of the creek, is the thirty unit Deadman Campground. At a point 0.4 miles east of the entrance to the Lower Deadman Campground, look for Forest Road 2S29 going off to the right. In 2.3 miles this Class I road will take you back to the paved Mammoth Scenic Loop Road. From there it is less than five miles back to Mammoth Lakes' Main Street.

There are other geologic points of interest to visit in the area north of Mammoth Lakes, accessible by the family car. There is the earthquake fault off Highway 203. It is an open crack in the earth's surface up to ten feet wide and sixty to seventy feet deep in places. At one time the Forest Service had a nature trail descending into the awesome crack, but the four major earthquakes of 6+ on the Richter Scale, occurring in May of 1980, caused them to close that portion. Visitors can now view the phenomenon only from the surface.

Another easily accessible geologic feature is Obsidian Dome, accessible by Forest Road 2S10 which goes west of Highway 395 at a point 0.3 miles north of Deadman Summit. Here, about 1400 A.D., a mass of molten rock pushed its way to the surface. The rock, rhyolite, was once quarried and sold under the trade name of "Featherock".

Obsidian can be found in great abundance along Glass and Deadman Creeks.

26

Deadman Pass

Primary Attraction:	This short outing offers spectacular views of Mammoth Mountain, the Minarets, and the volcanic field south of Mono Lake.
Time Required:	This is a one hour round trip from Minaret Vista, two hours round trip from downtown Mammoth Lakes.
Miles Involved:	The end of the trail is slightly over two miles from Minaret Vista.
Degree of Difficulty:	The road is generally no worse than Class II, but soft pumice makes a few places Class III.

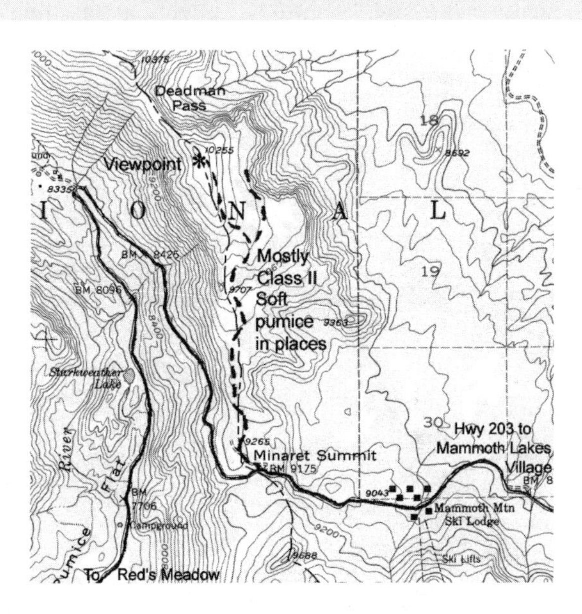

One of the shortest, but nevertheless, spectacular SUV trails in the Mammoth Lakes area is the jeep trail along the Sierra crest between Minaret Summit and Deadman Pass.

Our journey to this alpine wonderland begins in downtown Mammoth Lakes. Take State Route 203 from Mammoth Lakes Village five miles up to the Mammoth Mountain ski area. Because of the rain shadow effect, most ski resorts in the Sierra Nevada are situated on the western slope of the range, where they benefit from conditions of maximum snowfall. The Mammoth Mountain development can break this rule of nature, because of its close proximity to 9,200' foot Mammoth Pass where winter storm clouds can easily slip over the crest before dropping their moisture. Considering the fact that the Mammoth Mountain ski area is the only major ski development so far south in the Sierra Nevada, it gets a lot of snow.

The greatest snowfall that anyone can remember started on January 19, 1969, and continued for ten days thereafter. An unending series of storms came out of the Gulf of Alaska and pelted the mountain day after day. Three feet of snow would fall in a single night. The facilities were closed after a couple of days, because the chairlifts were no longer riding high above the snow. The snow was piled so high that two story A-frame cabins across the road from the chairlifts were completely buried. Many buildings suffered structural damage from the excessive weight of the snow. Fortunately these winters of extraordinary snowfall occur only once every decade or two. But even on a normal year, Mammoth Mountain receives sufficient snowfall that ski races are regularly scheduled over the July 4th holiday. When you pass this way in July or August, try to imagine what the scene looks like in January and February.

The author took this photo at Mammoth Mountain in May of 1969 just as parked vehicles buried in the snow since January were being discovered and dug out.

Continue past the ski resort another mile to Minaret Summit. Here a paved road turns right for a short distance to an attractive display put up by the U.S. Forest Service. The elevation here is 9175 feet. Markers at this vista point out the various features on the High Sierra skyline in a 180° arc to the west. There is also a self-guiding nature trail to acquaint the visitor with some of the natural history of this sub-alpine ridge.

Note your odometer reading as you turn right off of State Route 203 onto the Minaret Vista viewpoint road. Within two hundred feet an unmarked dirt road leads off to the right through the forest of lodgepole pine. Here many of the trees have trunks twisted and contorted by the weight of the winter snow. Simply follow the tire tracks and soon you will be heading north along the eastern side of the Sierra crest. The Class II road winds its way northward, alternating between forest and open pumice flats. Here and there may be a few Class III steep spots, where it is difficult to gain traction in the loose volcanic pumice. Nevertheless, the route is not difficult and even appeals to mountain bikers.

At a point 1.9 miles from the pavement, the jeep trail forks. The right fork dead-ends within a half-mile. Take the left fork that climbs the steep hillside. Once on top, the route again straddles the crest of the Sierra Nevada. Your left wheels are in the San Joaquin River watershed, while your right wheels are in the Owens River watershed. The snow and rainwater that fall on the western side of this ridge eventually end up in the San Joaquin Valley near Fresno, where they are used by agriculture to grow food and fiber. That which falls on the eastern side eventually flows into the Owens River, and then on to Los Angeles, where it is used to flush toilets. The views along this ridge are far better than those back at the Minaret Vista Viewpoint. Here nothing obstructs your vision for 360 degrees.

To the west is the dramatic skyline dominated by 13,157' Mt. Ritter. Immediately to the north of Ritter is 12,945' Banner Peak, and further north still is 12,311' Mt. Davis. To the south of Mt. Ritter are the saw-tooth spires of the Minarets. These high peaks to the west are not the light colored granite so typical in the Sierra. Instead, these are Mesozoic volcanics, about the same age as the Sierra granite, but formed in a very different way. Whereas the granite was formed deep within the earth and cooled slowly, these volcanics poured out onto the surface before cooling.

Looking down the San Joaquin River Valley past Agnew Meadow one can clearly see the scars left by the "Rainbow Fire", which was started by a lightning strike on August 20, 1992. The fire burned uncontained for ten days destroying 8,765 acres in the area west of Red's Meadows.

Farther to the south is also 11,053' Mammoth Mountain, with gondolas and ski lifts going to the very summit. Geologically, Mammoth Mountain is a volcano that consists of a series of at least ten lava flows. It sits on the southwestern edge of the Long Valley Caldera. Starting about 190,000 years ago, well after the Long Valley Caldera blew its top, lava began to ooze out of the earth here, a process that went on until about 50,000 years ago. Composed mostly of rhyolite and dacite, this volcano still shows some signs of life. About 10,000 years ago there was a relatively minor eruption of cinder on its south flank at a place called Red Cones. Ash from that eruption can still be found on Kaiser Pass and Mount Givens, at the start of the Ershim-Dusy Jeep Trail (see *High Sierra SUV Trails Volume II, The Western Slope*). Steam fumaroles still appear on Mammoth Mountain from time to time. Beginning in 1978 the Mammoth Mountain area began to experience a series of jarring earthquakes that reached their peak in 1980 with shocks exceeding 6.0 on the Richter Scale. They continue to this day on a lesser and more irregular basis. In recent years, subterranean volcanic activity has also released carbon dioxide gas that has been killing trees in the Horseshoe Lake area. Will the mountain erupt again? Probably, but nobody knows when that is likely to occur. The good folks of Mammoth Lakes are reluctant to talk about the threat for fear that it will depress property values.

San Joaquin Ridge with Mammoth Mountain in the background.

Turning to the east, one can see all the way past the 14,000-foot peaks of the White Mountains into Nevada, some fifty to seventy-five miles away. To the northeast, one gains some idea as to the vastness of the forest that blankets this area. Easily seen is the line of obsidian domes, pushed up from a single crack in the earth's mantle. These are quite new in geologic terms. One, appropriately named Obsidian Dome, is thought to be only six hundred years old. A half dozen volcanic cinder cones also stand out. Some are perfectly symmetrical. One cone has had one side blown out.

The ash from this cinder cone was blown to one side.

The route continues upward to dead-end in a clump of hardy whitebark pines at an elevation of 10,255 feet. Just below, and a quarter of a mile to the north, is Deadman Pass, the natural gap in the ridge used as a passageway for man and wildlife since the end of the last Ice Age. The volcanic rocks exposed here on this highpoint are a silica-rich type of latite, appropriately called quartz latite. They are Pliocene in age, and they have an interesting story to tell.

A few decades back, scientists believed that our recent Ice Age began at the start of the Pleistocene Epoch, about one million years ago. A funny thing happened here at the end of the jeep trail, however. Geologists dating the glacial till here discovered it was at least 2.7 million years old, and possibly as old as 3.1 million years. These dates were established by potassium-argon dating of both the andesite under the till, as well as the quartz latite rocks overlying the glacial deposits. So, if the quartz latite is 2.7 million years old, and if it lies on top of glacial till, then the glacial till must be older. The significance of this startling discovery is that the so-called "Pleistocene glaciation" actually started in the Pliocene, perhaps two million years earlier than previously thought. While such scientific discoveries on Deadman Pass may impress only a few, the scenic view will impress everyone.

27

Laurel Lakes

Primary Attraction:	This is a spectacular trip in the high country offering fishing, interesting geology, wildflowers, beautiful fall colors, and outstanding scenery any time of the year.
Time Required:	While this outing can be done in half a day, you are shortchanging yourself if you don't allow a full day.
Miles Involved:	The distance from downtown Mammoth Lakes to upper Laurel Lake is less than eleven miles. The rough road portion is five miles in length.
Degree of Difficulty:	The road is steep and rocky, often with poor traction, but no more difficult than Class III. Lingering snowdrifts can block the higher portions of the road early in the summer.

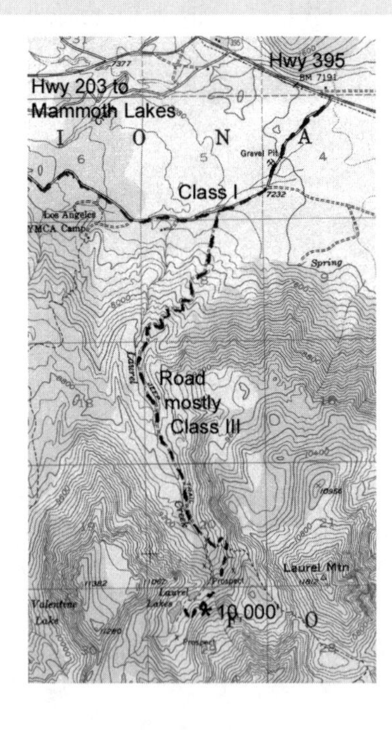

During the Korean War years of the early 1950s, tungsten, vanadium, and molybdenum were in great demand to alloy with steel. Minerals containing these metals had long been mined in Pine Creek Canyon from "metamorphic roof pendants", very old Paleozoic rocks that existed long before the Sierra granite was pushed up from deep within the earth's crust. Anywhere these old metamorphic rocks were exposed, there were prospectors out combing the mountainsides looking for traces of these valuable metals.

Rough access roads to tungsten prospects were carved out of the canyons of Bishop Creek, Rock Creek, Hilton Creek, McGee Creek, and Laurel Creek. When the John Muir Wilderness was established in 1964, the existing jeep trails to old mines and prospects in McGee Creek and Hilton Creek were included in the new *Wilderness Area,* and thus forever closed. In the case of Laurel Creek Canyon, however, the wilderness boundary was drawn around potential mineral deposits. The old access trails built by tungsten prospectors in the mid-1950s remain. For two decades a locked gate denied public access to the high country. That entry control has now been removed and anyone can use the road, providing they have a suitable vehicle.

From the U.S. Forest Service Visitor Center in Mammoth Lakes, take State Route 203 eastward a couple of mines to U.S. Highway 395, and then turn right in the direction of Bishop. Go only 1.4 miles; turn right again onto the Sherwin Creek Road. Follow this graded road in the direction of Old Mammoth for another 1.4 miles. Here, on the left, a dirt road heads straight up the hillside to the south. A forest service sign indicates this is road 4S86 and it is recommended for high clearance vehicles only. This is the road to Laurel Lakes; turn left here.

In about a half mile, the road begins to steeply ascend large rounded piles of gravel. These mounds are the terminal moraine of the Laurel Creek Glacier, that got as low as the canyon's mouth during the height of the Tioga Phase of the Pleistocene glaciation some 25,000 years ago. These mountains must have been an awesome sight in those prehistoric times, as there were glaciers spilling out of all of these canyons. A similar glacier in Rock Creek Canyon protruded out nearly to Tom's Place.

At the first switchback, note the cluster of six-foot shrubs on the right. These are Red Cherries, *Prunus emarginata,* often called Bitter Cherry. Normally these hardy shrubs like moist stream banks, but for some reason these seem to be thriving in the dry sandy soil of this moraine. In the fall, the plant is conspicuous by its abundance of small bright red berries. Native Americans found the fruit too bitter to eat, although many birds seem to enjoy them.

The first switchback is also the place you may wish to engage your four-wheel drive. Although one can continue another couple of miles in two-wheel drive, the grades are steep, the surface rocky, and the traction poor. It is simply easier on your rear tires if you direct power to all wheels. After a mile, the top of the moraine is reached and the road soon enters Laurel Creek Canyon. At a point 2.2 miles from the Sherwin Creek Road, a short side road right drops down to a small meadow area, where Laurel Creek is lined with aspen trees. This meadow is very nice in early October when the aspen leaves turn from green to hues of golden yellow and red.

You may wonder why the leaves in some aspen groves turn bright yellow, while others turn more golden hues, and still others have leaves of rusty brown or vivid reddish-orange. Anne Halford, a botanist in the BLM's Bishop office, explains the process this way: It is a matter of complex plant physiology. The cells of each leaf contain various pigments. Chlorophyll, the most common, produces the dominate green color. But hidden beneath the dominant chlorophyll other pigments are present, too. There are xanthophylls which produce yellow, and carotenoids which produce oranges and reds. With the shorter daylight hours and cooler temperatures of fall, the chlorophylls slow down their food production for the tree. They break down and the greens begin to disappear. In their place, the other pigments are able to emerge, and the tree leaves turn from green to yellow, or russet or red. Just which of these hues dominates depends on the tree's response to both moisture and temperature. If the period of late September through early October has warm sunny days followed by cool nights below 45 degrees, then the sugars produced in the leaves during the daylight hours are trapped there. Under these conditions a red pigment, anthocyanin is formed from the sugars and the leaves turn bright orange and red. But if the fall weather is cool and rainy, or if the nights are relatively warm, the sugars are still able to move from the leaves into the tree branches. Under these conditions, the fall colors are not nearly as intense.

During the Plio-Pleistocene Ice Age, massive glaciers filled Laurel Canyon several times.

Not only is this part of the canyon attractive to look at, it also has the best campsites in the canyon. There is ample room for an entire jeep club. The elevation here is about 8,400 feet.

The rocky road continues to climb high on the canyon's east side. In early to mid summer the slopes are alive with lupine, Indian paintbrush, scarlet pentstemon, and Western pennyroyal. Later in the summer and into fall, one cannot help but notice the colorful yellow flower clusters of the ubiquitous rabbit brush and the showy white blossoms of the prickly poppy.

The rocks here in this portion of the canyon are those old Paleozoic metamorphic rocks mentioned previously. They are part of a band that stretches from Laurel Canyon on the west, all the way east to Bishop Creek Canyon and beyond. It was in portions of these rocks that gold was found near Lake Mary, and tungsten was found in Pine Creek. Such peaks as 12,268' Mt. Morrison, 13,005' Mt. Morgan and 13,163' Red Slate Mountain are found in these formations.

At a point 3.7 miles in from the Sherwin Creek Road, there is a switchback that suddenly points you north. The new vista is sudden and stunning. Far below is the town of Mammoth Lakes, and beyond is the Sierra crest at the eastern side of Yosemite National Park. This is certainly a spot to stop and enjoy the view. High above is 11,812' Laurel Mountain, and at the head of the canyon is 12,544' Bloody Mountain.

On the otherwise narrow road, a relatively wide spot 4.4 miles in marks the beginning of a foot trail that steeply climbs the side of Laurel Mountain to eventually reach a trio of lady's lakes, Genevieve, Dorothy and Mildred. They are just across the divide in Convict Creek Canyon.

Continuing up the road, one soon has a view of a much closer lake. To the right, in the canyon bottom below, is the Lower Laurel Lake. Off to the north is an exceptional view of the Mono Craters area, where volcanoes have recently made their imprint on the landscape. There is ample evidence to suggest that Mother Nature is not yet through with sculpting this part of Mono County.

Soon the road tops out on a spur at an elevation of 10,050 feet. Stop here for a moment and enjoy all the eye candy around you. Ahead is the well-preserved glacial cirque that gave birth to the Laurel Creek Glacier. Below is Upper Laurel Lake, the larger of the two lakes. The contact between the dark reddish-brown Paleozoic metamorphic rocks and the white Cretaceous granite is very evident at the upper edge of Upper Laurel Lake.

The road climbs to 10,050 feet.

The switchbacks

Upper Laurel Lake

Lower Laurel Lake

The road now steeply descends a series of switchbacks, two hundred feet down to Upper Laurel Lake. The first of these hairpin turns is so sharp that it is necessary to back up several times in order to get around it. It is at this first turn that another hiking trail starts up the side of Bloody Mountain. This footpath was once a jeep trail, built in 1955 to gain access to the Hard Point Prospect situated on the steep north side of Bloody Peak. The mineralized zone containing the various tungsten minerals was exposed on a virtual cliff face. The mining claims were accessible only by ladders and ropes anchored into the rock. Because of the obvious access problems, and the quantity and quality of the orebody, no mining was ever done. The jeep trail is no longer passable, but if you take an hour to walk over to the base of the cliff below the prospect, you might find specimens of scheelite, powellite, and molybdenite that have fallen down from above.

Finally, 5.1 miles from the Sherwin Creek Road, the jeep trail ends at the water's edge of Upper Laurel Lake. At 9,850 feet in elevation, only a few hardy Whitebark pines grow here. There are a few rocky campsites, used by an occasional fisherman, but most folks camp lower in the canyon.

In the late 1950s the State Department of Fish and Game had closed the Laurel Lakes to fishing. Their isolated location and ease of blocking the road made these waters ideal breeding ground for the raising of Golden trout. That experiment has shifted back to the Kern Plateau, and the jeep road once again has been opened to the public, and fishing can resume.

The rugged scenic beauty of Laurel Creek Canyon should place it high on any off-roader's list of places to visit.

Bishop in 1886 (Photo courtesy County of Inyo, Eastern Calif. Museum)

Bishop today

When in Bishop, be sure to visit the Laws Railroad Museum just five miles north of town off of Highway 6.

Chapter VIII
Trails Out Of Bishop
(Inyo National Forest)

Bishop sits deep in the Owens Valley astride U.S. Highway 395 connecting San Diego, Reno, and Alturas. Its early days were associated with farming and ranching. Then in the 1920s, the City of Los Angeles bought up most of the land and water rights in the Owens Valley, and built an aqueduct to send all that water south. Folks have been arguing about it ever since.

With a population of about 6,000, Bishop and its environs are certainly noted as a center for outdoorsmen. Hunting, fishing, camping, backpacking, and photography are all pursuits that bring tourists through Bishop. The town has complete tourist facilities and is the headquarters for the Inyo National Forest. There are campgrounds aplenty in the Bishop area. The nearest one is at Schober Lane, a mile south of town on Highway 395. An Inyo County campground at the old millpond can be found just off Highway 395 five miles west of town. The U.S. Forest Service has seven campgrounds in the very scenic Bishop Creek Canyon, just up State Highway 168 southwest of town.

History and railroad buffs will want to take a six-mile side trip up U.S. Highway 6 to the Laws Railroad Museum on the old Carson & Colorado Railroad (later the Southern Pacific). This railroad once went north to connect with the Virginia & Truckee Railroad at Mound House, Nevada, near Carson City. In the other direction the railroad went as far as Keeler in the southern end of the Owens Valley. Laws Station serviced this narrow gauge line between March of 1883 and April of 1960.

The White Mountain Ranger Station on North Main Street
is the place to go for up to date road information.

28

Wheeler Crest

Primary Attraction:	This outing offers outstanding high mountain scenery, coupled with fine examples of glacial geology.
Time Required:	This is a full day's excursion out of Bishop.
Miles Involved:	It is nine miles from the Swall Meadows Road to the trail's end at the wilderness boundary, about 28 miles from downtown Bishop.
Degree of Difficulty:	The roads are Class II for the first four miles, then generally Class III for the remaining five miles.

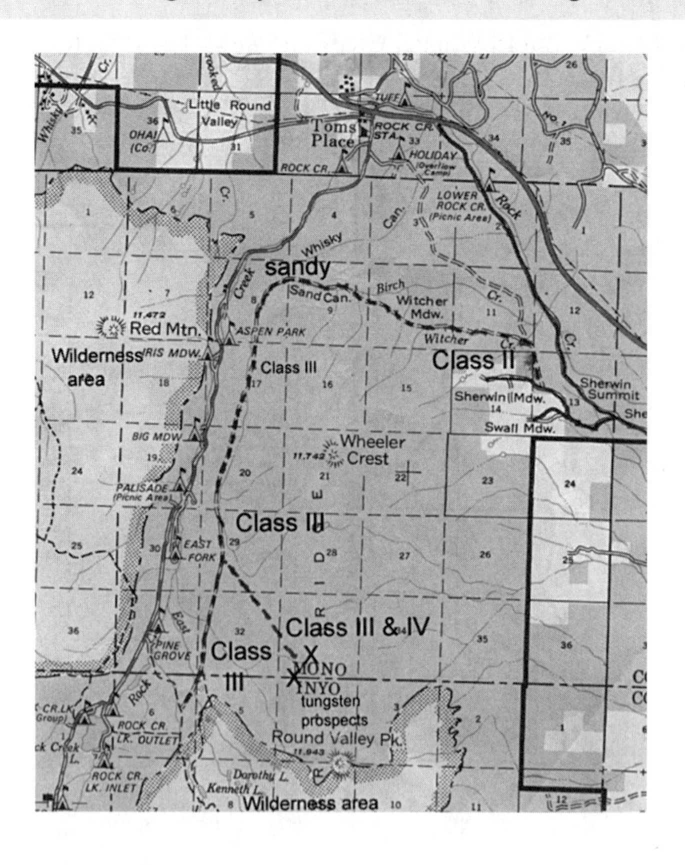

During the summer months, the U.S. Forest Service campgrounds along upper Rock Creek are often filled to their capacity, and great numbers of people are spread out all over the canyon floor. Less than a mile away, however, there is a secret wonderland, unknown to the masses and accessible only to four-wheelers. Here, midway up the east wall of Rock Creek Canyon, there are no crowds and primitive campsites are always abundant.

From the intersection of Main and Line Streets in downtown Bishop, take U.S. Highway 395 out of Bishop, northbound in the direction of Mammoth Lakes. The White Mountain Ranger Station is a half-mile north on the right, a good place to stop and ask about current road conditions. Twelve miles beyond look for the Paradise Road on the left. Turn left here, and then right, after 0.2 miles, onto the Lower Rock Creek Road. This road will take you past Paradise Camp and up through a housing subdivision. At a point 6.6 miles from Highway 395 turn left onto the Swall Meadows Road. Note your odometer reading here.

Keep right on the Sky Meadows Road at the fork 0.6 miles in. A half-mile beyond look for an unmarked dirt road going off to the right; turn here. The road passes through a gravel borrow pit and swings to the right. In another 0.7 miles, this Class II road will ford Witcher Creek and fork. The right fork, Forest Road 4S54, goes to Tom's Place on old Highway 395; stay to the left. In another half-mile the road forks again; again stay to the left. In another 0.8 miles yet a third fork in the road is encountered; again keep to the left. The right fork goes to Witcher Meadow, the first of the nice places to camp. The Jeffrey pine forest is now entered and soon the road drops down into Sand Canyon. At the bottom of the canyon is Birch Creek. For a tenth of a mile the road shares the streambed with a thicket of willow, aspen, and wild roses; however, the route remains Class II.

At the head of Birch Creek, 4.6 miles from the Lower Rock Creek Road, it is time to engage your four-wheel drive. The road ahead is loose sand, and the grade is steeper than it looks. The top of Sand Canyon is reached at the 5.6 mile-point, and here the road turns to the south. At this point you enter Rock Creek Canyon. Stop for a moment, walk a few feet through the desert mahogany to the right, and look about. The elevation here is about 9000 feet. To the north, Crowley Lake is sitting in the bottom of the Long Valley Caldera, a long ago collapsed volcano. Up the canyon to the south is 13, 748' Mount Morgan and behind it, from left to right, are more thirteen thousand footers, Mounts Julius Ceasar, Abbot, and Mills.

Rock Creek Canyon was repeatedly scoured by the massive glaciers during the seven major advances of ice of the Plio-Pleistocene Ice Age. The jeep trail you are on runs along the top of a long lateral moraine, perched high on the canyon's east wall. This elongated pile of unsorted gravel was pushed out to the side of a Tahoe stage glacier as the river of ice slowly crept down Rock Creek Canyon. At its peak, the glacier in Rock Creek Canyon was fifteen miles long and extended all the way to Tom's Place on Highway 395.

The Wheeler Crest trail

The road soon leaves the brush and again enters the cool pine forest. Thirteen miles from the Sky Meadows Road, the jeep trail comes to a beautiful mountain meadow. The meadow is beautiful only because others before you stayed on the roadway and have not torn it up with their lugged tires. There are several dry, but otherwise nice, campsites here. While the main road continues south, a faint jeep trail goes left and starts eastward across the meadows. On the other side, a Class IV route begins to climb the western face of Wheeler Ridge. It is about a mile and a half of steep grades and rough four-wheeling to the top, but the trip is worth the effort. Once on top, the jeep trail crosses the crest of the ridge at 11,000 feet and drops to a small, unnamed lake (no fish). The jeep trail continues out to the eastern face, where it turns southward. Here are spectacular views of the Bishop-Round Valley area, and you can look all the way south into the Buttermilk Country (see Excursion #29). The road forks, but both branches soon dead-end. This road was originally put in to reach some tungsten claims discovered near Round Valley Peak in 1939. The rock contained only small amounts of scheelite, however, and the claims were never mined.

Meanwhile back at the meadow, the main road, if it can be called that, continues up Rock Creek Canyon for another two miles. The trail ends a few hundred yards short of a beautiful unnamed lake. This road was originally established during World War I to reach tungsten mines above Morgan Creek. At that time, the road continued and dropped down into Rock Creek Lake. It now ends at the edge of the John Muir Wilderness, where motor vehicles are prohibited. If you wish to see the country behind the wilderness sign, an easy hiking trail goes on to Dorothy and Kenneth Lakes, just a mile beyond. With a little more effort, Francis and Tamarack Lakes are also easily reached. And what of the crowds? They are far below and out of sight.

Unnamed lake at the end of the jeep trail.

29

The Buttermilk Country

Special Features: This loop road takes you to the base of three thirteen thousand foot peaks, Mt. Tom, Basin Mountain and Mt. Humphreys. Here the Sierra escarpment stands out and can be seen like nowhere else.

Time Required: This outing can be done in a half-day out of Bishop.

Miles Involved: The entire loop from downtown Bishop and return is 35 miles.

Degree of Difficulty: The 21 mile dirt road portions are generally no more difficult than Class II, except for the three mile side-trip to Upper Birch Creek of which only two miles are Class III.

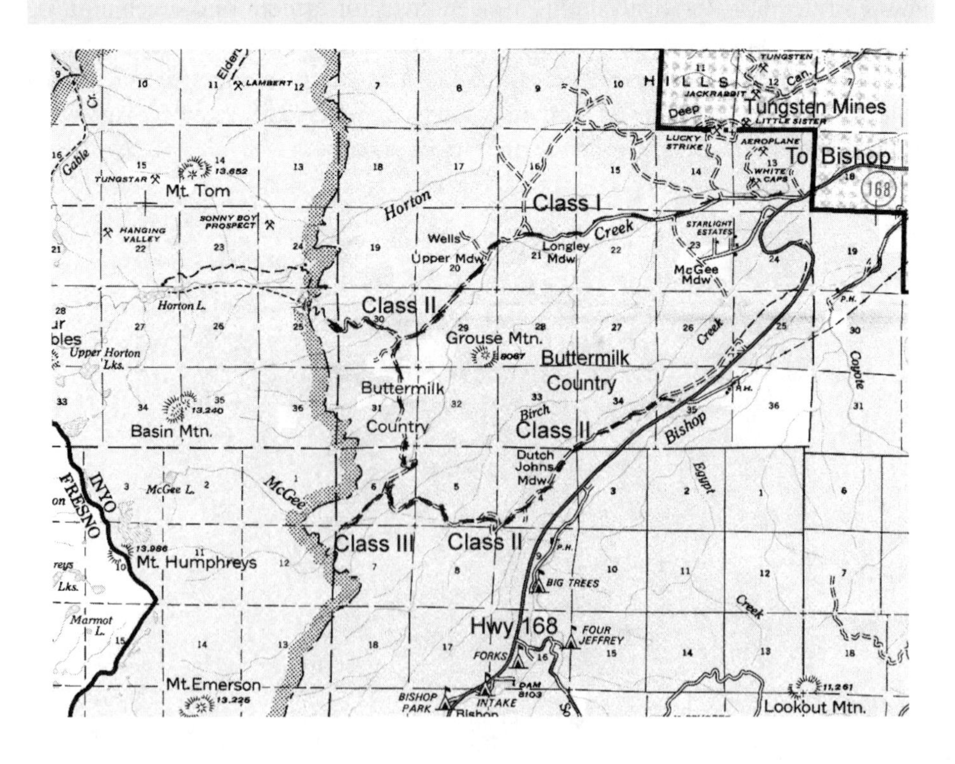

As long as man has been grazing cows in the Owens Valley, the Buttermilk Country has been cattle country. According to Genny Schumacher, the Buttermilk Country got its name from a dairy where teamsters would stop in the 1870s. Today it is an important winter range for the many mule deer that migrate down out of the high country each fall.

From the intersection of Line and Main Streets in downtown Bishop, note your odometer reading and then take West Line Street westward toward the High Sierra. This is also State Route 168. At a point 7.3 miles from downtown Bishop, look for a sign indicating Buttermilk Road on the right. Leave Highway 168 here, turning westward on the wide graded road. Straight ahead 13,652' Mt. Tom fills the windshield with its overpowering presence.

Soon you will enter the Inyo National Forest, although the only trees to be seen in this arid land are the cottonwoods that line McGee Creek off to the right. Also to the right are the Tungsten Hills, so named for that sometimes precious metal found there. The White Caps Mine is low on the hillside to the right about a half-mile in off of Highway 168. Above it, on the crest of the hills, are the Aeroplane Mine, the Little Sister Mine, and the Lucky Strike Mine. All these mines tapped into orebodies of scheelite (calcium tungstate) embedded in a hard metamorphic tactite. They last operated during WWII, when tungsten was a strategic material needed to harden steel for armour and other military purposes.

The high standard dirt road maintained by the county makes its way westward, passing through hills of well-weathered granite. Along the way, there are a number of nice, but unimproved campsites where one can stay for a few days without any charge. At a point 3.6 miles in from the highway, a cattle guard is crossed. On the other side are the blackened stumps left in the aftermath of a wildland fire, which burned through here in the year 2000. The road now deteriorates to Class I, with a few Class II rocky sections. In two more miles the road will mostly be Class II.

It takes years for the vegetation to recover from devastating fires like this.

A second area of past wildfire is encountered at a point six miles in from Highway 168. This was a part of a different fire occurring in 1999. Notice the difference in the vegetative regrowth between the two fires. In the first months after the fire, there is nothing but a desolate landscape of bare desert mahogany stumps. In the first year following the fire, the first plants to return are the white prickly poppy and the yellow rabbit brush. In another year or two, as other species regain a foothold, the poppy will disappear and the rabbit brush will take on a more diminutive role.

Prickley poppy *Argemone munita* Rabbitbrush *Chrysothamnus nausesous*

At this six mile point, the twin tire tracks of Forest Road 7S01 go off to the right, only to end in less than a mile at a locked gate. At one time the road continued well past the gate to climb up Horton Creek Canyon. The road ended at an elevation of 10,000 feet at Horton Lake. From here a tractor trail climbed the north side of the canyon to the Hanging Valley Tungsten Mine at an elevation of 11,500 feet. If you look close, to the northwest you can see the road scar ascending a pass on the north side of Horton Creek Canyon.

The Hanging Valley Mine camp and mine above Horton Lake.

Mt. Tom was first climbed as early as 1860 by Thomas Clark. One hundred plus years later in the days of my youth, I, too, climbed to the top of 13,652' Mt. Tom using the old mine road as far as I could. The ascent was not technically difficult, but from the locked gate it did involve an elevation gain of nearly 6,000 feet. It turned out to be just a long day in the sun without much shade.

You may also notice a zigzag scar ascending 13,240' Basin Mountain straight to the west. Sixty years ago this road provided access to other tungsten prospects. Even if these old mining roads were still passable, which they are not, they would be closed, because they are within the John Muir Wilderness created by Congress in 1964 (and later enlarged in 1984). The first recorded ascent of Basin Mountain did not come until September 15th, 1937, when veteran mountaineer Norman Clyde made the ascent from Horton Lake.

Behind the Horton Creek turnoff, the Buttermilk Road now turns in a more southerly direction. A small stream is easily forded, and soon the road descends a lateral glacial moraine into the forest of Jeffrey pine and aspen that line the course of McGee Creek. (This McGee Creek should not to be confused with another stream of the same name just up Highway 395 in Mono County.) Here among the willows and wild roses are some very nice, but unimproved campsites.

After fording McGee Creek, the road turns east as it climbs the lateral moraine on the opposite side. From here there are unobstructed views north of the lower Buttermilk Country and beyond into Round Valley at the foot of the Sherwin Grade. Once on top of the moraine, the road makes a hairpin turn and heads southwest.

At a point 8.3 miles in from Highway 168 is an important road intersection. The Buttermilk Road, Forest Road 7S01, goes to the left. We will want to go that way, but before doing so, let's first explore Forest Road 8S17 to the right. **Do not attempt this side-trip unless you have four-wheel drive.**

Forest Road 8S17 continues to climb up the moraine. (After 0.2 miles disregard the road to the left, which rejoins 7S01.) Straight ahead is 13,986' Mt. Humphreys, named by the Whitney expedition to honor A. A. Humphreys, a distinguished soldier and engineer. I have also climbed Mt. Humphreys, but it was much more of a challenge than Mt. Tom. I approached the peak from the south, by way of Paiute Pass, camping at Marmot Lake. Whereas the summit of Mt. Tom was a walk in the park, Mt. Humphreys had a formidable summit block with some scary exposure.

As the road takes you ever higher, soon more pleasant campsites will appear along Birch Creek to the left. A mile beyond the intersection, the steep grades coupled with poor traction require the use of four-wheel drive. The road leaves Birch Creek, steeply climbing the hillside to the right. A small valley is entered at a point 1.5 miles from the last intersection. The elevation here is 8,500 feet. Here two roads go off to the left, and two go off to the right; all soon dead-end. The first road to the left and the first road to the right climb a little to end at tall vents in the 14-inch penstock built here by the Southern California Edison Company. SCE operates a series of hydroelectric plants in Bishop Creek Canyon, and this modest pipe helps supply that system with water.

The road straight ahead ends in a quarter of a mile, while the second road to the left ascends a small valley to end in a half-mile at 8,600 feet, the high point of this route. For the young and the restless, it is possible for a strong hiker to walk across to the McGee Creek drainage just to the north, and then make a trail-less ascent 2,000 feet up the canyon to pretty McGee Lake. A small glacier on the northern slope of Mt. Humphreys feeds it.

Mount Humphreys was first climbed on July 18, 1894, by brothers Edward and James Hutchinson. Like me, many years later, they approached the mountain from the west. But it has also been climbed many times from the east by routes pioneered in the 1920s and 1930s by Norman Clyde and others.

But enough of this nostalgia. Let us now go back down the hillside, returning to the intersections of Forest Roads 8S17 and 7S01. Here we turn right, and soon we will enter the aspen and Jeffrey pine belt along Birch Creek. The road passes a small meadow on the left, leaves the riparian habitat, and once again returns to the open sagebrush country. At a point 2.2 miles from the intersection of roads 8S17 and 7S01, a "T" intersection is reached. Go left (the right fork soon comes to a locked gate).

The road improves a little, but remains Class II as is makes its way down the top of an enormous lateral moraine. At a point 2.5 miles from the "T" intersection, the road passes a large green pipe that is four feet across. This penstock is part of the Southern California Edison Company Bishop Creek Hydroelectric Project. It delivers water to Power Plant #3, near the mouth of the canyon.

At the valve structure on the penstock, stop and look into Bishop Creek Canyon below. Try to imagine what this place might have looked like 70,000 years ago during the Tahoe phase of the Plio-Pliestocene Ice Age. It must have been an awesome sight. In those times, the slow moving river of ice creeping down this canyon was sixteen miles long, up to a mile wide in places, and sometimes one thousand feet thick. Along its sides gravel was pushed outwards and upwards, leaving the ridge of gravel you are now standing on.

At a point four miles below the "T" intersection, the dirt road rejoins Highway 168. From here it is but two and a half miles back down to the Buttermilk Road where you first started, and from there just seven miles back to downtown Bishop.

The Buttermilk Country

30

Coyote Creek

Primary Attraction:	This route provides old mines and outstanding high altitude scenery.
Time Required:	This is an all day outing out of Bishop.
Miles Involved:	It is nearly twenty miles of dirt road from the pavement at Reata Road to the end of the trail at the Brackett prospect.
Degree of Difficulty:	Much of the route is Class II, but with enough Class III to keep things interesting.

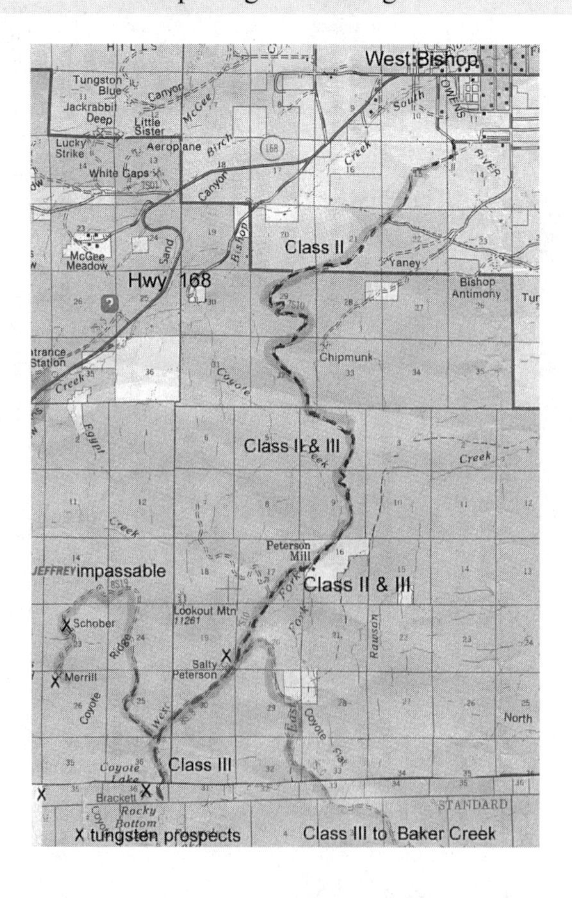

While long known to the residents of Bishop, the Coyote Flats area has been unnoticed by the hundreds of thousands of tourists, who annually pour into the vacation spots of the Eastern Sierra. Because of poor roads, little publicity, and an unmarked starting point, the recreation pressure on this twenty square mile area has been relatively light. Yet in terms of hunting, fishing, camping, and other outdoor activities, the area has much to offer. Access to this high plateau is over roads that are generally Class II. Coyote Creek makes a great day's outing.

To find Coyote Flats, take West Line Street 2.6 miles west of downtown Bishop. Turn left at Reata Road, and continue south 0.8 miles. Here the road turns southeast at a 45-degree angle. Turn with the road, and continue another 0.3 miles. At this second bend in Reata Road, do not follow it around to the east, but rather turn right on the graded dirt road. You may wish to note your odometer reading here. Go south 0.2 miles. Shortly before you reach the electrical substation, another graded dirt road will angle off to the right. Turn right here, passing beneath a double set of high voltage power lines. The Class I dirt road is a little sandy for the next three miles, but that should present no problem.

After a couple miles of washboard surface, the road enters a wide canyon. The Inyo National Forest boundary is three and a half miles from the pavement. Shortly thereafter a road can be seen switchbacking up the mountainside to the south. This is our route, Forest Road 7S10. Three and a half miles from Reata Road, the road begins to climb steeply. You may wish to engage your four-wheel drive at the base of the first switchback. While not absolutely necessary, it will provide better traction on the steep grades. When Salty Peterson built this road in 1942, he didn't fool around with easy grades. Sandy at first, the road climbs a series of switchbacks for nearly a mile, and then turns rough as it crosses an outcrop of reddish-brown basalt rock. For the next couple of miles, the road will cross two different types of rocks. Where the dark lava is encountered, the road is rough and rocky. Where the light colored granitic rocks are encountered, the road tends to be sandy.

The Piñon pine forest begins at an elevation of about 7,000 feet. After winding around the hillsides for a couple of miles, yet a second set of Class III switchbacks is encountered. At the top of these is your first view of Coyote Creek down in the canyon to your right. In the next mile or two, several roads branch off to the left. They were put in by ranchers and prospectors, and all dead-end. The main road stays to the right, where it descends to ford the creek. At a point nearly eleven miles from the pavement, the ruins of Salty Peterson's mill are reached. During the early days of World War II when tungsten was a strategic commodity, A. H. Peterson built this road to access tungsten deposits.

Of the three buildings that were here at the mill site, two have collapsed, and the one which remains won't last much longer. The actual mill was on right side of the road. It was used to test and treat small lots of tungsten ore from nearby prospects. There never was any significant production.

The road passes a spring above the mill site and continues to climb. A set of tracks turning off to the right leads to the Munsinger, Hilltop and Little Egypt tungsten claims. All were prospected and explored, but none were ever deemed worth mining. At a point twelve miles from the pavement, you come to a major fork in the Coyote Flats Road. The left fork, 7S10 goes south to Baker Creek (see Excursion #31).

Coyote Flats in early summer.

To follow Coyote Creek, continue right on 8S18. The road continues up the valley, keeping north of the stream. After a mile, you will pass Salty Peterson's mine on the right. The scheelite orebody, containing about 2% tungsten, was mined from a zone four feet wide by sixty feet long. Most of these tungsten deposits occurred at the contact between marble and highly metamorphosed tactite or hornfels. Here at the Peterson mine, a wedge of granodiorite complicates the geologic picture.

The Coyote Creek Road forks at a point 1.4 miles beyond the mine. The right fork turns north and after 0.4 miles splits again. The left fork dead ends on Coyote Ridge. The right branch continues north, and climbs the western flank of Lookout Mountain. Then it swings west, and starts a steep Class III descent into the Bishop Creek drainage. A cabin site is passed 3.5 miles from the last fork. The Schober Mine is but 0.8 miles around the hill. While there is not much left to look at, the Schober Mine was the only profitable tungsten mine in the Coyote

Flats area. Discovered by Harold Schober in 1940, it was sold to the El Diablo Mining Company. They built a three and a half mile road up from the Circle S Ranch on the South Fork of Bishop Creek, and carried out mining operations in 1942 and 1943. The good ore ran out in 1943, and the mine shut down. The El Diablo road up from Bishop Creek washed out in 1946, and it remains impassable to this day. The Class III Coyote Flat road continues for another mile past the Schober Mine, to dead end at the Merrill prospect.

Back on Coyote Creek (1.4 miles above the Salty Peterson Mine) the left fork turns south and soon enters the forest. There are several hunters' camps in this area. Within a mile you will reach Coyote Lake. Only in the spring does this lake have surface water flowing from it. Usually the lake seems to have no inlet or outlet.

The Class III road continues southward, climbing the ridge overlooking Coyote Lake. Then it doubles back and dead-ends at the Brackett prospect at an elevation of 10,800 feet. From the last switchback, you can walk a short distance to look down on Rocky Bottom Lake. Hikers can scramble the short distance up the ridge, and then make an easy two-mile hike south to climb The Hunchback, a 12,226' peak. In 1948, a U.S. Geological Survey crew took a jeep within 250 feet of the summit! Please respect the fragile alpine ecology and do not try to repeat that stunt.

Coyote Flats in late summer.

31

Baker Creek

Primary Attraction:	More high altitude mountain scenery with great close-up views of the Palisades group of peaks.
Time Required:	This is an all day outing out of Bishop, especially if you fish.
Miles Involved:	It is six miles beyond the Coyote Creek turnoff to Baker Creek.
Degree of Difficulty:	Once you get up onto Coyote Flat, the road over to Baker Creek is mostly Class II, and generally no worse than Class III.

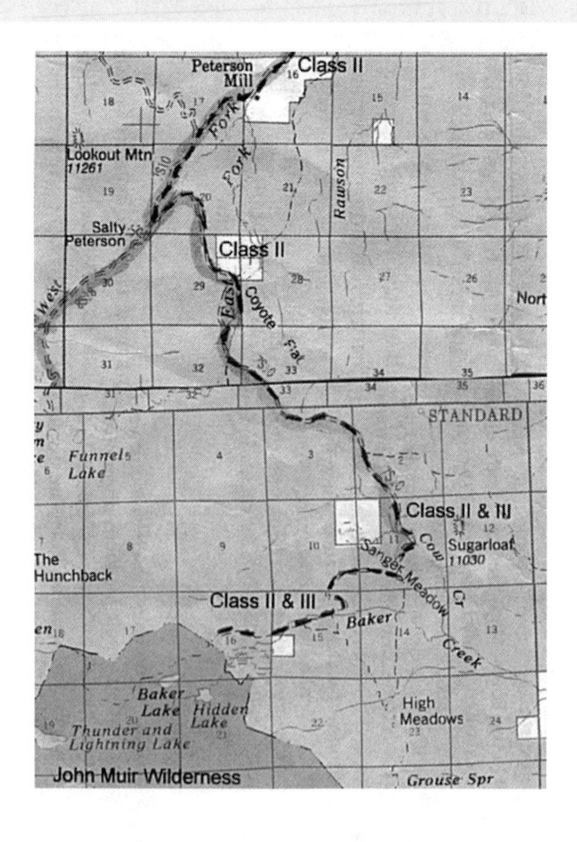

To reach Baker Creek, start up the Coyote Creek Road as described in Excursion #30. At a point 1.3 miles above the Peterson mill site, the road forks. For Baker Creek, go left. The road fords Coyote Creek and starts south, entering a wide valley known as Coyote Flats. The elevation here is almost 10,000 feet, so don't be surprised if you and your car don't seem to have the pep that you do in other places. Historically, the area has been used for summer grazing of sheep and cattle. At one time an old rancher's cabin was passed after a mile and a half. When I last scouted this excursion in 1999, I noticed the structure was no longer there. At a point 0.4 miles south of the cabin site, a jeep trail branches off to the right. Funnel Lake is reached after following this Class III route for 2.4 miles. Here, an unimproved campsite is used by the occasional hunter or fisherman.

The main route to Baker Creek continues southward across the length of Coyote Flats. In the late 1960s, an airstrip and hanger were built here by the Department of Defense, ostensibly to test the high altitude characteristics of helicopters and other aircraft. After seeing strange lights up here at night, the good folks in Bishop couldn't help but wonder what the military was really up to. Those facilities have now been removed.

A muddy spot in the road at the base of Sugarloaf Peak can cause problems in early summer. Once beyond that, Cow Creek is easily forded. The road climbs a little, passes through a drift fence (please close the gate behind you) and continues south. At a point six miles south of Coyote Creek, the road forks on the crest of a hill. From this point one gets a good view of Palisade Glacier just seven air miles to the south. Also to the south, but just below you, is Baker Creek. To go there, take the left fork. It descends 0.7 miles to several unimproved campsites in the "beaver pond" area. From here a little used hiking trail crosses the creek and continues south, climbing to High Meadows, before descending to Logging Flat at the Big Pine Creek trailhead. Meanwhile back on the ridge, the right fork turns westward and makes its way up a glacial moraine. Sections of this road are Class III. The jeep trail dead-ends after a couple of miles at a wooded campsite overlooking the upper meadows. Just beyond the spring is the boundary of the John Muir Wilderness. Here a hiking trail starts west crossing Baker Pass to drop down into Green and Brown Lakes, and eventually coming out at Parcher's Camp on the South Fork of Bishop Creek. Those not interested in such an ambitious hike can follow this same trail for only a mile to reach Baker and Hidden Lakes. Thunder and Lightning Lake is another mile beyond. The trout are generally small, but abundant anywhere along the Baker Creek drainage.

Baker Creek

Baker Lake

Chapter IX
Trails Out of Big Pine
(Inyo National Forest)

For the outdoorsman Big Pine, California, is synonymous with hunting and fishing in the High Sierra or possibly mountaineering in the Palisades. With the passage of the 1994 California Desert Protection Act, which created Death Valley National Park and greatly expanded its boundaries to the west, Big Pine has also become the jumping-off place for hundreds of square miles in the northwest corner of the park (see *Death Valley SUV Trails*). Big Pine is also the starting point for backcountry trips in the White and Inyo Mountains east of Big Pine (see *Inyo-Mono SUV Trails*).

Big Pine's roots go back to 1869. Once the Owens Valley Indian Wars were over, small farming communities began to develop up and down the valley, and Big Pine was one of them. The community got a big boost in 1877-78, when an irrigation ditch system better distributed the waters of the Owens River, and farms flourished. That all came to an end in 1924 as the City of Los Angeles acquired the water rights and the ditches dried up. Big Pine became relegated to being a bedroom community of its larger cousin, Bishop, just fourteen miles to the north.

Nevertheless, 1200 people still call Big Pine home. It has a market, two sporting goods stores, four places to eat and four motels. It also has a couple of service stations.

Downtown Big Pine today

Big Pine in 1919
(Photo courtesy Laws Railroad Museum)

Big Pine's Butler Hotel circa 1920
(Photo from the author's collection)

32

Glacier View

Primary Attraction:	This excursion provides outstanding high country scenery with great views of the Palisades Glaciers.
Time Required:	This is an all day outing out of Big Pine.
Miles Involved:	It is only eleven miles from Big Pine to the road's end above Onion Creek.
Degree of Difficulty:	The first 2.5 miles of dirt road are Class II, but the remaining 5.5 miles are Class III, much of it requiring low range gears.
Special Note:	The lower loop of this route can usually be done all year around.

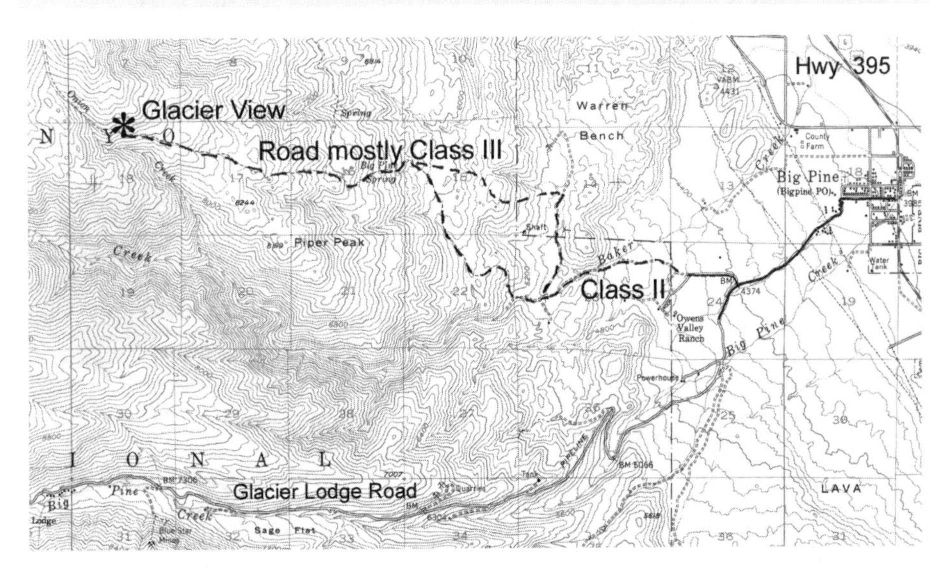

There are 497 glaciers in the Sierra Nevada. Not only are the three Palisade Glaciers today's southerly most glaciers in the United States, but the largest of the three, the one that lies to the east, is also the largest glacier in the Sierra

Nevada. Its ice covers something just less than a square mile. The icy trio lies tucked against the northern base of a string of rugged thirteen and fourteen thousand foot peaks in the headwaters of Big Pine Creek. The glaciers are but distant specs when seen from the Owens Valley, and even the road going ten miles up Big Pine Canyon does not adequately reveal their presence.

In order to see these glaciers close up, one must hike six miles up Big Pine Creek to Fourth Lake, while climbing some 2,200 feet in the process. While I have made that walk many times, and can certainly recommend it, there are alternative viewpoints that do not require such strenuous exertion. One fine viewpoint is from the headwaters of Baker Creek (see Excursion #31). Another is from a point overlooking Onion Creek, a place I call Glacier View.

To find the road to Glacier View, take Crocker Street west from downtown Big Pine. Note your odometer reading as you leave Highway 395. Upon leaving town Crocker Street turns into Glacier Lodge Road, as the highway swings to the left and passes beneath a double set of high power lines. Heading southwest along the roadway, there is a grand view of the Sierra skyline straight ahead. Left to right, we can see 12,790' Goodale Mountain, and behind it and slightly to the right is 13,397' Cardinal Mountain. Farther to the right is 13,665' Birch Mountain. Looking more westward we can see 14,040' Disappointment Peak and below it, middle Palisade Glacier.

Turn right onto the paved Sugarloaf Road at a point 1.6 miles from Highway 395. After 0.6 miles turn right onto Arc Road, a graded dirt road. A borrow pit is passed on the left, and a side road right goes over to Baker Creek on the right, but continue heading westward on the main road. Slightly more than three miles from Highway 395, the road crosses the Baker Creek culvert. This is the lower portion of the same Baker Creek described in Excursion #31. Here the stream is lined with cottonwoods, water birch, willows, and wild roses.

The grading ends at the 3.2-mile point from Highway 395, but a narrow Class II road passes through the drift fence and continues on. The road forks at 3.5 miles. You may return via the left fork ahead, but for the moment take the right fork, which turns north and heads up a broad flat shelf known as Warren Bench. This is important winter range for deer forced down out of the mountains by snow. Another fork is encountered at 3.7 miles; again go right.

The well-weathered igneous rocks all around you are part of the great Sierra Nevada batholith that was pushed up from the bowels of the earth during Jurassic and Cretaceous times. Related granite rocks of late Mesozoic age can be seen atop Mount Whitney, in the cliffs of Yosemite Valley and in the glacier scoured Desolation Basin west of Lake Tahoe. It was tungsten prospectors who put these roads in many years ago, but alas their efforts were for naught.

Our Class II road forks at a point 4.4 miles from Highway 395. The right fork goes onto some prospect holes. Take the left fork that, within a quarter of a mile, will begin to climb the rocky hillside to the west. It is here that you should engage your four-wheel drive and drop the transmission into low range. You will need them both for the next five miles.

The roadway, now Class III, climbs steeply up the mountainside. The steep grade ends at the 5.1 mile point, and just beyond there is a nice view of Warren Lake down in the floor of the Owens Valley. A ridgetop is crested at 5.5 miles, and here tracks go off to the left to return to the 3.7-mile point mentioned previously. Stay to the right. Our road now drops down into a small valley, where, at 6.1 miles, yet another road goes to the left. The left fork is an alternate return route, which we will choose on the way back from Glacier View. If you are out for a drive in the winter when snows still cover the high country, a left turn here would be in order. But for Glacier View, stay right and begin yet another steep ascent. This time the road is sandy in places, but it always remains Class III. The spot of green in the gulch to the left is Big Pine Spring. Behind and to the left are nice views down upon the town of Big Pine.

At 6.9 miles from Highway 395, the road forks again. Either fork will take you to Glacier View, but we will choose the slightly easier left fork for a tenth of a mile, and then go to the right. At 7.8 miles there is a very sandy uphill portion. Before you air down your tires, try get up some speed and simply force your way through. It took me several attempts before I was able to make it.

The road to Glacier View.

Trees begin to appear at the 8.2-mile point. If you come this way late in the spring, you may notice a curious web on various shrubs such as ceanothus and bitterbrush. In the springtime, when conditions are just right, clusters of dense spiderweb-like sacks appear on the plant. Each of these sacks is teeming with inch long caterpillars, which have just emerged from their cocoons. This is how life begins for the Tent caterpillar, *Malacosoma americana,* or *M. pluviale.* The caterpillar will soon turn into a brown moth.

The cocoon of the Tent caterpillar.

At 8.8 miles there is yet another steep rocky grade followed by a small meadow area, and then yet another steep climb and another meadow area. At 9.9 miles a ridgetop is reached, and now we have a hint of views yet to come. Drivers should not be distracted by the scenery, however, as a short section approaching Class IV lies directly ahead. Stay to the left at the top. Finally at 10.2 miles from Highway 395, you come to the top of a ridge looking down upon Onion Creek. This is what I call "Glacier View". The elevation here is roughly 9,200 feet, meaning that we have climbed a vertical mile since leaving Big Pine. At one time the jeep trail continued on, first dropping down into Onion Creek and then climbing again as it headed north to circle around the north side of prominent Sugarloaf Peak, to rejoin the jeep trail coming up from Bishop on Coyote Flat. The next few miles have become impassible in recent years, so here is where we must stop. Break out a picnic lunch and enjoy the scenery.

The view of the rugged rock spires that make up the Palisades to the west is simply outstanding. Looking south of our position we see 11,896' Kid Mountain and well behind it and slightly to the left, 13,665' Birch Mountain.

Now turning southwest to look left to right at the Palisades skyline, we can first see 11,630' Mt. Alice, 12,999' Temple Craig, 14,162' Mt. Sill, 14,242' North Palisade, 14,040' Thunderbolt Peak, 13,768' Mt. Winchell, and finally 13,891' Mt. Agassiz.

The view looking west toward Glacier View.

If you want to read more about these rugged spires and the man who first climbed them, find a copy of *Norman Clyde and the High Sierra.* It was originally published by La Siesta Press, and more recently reprinted by Spotted Dog Press in Bishop.

During the Plio-Pliestocene Ice Age, the climate of the earth cooled and warmed again nearly a dozen times, with at least four major cooling episodes that caused enormous accumulations of ice to build up in the Sierra Nevada Range. The last major advance of the ice, called the Tioga phase of the Wisconsin period, peaked about 20,000 years ago. As the earth warmed again, that glacial ice began to melt and the glaciers retreated for the next 8,000 to 10,000 years. It is even likely that sufficient warming occurred so that the Sierra glaciers melted completely away. Then about three hundred years ago, the climate cooled again, just enough to start a "little iceage". This cooling trend lasted about fifty years and things have been warming up ever since. Thus it is thought that most of the existing glaciers in the Sierra Nevada today are only three hundred years old, remnants of those cooler times. Throughout the world, and particularly in the Alps, there has been a dramatic melting of glacial ice in the last two hundred years. If the trend continues, and that appears likely in the near term, it is conceivable that all the glaciers in the Sierra will be gone in another few hundred years.

In terms of geologic time, however, that is but the blink of an eye. In the last 1.2 million years, the earth has been in seemingly endless cycles of cooling and warming. Cold cycles have lasted 20,000 to 100,000 years, with intervening warm cycles of 20,000 to 100,000 years. It is entirely possible that the earth is currently in one of those interglacial warm periods. Indeed, we may still be in the Pleistocene Ice Age without even realizing it. It is politically popular these days to blame man, industry, and the automobile for current global warming trends. No mention is ever made that a cooling and warming cycle has been going on for the last million years. It seems likely to believe that our current warming trend would be in progress whether man inhabited the earth or not. Nevertheless, the concern over "global warming" has been a steady source of grant money for many scientists. It is in their own self-interest to perpetuate the atmosphere of fear and crises surrounding the problem. In truth, however, nobody really knows whether the current global warming trend is natural or man made.

Close-up view of the Palisade Glacier taken in September when the bergschrund at the top of the glacier is open and exposed.

Once you have had your fill of the scenery, and perhaps walked down to Onion Creek to wet a line, return down the mountainside the same way you came up. If you turn right at the 6.1-mile point you passed coming up, that road will in two miles take you back to the fork in the road at 3.5 miles. Along the way the road winds its way through "The Boulder Patch", a picturesque maze of well-weathered granite rocks.

A trip to Glacier View should rank high on every four-wheeler's list of things to do in the Owens Valley.

Chapter X

Trails Out of Independence

(Inyo National Forest)

Independence is the Inyo County Seat, but it remains a sleepy little hamlet hardly affected by the steady stream of tourists and recreation seekers heading up and down U.S. Highway 395. While it is possible to fill your gas tank, get a room, buy some groceries, or get something hot to eat, most people pass right through without stopping. That is a shame because the Eastern California Museum at 155 Grant Street does a very nice job in explaining the history of Inyo County, and should not be missed. Other nearby historical attractions are the home of writer Mary Austin (at the corner of Market and Grant Streets) and the reconstructed Army Commander's House (relocated to Edwards and Main Streets).

History tells us that one Charles Putnam settled on Little Pine Creek in 1861. Putnam built a sturdy stone house, and operated a modest trading post out of it. Soon others were settling along the creek, and the site became known as Little Pine. There were Indian troubles in the Owens Valley, however, and Putnam's store was fortified against a possible attack. In 1862 the U.S. Army came and established a camp about a mile away. The fort was established on July 4th, 1862, and appropriately took the name Camp Independence. Its immediate purpose was to pacify the Indian deprivations in the valley, but the Union soldiers' presence also dampened the enthusiasm of local Confederate sympathizers, of which there were many. By 1866 the settlement had two stores, a hotel, a blacksmith shop and four saloons. A plot map of lots and streets was drawn up and the town's name was changed from Little Pine to Independence. About this same time there was a mass exodus from the nearby communities of Bend City and San Carlos. A few months later when Inyo County was established, Independence became the county seat.

The first courthouse, a two story brick building, had been in use only two years, when it was destroyed in the great earthquake of March 26, 1872. The second courthouse burned. What you see today is the fourth one, dating from 1920. The most famous prisoner to be brought here for legal proceedings was Charles Manson, who was arrested on October 12, 1969, and brought to Independence pending the filing of a long laundry list of criminal charges. These were later amended include the Tate-LaBianca murders, for which he and his followers were convicted.

Independence of yesteryear
(County of Inyo, Eastern California Museum photo)

Independence of today

The Eastern California Museum

33

Armstrong Canyon

Special Features:	This is an interesting excursion up the eastern escarpment of the Sierra Nevada, which takes one through the range's entire spectrum of geologic history.
Time Required:	This outing deserves the entire day.
Miles Involved:	The distance from downtown Independence to the road's end in Armstrong Canyon is twenty miles.
Degree of Difficulty:	Of the eight miles of dirt road, most are Class II, but because of the steep grades and sometimes-loose traction, four-wheel drive is recommended for the last five miles. At its worse, the road can be considered an easy Class III. In a few places the trail squeezes between large rocks. Here the driver may wish to have a passenger get out and guide the driver through.

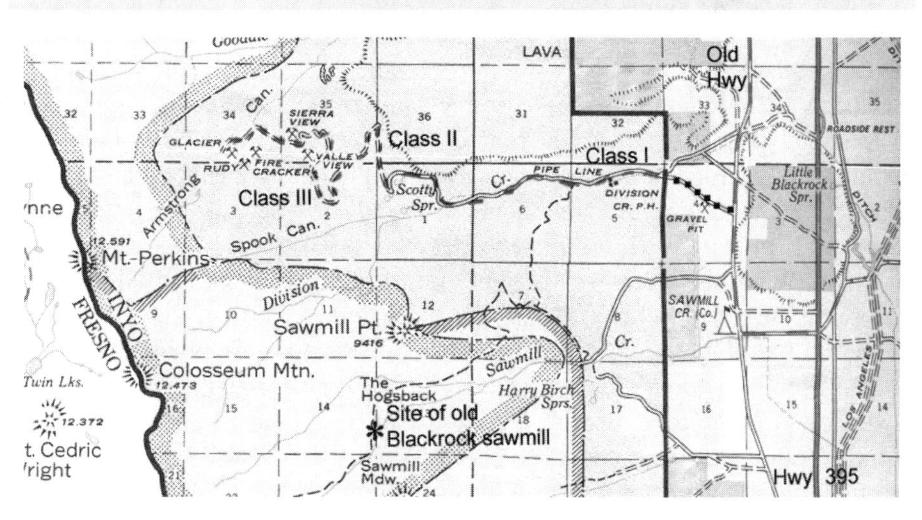

There would not be a road into Armstrong Canyon at all were it not for industry's need to harden steel. During the late 1930s, as the nation was rebuilding its manufacturing capacity after the Great Depression, the metal tungsten was one of those alloys which was starting to be in great demand. The principal ore of tungsten, the mineral scheelite had been found in Pine Creek Canyon, on Coyote Creek above Bishop (see Excursion #30) and on the slopes of Mt. Morgan above Rock Creek (see Excursion #28). From these deposits, prospectors knew that the valuable metal was often found in the Sierra Nevada in the contact zone between the very old metamorphic rocks comprising the ancient core of the range, and the younger igneous rocks which were pushed up from deep within the earth during Cretaceous times. Where exposed, these contact zones were of great interest to those searching for scheelite. One such zone was found high up in Armstrong Canyon. Scheelite was found, but the extent of the orebody could not be determined without probing the mountain with diamond drills with which to pull core samples. The heavy drilling equipment required the construction of a road. Thus it is that today's jeep trail had its origin with the quest for tungsten. As it turned out, the amount of tungsten extracted came nowhere close to paying the cost to build the road, but such is the gamble that the mining industry faces regularly.

To find the road into Armstrong Canyon, drive north out of Independence eight miles to where the Black Rock Springs Road crosses U.S. Highway 395. (For those coming from the north, this is 17.5 miles south of Big Pine). Turn left on Black Rock Springs Road and follow the pavement west 0.8 miles to where there is a "T" intersection. Turn right, on what was the old Highway 395 before today's alignment.

The road passes through a weathered lava flow. In slightly more than a mile, turn left on the paved Division Creek Road. A USFS sign indicates that this is the way to the Sawmill Pass Trail. As the road begins to ascend the alluvial fan, it is difficult not to notice the effects of volcanism all around you.

In slightly less than a mile, the road enters a burned area which will be along both sides of the road for the next three and a half miles. To the uninitiated it may seem strange that rangeland fires can even take place where the vegetation is so sparse and spread out. Unfortunately, however, it happens all too often in this arid land. When the humidity and fuel moistures are very low, any little spark can ignite the dry vegetation. If there is any wind at all, or if there is a slope above the fire, the countryside can be ablaze in minutes. Then add some time for the fire to be spotted and reported, and the time for adequate firefighting resources to come to the scene, and you can easily have hundreds of acres burning before the first suppression efforts have begun. We all need to be super careful with fire when we are traveling and camping in this arid land.

After a mile and a half, the paved portion of the Division Creek Road ends at the DWP's Division Creek Power Plant. Here a 12-inch pipeline coming down from Spook Canyon drives a small generator, which adds its modest contribution to the electrical grid in sending power southward to Southern California. You may wish to note your odometer reading here, as all future distance references will be made from this point. If you are calibrating an altimeter, the elevation here is 4,462 feet.

Beyond the powerhouse, the road now becomes Forest Road 12S01. It is of high standard graded dirt as it continues westward climbing steadily up the alluvial fan. In a half-mile, the parking area for the Sawmill Pass trailhead is encountered on the left. At one time the trail started on the south side of Sawmill Creek at Harry Birch Springs. With the relocation of the highway, the forest service moved the trailhead here.

Because of its steep, hot, dry, and exposed beginnings, coupled with its twelve mile length and nearly 7,000 feet of elevation gain, the Sawmill Pass Trail is not one of the more popular access routes crossing the Sierra crest. Nevertheless, the trail does provide hikers with access to the Woods Lake Basin and the John Muir Trail. Cedar Grove in the depths of Kings Canyon is about a three-day hike to the west. Map features named Sawmill Pass, Point, Lake, Creek, and Meadow all derive their name from the Blackrock sawmill, which operated in the late 1860s in the next canyon to the south. Here, Jeffrey pine and some fir were cut into manageable lengths, and then dragged by oxen to a water-driven sawmill erected on the creek at about 8,400 feet. The logs were cut into lumber, which was then tied into bundles and sent sliding down a three-mile long flume, dropping 4,000 feet to the Owens Valley below. When I first hiked in here in the 1960s, I found portions of the century old flume remaining, but little remained of the sawmill itself.

The well-preserved flume structure of the Blackrock sawmill in 1968.

The dirt road into Armstrong Canyon is interesting, because along its short length of less than eight miles can be found rocks representing all stages of the

Sierra Nevada's geologic history. Beyond the trailhead the devastating effects of the wildland fire have removed all the vegetation, clearly exposing the millions of rounded white boulders of granite that have been carried by gravity and stream erosion out of Spook Canyon. Geologists would call this *Quaternary alluvium*, generally the youngest rock units shown on a geologic map. Alluvium reminds us that once uplifted, all mountains erode and wear back down to sea level. It is an ongoing process that requires only exposure to the elements, gravity and long periods of time. While appearing fresh, the Sierra Nevada range has actually undergone massive erosion. It has been estimated that more that 50,000 vertical feet of rock have been eroded away in the last twenty five million years! And where is that rock today? It can be found in the bottom of the San Joaquin Valley and, to a lesser degree, the Owens Valley.

All around us, but particularly to the left, we can see where the mudflows containing light colored granodiorite boulders have washed out over the dark basalt lava. If the alluvium is deposited upon the lava, then the lava must be the older of the two rock units. This reminds us that in certain places in the Sierra Nevada, volcanism was widespread. Vents deep within the earth have caused thousands of square miles of lava to spill out on top of the granite core of the range over a period of the last thirty million years. It just so happens that here, the volcanism was relatively recent in geologic terms. Some of these cinder cones may have erupted as recently as a mere 10,000 years ago. Long fault lines along both sides of the Owens Valley have caused the valley to drop, while the White and Inyo Mountains on the east and the Sierra Nevada range on the west have been thrust upwards. Along these faults, actually zones of weakness in the earth's crust, molten rock from far below has seeped upwards to the surface. In the case of the dark flows of basalt lava, this molten rock simply oozed out onto the surface, slowly flowing downhill as it cooled. In other nearby areas, notably just to the north, there were a lot of hot gasses mixed in with the molten rock. When these eruptions occurred, reddish brown cinders were produced, creating cinder cones around the vents. In places, these deposits of cinders lie on top of a basalt base, indicating this phase of volcanism was the latest and most recent. As we continue up the road, be watchful for rocks representing even older aspects of geologic history.

The road forks at a point two miles beyond the powerhouse. The better, once graded road goes to the left; however, it soon ends just beyond a small check dam that feeds the pipeline to the powerhouse. There is an unimproved place to camp here, and the pond created by the dam makes a good place to cool off in the heat of summer. For Armstrong Canyon, however, keep to the right at the fork. The road immediately crosses a culvert and deteriorates to Class I and II, as it heads for a spot of greenery less than a mile to the northwest. In 0.2 miles the road forks again. Stay left on the most heavily traveled route. Just less than three miles from the powerhouse is Scotty Spring, a shady oasis set amid the oaks and cottonwoods. There is another unimproved, but nevertheless inviting campsite here. Water seeps to the surface, because the springs sit right on top of the fault running along the eastern base of the Sierra Nevada range. The zone of crushed rock along the fault makes for easy passage of the water in finding its way to the surface.

The elevation at Scotty Spring is 5,700 feet. We have already climbed 1,800 feet since leaving old Highway 395, but the real climb is just ahead. It might be prudent to engage your four-wheel drive here, for while you might not technically need it, you are likely to feel more confident when facing the steep grades ahead.

Beyond Scotty Spring, the road is now certainly Class II, and possibly Class III in places. After a mile the road begins to cross the dark rocks of a lava flow that oozed out of the hillside above. This is an olivine rich basalt.

At the first switchback, there are nice views of the valley below. Within a quarter of a mile the lava is left behind, and we come to the third chapter in our geologic history lesson. Ahead, and high above, are the rocks of granodiorite so typical of the Sierra Nevada. These crystalline plutonic rocks are part of the igneous batholith that was pushed up from deep within the earth during Cretaceous times. These are closely related to the rocks that we see on Half Dome and El Capitan in Yosemite Valley. As the road climbs higher, watch for boulders with white aplite dikes running through them. If you were to hike the Sawmill Pass Trail over the crest, you would see that the granodiorite there has been penetrated with thousands of small dikes of dark rock.

With a gain in elevation, the vegetation also changes. On the floor of the Owens Valley low shrubs like sagebrush, shadscale and rabbit brush dominate the natural scene. As we climb higher we begin to see Mormon tea, *Ephedra viridis,* and larger shrubs such as Mountain Mahogany, *Cerococarpus betuloides,* as well as Desert Mahogany, *Cercocarpus ledifollius*. As uninviting as this dry vegetation may seem, this hillside is prime winter range for large numbers of deer. They move up and down the slope depending on the snow conditions.

A half-mile beyond the second switchback, nearly six miles from the powerhouse, the Valley View Mine is reached. The elevation here is 7,600 feet. It is at the Valley View Mine that one can get a close look at the fourth, and oldest rock unit exposed in the Sierra Nevada. Here can be seen the very old rocks which were in place long before the Sierra Nevada batholith squeezed upwards from the molten core of the earth. When the pluton rose through these rocks, those pre-existing rock units at the edges were simply pushed aside, while those directly under the magma were largely dissolved into the liquid granite. These original rocks have been so altered by heat and pressure that their original form (and age) is difficult to determine. The rocks we see today after this process of metamorphism, include schist, gneiss, tactite and hornfels.

The Valley View Mine

Miners dug a shaft and a tunnel to explore the contact zone between igneous and metamorphic rocks. An examination of the mine dumps will reveal green epidote and a little garnet, both common minerals of metamorphic rocks. Lots of pure white quartz is also present. To look for scheelite, the mineral being sought here, you must come at night with a battery powered "black light". Scheelite gives off a characteristic greenish fluorescent glow when it is exposed to ultraviolet light. Scheelite is the principal mineral from which the metal tungsten is derived. This metal, when alloyed with iron, produces a steel of exceptional hardness, which can be used for everything from drill bits to armor plating. The price of tungsten seems to go up and down with world conflict. It was high during World War II and the Korean War, and depressed during time of peace. State records show that the Division Creek Mine, apparently another name for the Valley View Mine, shipped fifteen tons of tungsten ore in 1939, before the road was built, and another fifteen tons in 1941, after the road was constructed up from Scotty Spring. In the early 1950s, another forty tons of ore was shipped. **Warning: stay out of the underground workings. The shoring has collapsed and they are dangerous**!

Climbing still, the road soon crosses the shoulder of the ridge and enters the Armstrong Canyon drainage. As you round this corner, there are views of the heavily forested Shingle Mill Bench a few miles to the north, another site of logging during the 1800s.

Finally, at a point 6.7 miles from the powerhouse, a three-way fork is reached. The right fork ends after one hundred yards, but it contains a view you will not wish to miss. From this lofty vantage point at 8,000 feet, there is a grand view down into the Owens Valley to the north. Just below can be seen a dozen volcanic cinder cones in various stages of preservation. Slightly to the left, and closer, one can see that a glacial moraine was left in Armstrong Canyon. It descends all the way to the top of the cinder deposits, about the 7,000-foot level. Obviously, the glacier must have descended the canyon at least that far. Because the moraine seems so fresh and has so little erosion, it was probably deposited during the last of the many glacial advances, the Tioga phase only 20,000 years ago. Geologist James Moore, who studied this area, found glacial deposits in Armstrong Canyon from two different stages of Pleistocene glaciation. The youngest are Tioga in age, but in places they over lie older Tahoe phase deposits (see Appendix "C").

The Armstrong Canyon Road provides one with a good view of many cinder cones on the floor of the Owens Valley.

The left fork of this three-way intersection is a Class III road that passes two large fir trees and then switchbacks steeply up the hillside a mile to the Firecracker Mine, situated at an elevation of 8,800 feet. You can drive up there if you wish, but the road is forever blocked by multiple rockslides beginning at a point 0.7 miles beyond this intersection. If you attempt it, you may have to back 0.2 miles down to the second switchback to turn around. The remains of the ore bunker below the Firecracker Mine suggest that this mine, too, might have shipped a little ore out. The 15-minute Mount Pichot quadrangle shows the Pinnacle Mine above the Firecracker, but no road ever went that high. More likely it was just a prospect hole rather than a real mine.

The collapsed ore bunker of the Firecracker Mine.

Select the middle fork to continue on into Armstrong Canyon. The tracks contour around the hillside, and within a mile enter a basin within Armstrong Canyon. Soon they abruptly dead-end at a two-acre flat spot on top of a glacial moraine. The elevation here is about 8,400 feet. Although without water, this flat is covered with some very large pine and fir trees, making it a very pleasant place to camp. The topographic map shows the Rudy and Glacier mines nearby in this basin, but scree sliding down from the steep canyon walls has apparently buried any trace of man's search for tungsten.

Towering above the glacial cirque at the head of Perkins Canyon is 12,591' Mount Perkins. I have never climbed this particular summit, but the trail-less route up Armstrong Canyon appears to be a viable alternative to the usual route from the basin below Pinchot Pass.

The road ends at this beautiful flat.

34

Valley Viewpoint

Special Features:	This is a short, but scenic excursion to a highpoint offering nice views west into the Owens Valley and the Inyo Range beyond.
Time Required:	This outing only takes an hour to complete.
Miles Involved:	The roundtrip distance from downtown Independence to the viewpoint and return is only fourteen miles.
Degree of Difficulty:	Of the three miles of dirt road, most of the route is Class II, but because of the steep downgrades, you may wish to remain in four-wheel drive until reaching the pavement again.

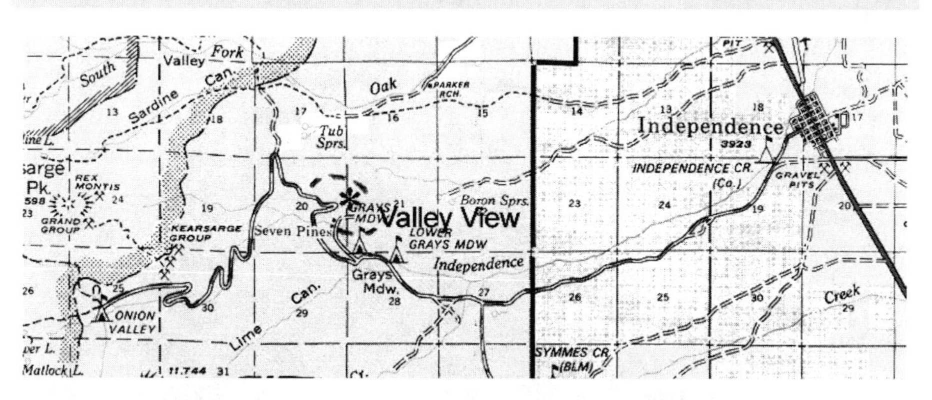

This backroad odyssey begins at the intersection of U.S. Highway 395 and Market Street in downtown Independence. Signs on Highway 395 indicate that Market Street goes to Onion Valley and the Kearsarge Pass trailhead some thirteen miles up the canyon to the west. Note your odometer reading as you turn off Highway 395 onto Market Street. Soon town is left behind and the highway, now the Onion Valley Road, is gradually making its way up the bajada toward the great Sierra Nevada escarpment.

At a point 4.3 miles west of Highway 395, Foothill Road, a good graded side road to the left, goes six miles south to the Shepherd Pass trailhead. Of the two trail passes over the Sierra crest out of Independence, Shepherd Pass is by far the most difficult. By taking it, the backpacker must start at 6000 feet in elevation, then climb 6,000 feet in nine and a half miles to reach 12,050' Shepherd Pass. Kearsarge Pass, on the other hand, is the easiest of the trans-Sierra passes for the hiker. It starts at 8800 feet where the road ends in Onion Valley and climbs only 3000 feet in four miles to 11,823' Kearsarge Pass. Compared to Shepherd Pass, Kearsarge Pass is a piece of cake.

Continuing on up the Onion Valley Road, the Lower Grays Campground is passed on the right, soon followed by the Upper Grays Meadow Campground. At a point six miles from Highway 395, the Onion Valley Road passes the entrance to the 7 Pines Summer Home Tract also on the right. This is where we will return to civilization and end our dirt road adventure.

For the moment we will continue on up the Onion Valley Road, which makes a couple of steep switchbacks. At the seven-mile point look to the left at the lateral moraines left at the edges of Pleistocene glaciers coming down the canyon. If we had been standing here 70,000 years ago, we would have seen an awesome sight. From this vantage point one can also see the remnants of old rock retaining walls marking the site of an old millsite along the first Onion Valley Road.

At a point 7.4 miles from Highway 395, a short road left leads to an ore mill whose tin roof and walls are visible from the roadway. Curiously while the building is probably no older than sixty to seventy years old, it contains an arrastra, a crude device used to crush ore. They were generally replaced by more modern milling technology one hundred years ago.

The ore mill

Gold and silver were first found in steep cliffs above Grays Meadow by a man named Thomas Hill in 1864. Some of the ore was very rich and the find did not go unnoticed. By 1886 there were a half a dozen mines working, each clinging precariously to the canyon's north wall, high above Onion Valley. In the canyon floor below, a ten stamp mill was in operation. The mines had names such as Virginia, Rex Montis, Kearsarge, Phoenix, and Grand, and were accessible only by steep mule trails. All that activity came to a crashing halt in the winter of 1867, when an avalanche came rumbling down from the heights of Kearsarge Peak, destroying eleven cabins and killing one man. Mining resumed again, but most of the mines were abandoned by 1870. In the years since then, scree and rock slides have pretty much obliterated all traces of the mines and the trails which led up them.

The Kearsarge Mine's stamp mill in 1871.
(Photo courtesy County of Inyo, Eastern California Museum)

About a two hundred yards above the turnoff to the mill, the Onion Valley Road crosses a broad flat area where the old road turns off to the left. This is where we will leave the pavement, but we will go to the right, not the left. Recheck your odometer reading, engage your four-wheel drive, and put your transmission in low range. Immediately after leaving the pavement there is a short section of Class III road. It steeply climbs the embankment, but soon moderates in severity. The road forks after only 0.3 miles. The left fork quickly dead-ends at some prospect holes; stay right at this intersection. At a point a half-mile off the pavement, the now Class II road climbs to the rounded summit of a hill. This is the place I call "Valley View", because from this point there is a sweeping panorama eastward of the Owens Valley and the Inyo Mountains on the other side. Behind you to the west, the Sierra Crest stands out. If you are up here in the early morning hours, the Sierra peaks remind one why they are called *The Range of Light.* If you come up here late in the afternoon, it is the White and Inyo mountains that stand out in the sunshine. What time is best? I really don't know, try mid-day as a compromise, although the light tends to be flat then.

The road to Valley View.

One thing you should not compromise on, however, is the time of year. While this excursion can usually be done throughout the year, often even in the dead of winter, try to time your visit for May, when the spring wildflowers are out in great profusion. The vibrant blue of the lupine seems to be in competition with the deep blue flowers of the Great Basin sage. As colorful as those shrubs are, they pale when compared to the unique blood red crimson of the Indian paintbrush.

The road continues on, dropping steeply down the eastern side of the hilltop. Although four-wheel drive is no longer needed, it is better to utilize the braking power of the engine and transmission with four wheels to hold you back rather than only two. After only 0.3 miles the steep downgrade ends, and the tracks make a sharp turn to the right. At a point one mile since leaving the pavement there is a "T" intersection. The U.S. Forest Service has closed the right fork; turn left. The road improves to Class II and in a half-mile, makes a sharp hairpin turn to the right.

At 2.2 miles since leaving the pavement, the road becomes Class I and patches of old asphalt suggest that this was once the main Onion Valley Road. Follow the road through the 7 Pines Summer Home Track. Three miles since leaving the pavement you will return to the modern Onion Valley Road. By turning right it is but seven miles up to the Onion Valley Trailhead. By turning left it is only six miles back to Independence.

Chapter XI
Trails Out of Lone Pine
(Inyo National Forest)

Lone Pine's beginning goes back to the Civil War years of 1862-63, when it became a ranching and farming community, a supplier to the mines scattered about to the east. At that time water from the Owens River had not yet been diverted (some say stolen) by the City of Los Angeles, and the floor of the Owens Valley was a green and fertile place.

The peaceful tranquility of the community was broken at 2:30 a.m. on March 26, 1872, when a major earthquake suddenly struck without warning. The town was nearly destroyed. In a matter of seconds Metsan's General Store and Juan Ybaceta's Union Market were flattened. Worse yet, the Munzinger & Lubken Brewery was reduced to rubble. Twenty-nine of Lone Pine's citizens were found dead under the rubble of collapsed adobe buildings. A twenty-foot fault scarp left by that earthquake can still be seen at the north edge of town. For a better understanding of Lone Pine's past, you may wish to visit the small Southern Inyo Museum. Sponsored by the New Coso Heritage Society, it is located just a half block off Highway 395 at 127 Bush Street.

Lone Pine today, although still a small community of only 2100 people, caters to tourists moving up and down US Highway 395. There are eight motels, several restaurants, four service stations, a market, two auto parts stores and even a small hospital. There are also several campgrounds nearby, just off the road to Whitney Portal. Be sure to stop at the Inter Agency Visitor Center just south of town at the junction of U.S. Highway 395 and State Route 136. Not only does it have some interesting displays, and a well-stocked bookshop, the staff will endeavor to provide the latest road information.

Lone Pine in the 1880s.
(Photo courtesy County of Inyo, Eastern California Museum)

For the very latest in road information, stop at the Inter Agency Visitor Center just south of Lone Pine.

While you are in Lone Pine, check out the Southern Inyo Museum, at 127 Bush Street a half block off Highway 395.

35

The Haiwee Pass Trailhead

Special Features:	While this excursion can generally be done any time of the year, the chief reason to come in here is to see the first of the spring wildflowers. They begin to appear as early as March and April, and peak in May.
Time Required:	This outing can be done in half a day out of Lone Pine.
Miles Involved:	The distance from downtown Lone Pine to the road's end at the start of the Haiwee Pass Trail is about 37 miles.
Degree of Difficulty:	The three miles of dirt roads involved in this excursion are generally no worse than Class II.

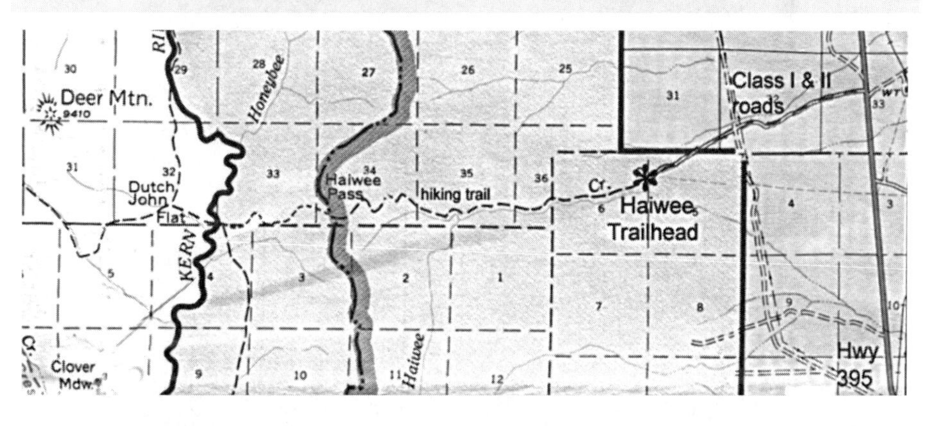

From downtown Lone Pine, take U.S. Highway 395 south 23 miles to the small community of Olancha. Remain southbound on Highway 395, but check your odometer at the intersection of Highway 395 and State Route 190. Note your odometer again as you pass Sage Flat Road, which is 6.3 miles south of your last checkpoint in Olancha. Go another 3.9 miles where a Class I dirt road on the right passes through a gate in the highway fence and starts westward towards the Sierra Nevada (if you are coming from the south, the turnoff left is fourteen miles north of Cinder Road). There may or may not be a sign indicating *Haiwee Pass*. The gate is usually closed, but unlocked. After passing through, please close it again. As sparse as the vegetation may seem, this is cattle country, and the busy highway is no place for cows.

The Joshua tree, *Yucca brevifolia*, is considered to be an "indicator plant" of the Mojave Desert. The presence of Joshua trees here, then, suggests that the lower Owens Valley at least is still within the Mojave Desert Province. Points farther north in the Owens Valley would be considered to be part of the Great Basin Desert, the largest of North America's eight deserts. If you take this road in the spring, as I suggest, the Joshua trees will have large, white showy flowers.

Joshua Trees are indicator plants of the Mojave Desert.

Cholla cactus is common throughout the American Southwest.

There will be many other plants blooming here in the springtime as well. Down on the valley floor, purple pentstemon, *Penstemon monoenis*, Desert aster, *Machaeranthera tortifolia*, and orange mallow, *Sidalcea oregana,* should be evident. As the road goes higher, into the mouth of the canyon, even more wildflowers may be blooming.

A mile in from the highway, a BLM *Watchable Wildlife* sign announces that this is key winter habitat for deer. Still Class I, the road passes beneath a double set of power lines and soon enters Inyo National Forest lands. By now you may be seeing lupine, *Lupinus*, and Indian paintbrush, *Castilleja.* Both plant families have many genera and have widespread distribution in the western states. At a point 2.4 miles from Highway 395, the road forks; stay left and soon you will come to a very large juniper tree, standing alone like a sentry. This was once the site of a pack station which catered to fishing parties going up onto the Kern Plateau. Here we found Yellowheads, *Trichopitilium incisum,* and a yellow composite which keyed out to be Bigelow coreopsis, *Coreopsis bigelovii.* We also found the aromatic bladder-sage, *Salazaria mexicana*, in bloom here.

Standing at the lone juniper and looking west at the Sierra Nevada, you may notice a broken line of greenery extending in a north-south direction along the base of the mountains. The vegetation is green in these spots, because of the presence of added moisture near the surface. That moisture finds its way to the surface through a narrow band of broken and shattered rocks along a fault zone at the base of the mountains.

The Sierra Nevada Range has been thrust upward by a "hinge-fault" mechanism. The western slope of the range rises very gradually from the Central Valley to the Sierra Crest. But here on the eastern flank, the mountains have been pushed steeply upwards creating the impressive Sierra escarpment. The tectonic forces at work deep within the earth go farther than that. While the eastern slope of the Sierra Nevada was being thrust upward, similar faults along the western base of the White and Inyo Mountains were also active. The result is that parallel faults along each edge of the Owens Valley have caused the valley floor to drop, while the mountains on either side have been pushed upwards. Geologists call this a "Horst and Grabben" structure.

From the lone juniper, the road becomes two tracks through the sage and deteriorates to Class II. A canyon is soon entered, and here trees line the channel of tiny Haiwee Creek. While Haiwee Creek flows all year long, the DWP puts its output into a pipe near the trailhead never to be seen again. The stream bank is lined with willows, grapevines and wild roses, all of which require a steady supply of water to survive. In the canyon you are also likely to see mint, clover, thistle, and the *piece du resistance,* prickly pear or beavertail cactus, *Opuntia basilaris.* The cactus has distinctive reddish-purple blossoms.

At a point three miles from Highway 395, the road ends at 4,800 feet, just where the Piñon trees begin. A little used hiking trail starts up the canyon, where after 4.5 miles it crosses 8,200' Haiwee Pass. Here the South Sierra Wilderness boundary is located. From the pass it is only 1.5 miles down to the South Fork of the Kern River. Around the Turn of the 20th Century, when ranchers in the Owens Valley started driving their cows up to the high country meadows, both Olancha Pass and Haiwee Pass were used for those annual cattle drives. The lush meadows of the Monache Mountain area provided plenty of summer feed. Backroad excursions in that area are described in *High Sierra SUV Trails Volume II-The Western Slope*.

The road into Haiwee Canyon.

Appendix A

A Glossary of Geologic Terms Used in the Text

Alluvial fan: the cone-shaped deposit of sand and gravel washed out of a canyon. (See photo on page 198.)

Andesite: a brown, reddish, or gray volcanic rock with a mineral composition equivalent of granite.

Ash: very fine rock particles thrown out by explosive volcanic eruptions.

Bajada: a series of coalescing alluvial fans along the base of a mountain range.

Basalt: a hard black volcanic rock, sometimes containing gas bubble holes.

Batholith: a large mass of igneous rocks still deep within the earth.

Bedrock: solid rock exposed at the surface of the ground.

Bergschrund: the crevasse at the head of a mountain glacier separating the ice and the rock of the mountainside. (See photo on page 174.)

Breccia (volcanic): angular fragments of volcanic rock held together by finer material.

Caldera: a basin formed when a volcano collapses into its magma chamber.

Cinder cone: the accumulated pile of ash and cinder at the mouth of a volcano. (See photos on pages 141 and 183.)

Cirque: a semi-circular basin near the top of a mountain, scooped out and formed by the ice at the head of a glacier.

Cobbles: rounded rocks measuring 2½" to 10" in diameter.

Conglomerate: fragments of rock, often water-worn and rounded, which have been cemented together by other mineral substances. (See photo on page 198.)

Dacite: a light-colored volcanic rock high in quartz (silica) and feldspar.

Dike: an intrusion of molten igneous rock into a crack or joint. (See photo on page 199.)

Epoch: a unit of geologic time within a "Period" (example: the Pleistocene Epoch of the Quaternary Period of the Cenozoic Era).

Era: the largest subdivision of geologic time (example: Mesozoic Era).

Exfoliation: the peeling off from granite of thin concentric layers, similar to an onionskin. (See photo on page 199.)

Fault: a crack in the earth's surface, with one side moving in relation to the other side.

Feldspar: a very common rock-forming mineral containing silica and aluminum oxides.

Fumerole: a volcanic gas vent.

Garnet: a very hard dark reddish-brown mineral, often in crystal form, found in igneous or metamorphic rock.

Glacier: an accumulation of snow that has compacted into ice, slowly moving down-slope or outward in response to gravity. (See photo on page 174.)

Glaciation: the formation and movement of ice masses.

Glacial erratic: a rock fragment caught in a glacier and transported from its original location by the moving ice, to later be deposited elsewhere when the glacier melts. (See photo on page 198.)

Glacial till: unconsolidated sediments of mud, sand, gravel and boulders left by a glacier or streams flowing from glaciers.

Gneiss: a very hard, often banded, metamorphic rock.

Granite: a coarse-grained igneous rock containing quartz, feldspar and mica as the principal minerals.

Granodiorite: an igneous rock of similar composition as granite, except it contains more plagioclase feldspar than granite.

Hornfels: a dense metamorphic rock, often formed when slate (another metamorphic rock) has come in contact with hot igneous rocks such as granite.

Ice Age: a long period of cold climate where snowfalls on the land accumulated vast areas of ice, because precipitation exceeded melting. Ice Ages have occurred as early as the pre-Cambrian and as recently as the Holocene Epochs.

Igneous rock: molten rock formed deep within the earth that has been forced to the surface.

Lava: magma that comes to the earth's surface by volcanic action.

Magma: deep-seated molten rock.

Metamorphic rock: rocks which have been altered from their original form after being exposed to high temperatures and great pressures deep within the earth.

Metamorphism: the alteration of older igneous or sedimentary rocks by great heat, pressure, or chemical changes, which results in changing the original rock into something different.

Mica: a group of minerals characterized by their separation into thin, shiny plates or flakes.

Monzonite: a granite-like igneous rock rich in both plagioclase and orthoclase feldspar and ferro-magnesium minerals, but having little quartz.

Moraine (lateral): unconsolidated sand, gravel, and boulders, which have been pushed out by the sides of a glacier. (See photo on page 199.)

Moraine (terminal): unconsolidated sand, gravel, and boulders, which have been pushed ahead of a glacier as the ice moves down-slope.

Obsidian: a black volcanic glass, which has formed by very rapid cooling of volcanic lava. (See photo on page 136.)

Orebody: a sufficient concentration of valuable minerals to warrant the expense of mining.

Patented claim: a mining claim of sufficient value that a legal process has been gone through which gives the owner not only mineral rights, but ownership of the land with all rights of use.

Period: a unit of geologic time within an Era (example: Jurassic period of Mesozoic Era).

Placer: sand or gravel deposits containing gold or other valuable minerals.

Pluton: A great mass of hot, fluid, igneous rock deep within the earth, that is being, or has been, pushed towards the surface

Potassium-argon dating: a method of dating rocks, based on the decay of the potassium-40 isotope to argon-40.

Prospect: a place where an economically valuable mineral has been found and explored for; however, no mining has (yet) taken place.

Pumice: a light-colored, light-weight frothy volcanic rock, often having enough air holes in it to permit it to float.

Pyroclastic: rock fragments formed by a volcanic explosion.

Quartz: a common rock-forming mineral of silicon dioxide commonly found in a crystalline state.

Quartz latite: a volcanic rock rich in feldspar and quartz.

Quartz monzonite: a granite-like rock, except it is rich in quartz as well as the feldspars.

Rhyolite: a volcanic rock similar in mineral composition to granite.

Richter scale: a system for measuring the intensity of earthquakes. It is a log-rhythmic scale, meaning each numerical increase represents a tenfold increase of intensity.

Roof pendant: older rocks (often metamorphosed) which lie above and often project down into a batholith.

Scheelite: the principal ore mineral of tungsten.

Schist: a metamorphic rock, rich in mica, that easily splits into plates or flakes.

Seismic: earthquakes or man-made vibrations of the earth.

Slate: a relatively fine grained metamorphic rock having well developed cleavage. (See photo on page 199.)

Sulfide: the presence of sulfur chemically bonded with other metallic minerals.

Tactite: a contact-metamorphosed calcareous rock.

Tailings: a pile of waste rock at a mine tunnel or shaft. May also be finely ground ore left over after the milling process has extracted the valuable minerals.

Till: see Glacial till.

Tuff: a rock formed from compacted volcanic ash.

Vein: any mineral deposit that has filled a fissure or fracture. A relatively few contain valuable minerals, but most do not.

Volcanic ash: fine rock material ejected from a volcano.

Weathering: decomposition of rock by exposure to the elements.

Zenolith: (sometimes called inclusion) a fragment of older pre-existing rock which has enclosed within igneous rock. (See photo on page 199.)

Alluvial Fan

Brecchia (volcanic)

Conglomerate

Glacial erratics

Dike

Exfoliation

Metamorphic Rock

Lateral moraine

Slate on Verdi Peak

Dark zenoliths in granite

Appendix B

Geologic Time Chart

Era	Period	Epoch	
Cenozoic	Quaternary	Holocene	
		Pleistocene	2-3
			12
	Tertiary	Pliocene	
		Miocene	26
		Oligocene	37-38
		Eocene	53-54
		Paleocene	
			65
Mesozoic	Cretaceous		
			136
	Jurassic		
			190-195
	Triassic		
			225
Paleozoic	Permian		
			280
	Pennsylvanian		
			310
	Mississippian		
			345
	Devonian		
			395
	Silurian		
			435
	Ordovician		
			500
	Cambrian		
			570
Proterozoic	Keweenawan		
	Huronian		1,000
Archeozoic	Timiskaming		
	Keewatin		1,800

Appendix C

The Plio-Pleistocene Ice Age

Epoch **(Present Time)**	Sierra Nevada Phase	Years Ago	Significance
	Matthes	700 to present	
Holocene	Recess Peak	2000 to 2600	Bow & arrow replaces atlatl. Grinding stones first used. Pottery introduced. All desert lakes are now mostly dry.
Neoglacial	Hilgard	9000 to 10,500	Earliest human artifacts found in Death and Panamint Valleys.
		15,000	High water in Lakes China, Searles Panamint, Manly & Rogers.
	Tioga	20,000	Maximum ice in the Sierra.
Wisconsin	Tenaya	45,000	Maximum ice in the Sierra.
	Tahoe	75,000	Greatest known water depths in inland lakes.
Pleistocene			
Illinoian	Mono Basin	130,000	
Kansan	Casa Diablo	400,000	Maximum ice in Sierra.
Nebraskan	Sherwin	700,000	
	McGee	2,600,000+	Continental glaciation begins in North America.
Late Pliocene			
	Deadman Pass	2,700,000 to 3,100,000	Oldest known Plio-Pliestocene glaciation in California.

Appendix D

Common Wild Flowers likely to be seen along Eastern Sierra Nevada SUV Trails

White or cream-colored flowers

Cow Parsnip, in wet areas, stems 4 feet to 6 feet high with large leaves and large white flower cluster.
Elderberry, large shrub to 8 feet, small white flower, produces blue fruit. (See photo on page 91.)
Prickly Poppy, in disturbed or burned areas, large showy white flowers. (See photo on page 156.)
Ceanothus(Whitethorn), large evergreen bush to 8 feet, spiny twigs, with masses of white flowers. (See photo on page 203.)
Nude Buckwheat, 1-3 feet high, all leaves at base, none on slender stems, petal color variable.
Corn Lily, common in wet meadows, stalk 3 to 6 feet high resembling a cornstalk.

Yellow or golden colored flowers

Western Wallflower, in dry areas, single stalk with golden yellow flower .
Mule Ears, in meadows, low shrub, many hairy leaves with few flowers. (See photo on page 50.)
Rabbitbrush, in disturbed and arid areas, bushes may be large, scented. (See photo on page 156.)
Monkeyflower, in wet meadows, low herb, paired oval leaves, yellow flowers in pairs.
Blazing Star, in dry areas, large showy five-petaled flowers open in evening, close in morning.

Red, pink, or orange colored flowers

Indian Paintbrush, very common with many species. (See photo on page 48.)
Scarlet Pentstemon, often in dry areas, flowers scarlet to vermilion. (See photo on page 76.)
Red Columbine, in moist areas, red flowers with yellow stamens. (See photo on page 48.)
Snowplant, single red stalk, no green leaves, grows in deep organic soil, prefers red fir forest.

Red, pink, or orange colored flowers (continued)

Fireweed, often in disturbed soil or after wildfire, stalks up to 6 feet, deep pink to magenta petals.

Pussy Paws, in dry sandy soil, rosette plant with prostrate flower stems, pink flowers.

Wildrose, common in wet areas along stream banks, stems spiny, pink flowers fragrant.

Desert Peach, large shrub to 6 feet, spiny branches, small flowers with 5 light pink petals.

Beavertail Cactus, arid areas, low, to 1 foot, no leaves, showy flowers, pink to reddish-purple.

Blue or purple colored flowers

Lupine, many species, widespread, flowers usually blue. (See photo on page 48.)

Larkspur, 2 to 4 feet, central stalk with purple flowers. (See photo on page 48.)

Shooting Star, in wet areas, unique purple flower with stamens exposed and petals backwards.

Western Mountain Aster, very common, blooms late, lavender petals around a yellow center.

Sierra Gentian, in wet meadows, funnel-shaped flowers of deep purple on naked stalks.

Showy Pentstemon, in dry areas, blue to violet flowers.

Pennyroyal, mint family, 9 to 18 inches high, pale lavender flowers, the leaves make an excellent tea.

Sierra Iris, in dry open forest below 6,000 feet, grows 1 foot high from bulb. (See photo below.)

Thistle, several species, stem 2 to 6 feet tall, spiny leaves, mostly near base, flower heads to 2 inches. (See photo below.)

Sierra Iris

Sierra Thistle

Ceanothus

Photos by Loris Mitchell

Appendix E

Collecting and Using Wild Berries

Currants, gooseberries, and elderberries, are high in vitamin C, phosphorus, and iron. All can all be used to make homemade pies, jellies, and sauces. In the case of elderberries, they can be crushed and fermented to make an acceptable table wine. **Warning: before eating any native plant product, be sure your plant identification is correct.**

Currants and elderberries can easily be picked by hand off the bush. In order to obtain a pail of currants, you may have to visit a dozen different shrubs. Lay down a poncho, a piece of plastic, or newspaper under the plant and shake the bush. If that does not produce the quantity of berries desired, hand pick the rest. Elderberries are best hand picked, but they grow so profusely that a single bush is likely to provide all your needs in just a matter of minutes. Gooseberries are somewhere in-between in ease of harvest. They have prickly spines covering the fruit that require special handling. The easiest way to pick gooseberries is to use a coffee can with a notch cut into it. Simply put the berry stem in the notch and using the can, pull the berry off the branch so that it drops down into the can.

A coffee can modified to pick gooseberries.

Now that you have a few quarts of fresh raw fruit, the next step is to take them home and prepare them. Here are some ideas:

Currant, Gooseberry or Elderberry Jelly

Wash and crush 2 quarts of fruit. Heat to boiling and pour hot fruit through a filter cloth in a colander. Measure 3 cups into a 6 - 8 quart pan. Add ¼ cup of lemon juice and reheat. Slowly add 1/3 cup of pectin mix while stirring. Heat to boiling. Add 4½ cups of sugar and again heat to boiling. Boil hard for two minutes, then remove from heat for 30 seconds. Skim and pour into canning jars and apply lid. Invert the jars for 1-2 minutes, then set them upright and put them in the pantry to cool.

Elderberry Syrup

To a quart of crushed elderberries add a cup of water and ¼ cup of sugar or honey. Simmer the mixture for 15 minutes, then strain and save the liquid. Add 2 more cups of water to the pulp and seeds and repeat the process. Combine the two liquids and add the juice from one lemon. Bring the liquid to a boil. While that is happening, make a thickening agent by mixing one tablespoon of cold water with one tablespoon of flour or cornstarch. Add the mixture to the simmering mixture and let cool. The resulting syrup is tasty used on pancakes and waffles.

Appendix F

Collecting and Using Piñon Nuts

Piñon nuts are very nutritious. They were a dietary staple of the Paiute as well as other Native American cultures throughout the Southwest. The Indians ate them both raw and roasted, and they often mixed ground piñon nuts with animal fat to make a calorie rich pemmican that was nourishing and easy to carry on long trips.

There are a dozen different species of piñon pine, but only four of them are found in North America north of the U.S.-Mexico border, and of those only one, the single leaf piñon, *Pinus monophylla,* is found in California. Identifying a piñon pine should be no problem to most people. It is the only pine tree in the Sierra Nevada that has a single needle attached to each branchlet. The other pines have their needles in two, threes, or fives.

Like wild berries, the cones from the piñon pine can be collected in our national forests without any permit, or other bureaucratic red tape, provided they are for home consumption and are not sold commercially.

September is the month to go "nutting", although in years of abundant cones October may be good, too. If you start in early September, the cones may not have opened yet, but do not let that deter you. Simply pick the cones off the tree and place them in a bag to take home. A long stick or pole with a hook on the end may help you pick cones from the higher branches that are beyond reach. If the cones are still green, they take more force to twist them off the branches than cones that have ripened and opened. If the cones have already opened, pick the cone apart and let the nuts drop into a pail or pot. It is also OK to pick the fresh dark brown seeds off the ground. If you don't get them, the rodents and Piñon Jays will.

The cones are sticky with pitch, and soon your hands and fingers will be also. I have found that most brands of mechanic's waterless hand soap quickly and easily cut the pitch.

Once you bring your hoard home, the real work begins. If the cones are green and have not yet opened, bring them indoors, spread them out on a tarp, and let them dry out. Depending on the room temperature, the cones will open in a week or two. Then shake the seeds out of the cones onto an opened newspaper. If stored in a dry, well-ventilated environment, the seeds can be stored for a year or more. Do not store them in a sealed container.

The next step is a bit of a bore, cracking the seed shell to get to the meaty nut inside. One method is to spread a light layer over a dishtowel or paper towel, put another towel over them, and then lightly roll a rolling pin over the top towel. Use just enough pressure to crack the shells without crushing the seeds inside. Another more tedious method is to use Vise Grips with the setting adjusted to the size that will just crack the shell.

Once you have the actual nuts separated from the shells, the next step is to roast them. We use a large cast iron skillet over our wood stove, but any a low heat source will do. They can also be put on a large cookie sheet and placed in the oven on low heat. Roasting time and temperature will depend on the residual moisture content of the nuts. If you are using an oven, try one hour at 200-225 degrees, but check them every twenty minutes. Once roasted, the nuts can be stored for months in sealed containers.

Now that you have your nuts, what to do with them? Unfortunately, the writers of most cookbooks would not know a pine nut if one suddenly appeared on their plate. Your imagination is likely to be more useful than most cookbooks. Here are some ideas:

Baked Goods: Add roasted piñon nuts to any variety of breads, cakes, and cookies, just as you might use walnuts. They are also yummy in fudge.

Beverages: I found a café in Albuquerque that adds finely ground piñon nuts to their coffee. I tried it at home and achieved the same "woodsy" flavor.

Cereals: Granola, museli, and any number of other breakfast cereals can benefit from a light sprinkling of piñon nuts.

Fish Dishes: Lightly sprinkle piñon nuts over fish. They particularly enhance the flavor of baked bass and fried trout.

Meat Dishes: Do you like pepper steak? Try lightly broken piñon nuts rather than peppercorns, or add them to meatloaf. Piñon nuts are also good on roasts.

Pasta: The Italians use Piñon nuts (Pignolata) mixed with basil leaves, garlic cloves and Parmesan cheese to make a tasty pesto.

Pilaf: Simply add your roasted piñon nuts to the rice.

Salads: Sprinkle the roasted nuts over a green salad in the same way that you might use sunflower seeds. In a Waldorf salad, use them in place of walnuts.

Appendix G

Tea For The Taking

While coffee is generally my favorite hot drink, I do from time to time, generally while sitting around the campfire, indulge in a cup of one of nature's free teas. There are a number of plants in the High Sierra that make a palatable tea. As you might imagine, the number of leaves (or stems in the case of ephedra) and the time left boiling determine the strength of the resulting brew. Some of these concoctions may have a medicinal value, while others may not. I should emphasize, however, **if you cannot recognize your native plants and know their properties, do not use them for human consumption.** Thus if you are armed with a copy of Jepson's *A Manual of the Flowering Plants of California,* or its successor, *A California Flora and Supplement* by Phillip Muntz, go forth into the mountains and harvest the tax-free bounties of nature!

Tea can be made from a number of wild herbs. The five listed below are perhaps the most common. Dried plant leaves tend to make a stronger brew than fresh ones, so adjust your quantity accordingly. Add boiling water to the leaves, letting the liquid steep for ten minutes or so. Add honey, sugar, and lemon to suit your own taste.

Ephedra, *Ephedra viridis,* is often called Squaw Tea, Mormon Tea, or Mexican Tea. This hardy shrub has at least eight species growing in California and Nevada. In the Sierra Nevada, it grows on the arid eastern slope anywhere from 4,000 to 9,000 feet. Select a plant with fresh green stems. Break off the tender young stems at the tips of the branches. Take some home to dry for later use, but they can also be used immediately. Straight ephedra is a bit bitter for my taste, so I add a dollop of honey or three teaspoons of granular brown sugar. Native Americans utilized this brew for several millennia, taking it for various intestinal and kidney ailments, as well as canker sores. **Warning: I cannot recommend this drink for people with cardiac problems. Ephedra contains the drug ephedrine, a heart stimulant.**

Western or Mountain Pennyroyal, *Monardella odoratissima,* is a member of the mint family which grows to the higher elevations in the eastern Sierra Nevada. Its fragrant leaves, either fresh or dried, can be boiled to make a delicious tea.

Wild Mint, *Mentha arvensis,* can be found in moist meadows and marshes below 7,500 feet. Like most members of the mint family, it has a square stem. Mint leaves, too, make a fragrant tea. In the Middle East, where mint tea is part of the social fabric of life, it is consumed from small glasses for just about any occasion. A cube of sugar enhances the flavor.

Labrador Tea, *Ledum glandulosum*, is sometimes called Trappers Tea. As its name implies, this forest shrub that likes to grow along moist stream banks, has leaves which emit a fragrant odor, and which can be used to make a tea. It is found primarily on the western slope at elevations of 5,000 to 9,000 feet. **Warning: Although I have never suffered any ill effects from drinking its nectar, the plant is said to be poisonous to livestock!**

Wild Rose, *Rosa californica*, has leaves that can also produce a pleasant campfire tea. The rose hips can also be used to make jelly.

Wild Rose

Appendix H

Equipment Checklist for Backcountry Vehicles

Documents

Current vehicle registration (required by State law)
Proof of current liability insurance (required by State law)
Campfire permit (free, obtain one annually)
Map of the specific area you are in, the more detailed the better.
Shop manual for vehicle involved

Personal Safety & Comfort Items

First Aid Kit (the bigger the better)
Extra medications used by anyone present
Water, 2 gallons per person
Pot, cooking, small
Canteens, with carrying case, 2 minimum
Lightweight day or fanny pack
Extra food (sealed MRE's are good for emergencies)
Warm clothing, jacket & hat for all
Compact disposable space blanket, 1 per person
Work gloves, 1 pair minimum
Flashlights, 2 minimum, with fresh or extra batteries
Citizens Band radio, or better yet, 2 meter radio transceiver
Compass
Swiss Army knife or equivalent (with can opener)
Fire extinguisher
Plastic tube tent
Matches (in waterproof container)
Whistle, shrill, emergency signaling
Toilet paper roll
Female sanitary pads, 2 each (can double as trauma dressings)
Notebook, small, with lead pencil
Highway flares, 2 minimum
Sun screen
Insect repellent
Poncho, 1 minimum
Tarp, plastic, small or medium size
Bucket, canvas, collapsible, (a required item in some National Forests)

Extrication Equipment

Shovel, folding GI type, or preferably long handle (required item in some National Forests)
Nylon tow strap
Hi-Lift jack
Hydraulic jack, 4 ton
Come-along, 4 ton rating (minimum)
Tire chains (may be a seasonal item)
Hatchet, or preferably, full size ax
Saw, small

Automotive Tools

Socket set, SAE & metric, recommended
Spark plug socket for above
Open end wrench set, SAE & metric
Crescent wrench set, 3 sizes recommended
Screwdriver set, slot and Phillips
Pliers assortment
Wire cutters
Hammer
Battery post & terminal cleaner
Battery jumper cables
Hack saw with extra blades
Lug wrench
Mini-air compressor
Small funnel
Tire pressure gauge

Spare Automotive Parts

Spark plugs, 2 minimum
Spark plug wire material
Coil
Points set with condenser
Brake fluid, 1 pint
Power steering fluid, 1 pint
Motor Oil, 2 quarts minimum
ATF Fluid, 1 quart

Oil filter
Fuse assortment
Fan belts of appropriate sizes
Tire boot & inner tube
Hose bandage tape

Field Expedient Supplies

Duct tape, 1 roll
Electrical tape, 1 roll
Bailing wire, 1 roll
Electrical wire, 1 small roll, 16 gauge
Sealant, radiator (Stop Leak)
Gasket sealant
Tube, siphon, 5' minimum
Cord, nylon, 50' minimum
Hand Cleaner (waterless)
Paper towel roll
Plastic trash sack

Optional Non-Essential Items which are nice to have along

Camera with film
Binoculars
Glass cleaner
Bar soap, small
Plastic bags, small, resealable
NOAA Weather radio receiver
GPS receiver
Spare fuel container with spout
Cellular telephone
Family radio service transceivers, one pair

Appendix I

Fuel Safety

Most backroad explorers feel more comfortable knowing they have a full tank of gas, with perhaps a little more held in reserve. While maintaining adequate fuel supplies is a legitimate concern in the remote places of Arizona, Nevada and Utah, it should not be a problem in the Eastern Sierra. Every backcountry destination described in this guide is but a few gallons from the nearest gas pump.

Nevertheless, if you feel you must carry some extra fuel, remember that any gasoline carried in any container, other than the vehicle's fuel tank, poses an increased fire hazard. The reader would be well advised to observe these simple Do's and Don'ts:

- **Don't** ever carry any fuel in a plastic container.
- **Do** secure any gas container so that it cannot tip over or bounce around. Utilize an appropriate external mounting bracket.
- **Don't** ever carry any fuel inside the passenger space of any vehicle. Not only is it an extreme fire hazard, but it is sure to leak, creating noxious fumes. The popular GI "Jerry Cans" are notorious for their leaking gaskets.
- **Do** carry an ABC fire extinguisher in your vehicle, the bigger the better, and be sure it is stowed within easy reach.
- **Don't** ever fill any supplemental fuel container while it is in the vehicle. Avoid static electricity by setting the container on the ground while filling it.
- **Do** transfer the extra fuel into your vehicle's gas tank as soon as you can.
- **Don't** forget to bring a pouring spout, preferably one with a screen filter to catch any large rust particles that might be in the gas can.

Carry extra gasoline in a metal container properly secured on the exterior of the vehicle.

Appendix J

Some Useful Addresses and Telephone Numbers

California Highway Conditions: 1-800-427-ROAD
Nevada Highway Conditions: (775) 793-1313

Trails Out of Reno

Supervisor's Office
Humboldt-Toiyabe National Forest
1200 Franklin Way
Sparks NV 89431
(775) 331-6444

Carson Ranger Station
Humboldt-Toiyabe National Forest
1536 So. Carson Street
Carson City NV 89701
(775) 884-8123

Carson City District Office
Bureau of Land Management
5665 Morgan Mill Road
Carson City NV 89701
(775) 885-6000

Trails Out of Truckee

Truckee Ranger Station
Tahoe National Forest
10342 Highway 89 North
(530) 587-3558

Truckee-Donner Chamber of Commerce
10065 Donner Pass Road
Truckee CA 96161
(530) 587-2757

Trails Out of South Lake Tahoe

Lake Tahoe Basin Management Unit
U,S, Forest Service
870 Emerald Bay Road, Suite 1
South Lake Tahoe CA 96150
(530) 573-2600

Lake Tahoe Visitor Center
U.S. Forest Service
Highway 89
Camp Richardson CA
(530) 573-2674

Trails Out of Markleville

Alpine County Museum
P.O. Box 517
Markleeville CA 96120
(530) 694-2317

Trails Out of Bridgeport

Bridgeport Ranger Station
Humboldt-Toiyabe National Forest
HCR-1, Box 1000 (just south of town on Hwy 395)
Bridgeport CA 93517
(760) 932-7070

Bridgeport Chamber of Commerce
P.O. Box 541
Bridgeport CA 93517
(760) 932-7500

Trails Out of Lee Vining

Mono Lake Ranger Station
Inyo National Forest
P.O. Box 429
Lee Vining CA
(760) 647-3000

Mono Basin Visitor Center
Inyo National Forest
Highway 395 North
Lee Vining CA 93541
(760) 647-3044

Mono Basin Historical Society
(Schoolhouse Museum)
1st Street at Mattly Ave
P.O. Box 31
Lee Vining CA 93541
(760) 647-6461

Trails Out of Lee Vining (continued)

Mono Lake Committee
Highway 395 at 3rd Street
Lee Vining CA 93541
(760) 647-6595

Trails Out of Mammoth Lakes

Inyo National Forest
Mammoth Ranger Station and Visitor Center
State Route 203
P.O. Box 148
Mammoth Lakes CA 93546
(760) 924-5500

Trails Out of Bishop

Supervisor's Office
Inyo National Forest
873 No. Main Street
Bishop CA 93514
(760) 873-2400

White Mountain Ranger Station
Inyo National Forest
798 No. Main Street
Bishop CA 93514
(760) 873-2500

Bishop Field Office
Bureau of Land Management
785 No. Main Street, Suite "E"
Bishop CA 93514
(760) 872-4881

Laws Railroad Museum
Silver Canyon Road east of Hwy 6
P.O. Box 363
Bishop CA 93514
(760) 873-5950

Bishop Area Chamber of Commerce
690 No. Main Street
Bishop CA 93514
(760) 873-8405

Trails Out of Big Pine

Big Pine Chamber of Commerce
126 So. Main Street
Big Pine CA 93513
(760) 938-2114

Trails Out of Independence

Eastern California Museum
155 Grant Street
Independence CA 93526
(760) 878-0258

Independence Chamber of Commerce
P.O. Box 397
Independence CA 93526
(760) 878-0084

Trails Out of Lone Pine

Lone Pine Ranger Station
Inyo National Forest
501 So. Main Street
P.O. Box 8
Lone Pine CA 93545
(760) 876-6200

Inter Agency Visitor Center
Highway 395 and State Route 136
P.O. Drawer "R"
Lone Pine CA 93545
(760) 876-6222

Lone Pine Chamber of Commerce
126 So. Main Street
P.O. Box 749
Lone Pine CA 93545
(760) 876-4444 or (877) 253-8981

References

Anon, *Alpine Heritage*, Bishop CA: Centennial Book Committee, 1964.

____, *Cultural and Historical Significance of the Lake Tahoe Region,* South Lake Tahoe CA: prepared for Tahoe Regional Planning Agency and the U.S. Forest Service, September 1971.

____, "Tungsten", *Mineral Information Service,* San Francisco CA: Vol. 9, No. 5, California Division of Mines, May 1, 1956.

Alt, David, and Donald W. Hyndman, *Roadside Geology of Northern and Central California,* Missoula MT: Mountain Press Publishing Co., 2000.

Bailey, Edgar H., editor, *Geology of Northern California,* San Francisco CA: Bulletin 190, California Division of Mines and Geology, 1966.

Bateman, Paul C., *Economic Geology of the Bishop Tungsten District,* San Francisco CA: California Division of Mines and Geology, 1956.

Berger, Karen, and Daniel Smith, *The Pacific Crest Trail,* Woodstock VT: Countryman Press, 2000.

Birman, Joseph H., *Glacial Geology Across the Crest of the Sierra Nevada, California,* New York: Special Paper No. 75, Geological Society of America, 1964.

Browne, Juanita Kennedy, *Nuggets of Nevada County History,* Nevada City CA: Nevada County Historical Society, 1983.

Calhoun, Margaret, *Pioneers of Mono Basin*, Lee Vining CA: Artemisia Press, 1984.

Clark, William B., *Gold Districts of California*, San Francisco CA: Bulletin 193, California Division of Mines and Geology, 1970.

____, *Mines and Mineral Resources of Alpine County California*, Sacramento CA: County Report #8, California Division of Mines and Geology, 1977.

Clarke, Charlotte Bringle, *Edible and Useful Plants of California,* Berkeley, Los Angeles, and London: University of California Press, 1977.

Constantine, Helen, *Plant Communities of the Mono Basin,* Lee Vining CA: Mono Lake Committee, Kutzavi Press, 1993.

Curry, Robert R., "California's Deadman Pass Glacial Till is Also Nearly 3,000,000 Years Old", *Mineral Information Service*, San Francisco CA: Vol. 21, No. 10, California Division of Mines and Geology, October 1968.

Dedecker, Mary, *Mines of the High Sierra*, Glendale CA: La Siesta Press, 1966.

Egan, Ferol, *Fremont, Explorer for a Restless Nation,* Garden City NY: Doubleday & Co., 1977.

DuBray, E.A., *Generalized Bedrock Geologic Map of the John Muir Wilderness, Fresno, Inyo, and Mono Counties, California,* Washington DC: U.S. Geological Survey Map MF-1185A, 1981.

____, with D.A. Dellinger, H.W. Oliver, M.F. Diggles, Frederick L. Johnson, Horace K. Thurber, Richard W. Morris, Thomas J. Peters, and David S. Lindsay, *Mineral Resource Potential of the John Muir Wilderness, Fresno, Inyo and Mono Counties California*, Washington DC: U.S. Geological Survey, Map MF-1185-C, 1982.

Ekman, A, et al, *Old Mines and Ghost Camps of California*, Fort Davis Texas: Frontier Book Co., 1970.

Farquhar, Francis P., *History of the Sierra Nevada*, Berkeley and Los Angeles: University of California Press, 1966.

Fremont, John Charles, *Report of the Exploring Expedition to the Rocky Mountains in the years 1842, and to Oregon and north California in the years 1843-44*, Washington DC: U.S. 28th Cong., 2nd session, House Ex. Doc. No. 166, 1845.

Gortner, Willis A., *The Martis Indians: Ancient Tribe Of The Sierra Nevada,* Woodside CA: Portola Press, 1986.

Grossi, Mark, "Sierra Frogs Fall Silent", *The Fresno Bee,* Fresno CA: The Fresno Bee, June 24, 2001.

Gudde, Erwin G., *California Place Names*, Berkeley CA: University of California Press, 1962.

____, *California Gold Camps*, Berkeley, Los Angeles, and London: University of California Press, 1975.

Harris, Stephen L., *Fire Mountains of the West,* Missoula MT: Mountain Press Publishing, 1988.

Hayden, Mike, *Guidebook To The Lake Tahoe Country, Volume II*, Los Angeles: Ward Ritchie Press, 1971.

Hill, Mary, *Geology of the Sierra Nevada,* Berkeley, Los Angeles, and London: University of California Press, 1975.

Hindes, Margaret G, *A Report on Indian Sites and Trails, Huntington Lake Region, California,* (unpublished).

Huber, N. King, and C. Dean Rinehart, *Geologic Map of the Devil's Postpile Quadrangle,* Washington DC : U.S. Geological Survey Map GQ-437, 1965.

____, with Paul C. Bateman and Clyde Wahrhaftig, *Geologic Map of Yosemite National Park and Vicinity, California,* Washington DC: U.S. Geological Survey Map I-1874, 1989.

Jaeger, Edmund C., *The North American Deserts,* Stanford CA: Stanford University Press, 1957.

Lanner, Ronald M., *The Piñon Pine*, Reno NV: University of Nevada Press, 1981.

Lekisch, Barbara, *Tahoe Place Names,* Lafayette CA: Great West Books, 1988.

Lewis, Oscar, *High Sierra Country*, New York: Duell, Slone & Pierce, 1955.

Matthes, Francois E., *Reconnaissance of the Geomorphology and Glacial Geology of the San Joaquin Basin, Sierra Nevada, California,* Washington DC: Professional Paper 329, U.S. Geological Survey, 1960.

Mills, Russ, "A Road From The Past", *Desert Magazine*, Palm Desert CA: Desert Magazine, March 1974.

Mitchell, Roger, *Inyo-Mono Jeep Trails*, Glendale CA: La Siesta Press, 1969.

____ *Eastern Sierra Jeep Trails,* Glendale, CA: La Siesta Press, 1971.

____ "Avalanche on Copper Mountain", *Desert Magazine*, Palm Desert CA: Desert Magazine, November 1975.

____ *Western Sierra Jeep Trails*, Glendale CA: La Siesta Press, 1976.

Moore, James G., *Geology of the Mount Pinchot Quadrangle, Southern Sierra Nevada California,* Washington DC: U.S. Geological Survey Bulletin 1130, Government Printing Office, 1963.

Nadeau, Remi, *Ghost Towns and Mining Camps of California,* Los Angeles CA: The Ward Ritchie Press, 1965.

____ *The Silver Seekers*, Santa Barbara CA: Crest Publishers, 1999.

Peattie, Donald Culrose, *A Natural History of Western Trees,* Boston MA: Houghton Mifflin Company, 1953.

Rinehart, C. Dean, and Donald Ross, *Geology and Mineral Deposits of the Mount Morrison Quadrangle Sierra Nevada, California,* Washington DC: U.S. Geological Survey Professional Paper 385, Government Printing Office, 1964.

Sampson, R.J., "Mineral Resources of Mono County", *California Journal of Mines and Geology,* San Francisco CA: Vol. 36, No. 2, California Division Mines and Geology, April 1940.

Schumacher, Genny, et al., *Mammoth Lakes Sierra,* San Francisco CA: The Sierra Club, 1962.

Scott, Edward B., *The Saga of Lake Tahoe,* Crystal Bay NV: Sierra-Tahoe Publishing, 1973.

Sharp, Robert P. and Allen F. Glazner, *Geology Underfoot in Death Valley and Owens Valley,* Missoula MT: Mountain Press Publishing Co., 1997.

Signor, John R., *Donner Pass, Southern Pacific's Sierra Crossing,* San Marino CA: Golden West Books, 1985.

Slemmons, David B., *Cenozoic Volcanism of the Central Sierra Nevada, California,* Reno NV: Mackay School of Mines Technical Report #4, (prepared for NASA), University of Nevada, 1966.

____, *Cenozoic Volcanism of the Central Sierra Nevada, California,* San Francisco CA: Bulletin 190, California Division of Mines and Geology, 1966.

Stone, Irving, *Men To Match My Mountains,* Garden City NY: Doubleday & Co., 1956.

Storer, Tracy and Robert Unsinger, *Sierra Nevada Natural History,* Berkeley, Los Angeles and London: University of California Press, 1963.

Teie, William C., *4 Wheeler's Guide to the Rubicon Trail,* Rescue CA: Deer Valley Press, 1998.

Thomas, John Hunter, and Dennis R. Parnell, *Native Shrubs of the Sierra Nevada,* Berkeley, Los Angeles and London: University of California Press, 1974.

Tortorich, Frank, Jr., *Gold Rush Trail,* Pine Grove CA: Wagon Wheel Tours, 1998.

Townley, John M., *The Lost Fremont Cannon Guidebook*, Reno NV: The Jamison Station Press, 1984.

Twain, Mark (aka Samuel Clemens), *Roughing It*, New York: reprinted as a Signet Classic by The New American Library of World Literature, 1962.

Voge, Harvey, editor, *A Climber's Guide To The High Sierra,* San Francisco CA: The Sierra Club, 1954.

Whitney, Stephen, *The Sierra Club Naturalist's Guide, Sierra Nevada*, San Francisco CA: The Sierra Club, 1979.

Williams, George III, *Mark Twain, His Adventures At Aurora and Mono Lake,* Riverside CA: Tree By The River Publishing, 1987.

Index

A California Flora, 208
A Manual of the Flowering Plants of California, 208
Addresses, 214-217
Adobe Valley, 117
Aeroplane Mine, 155
Agnew Meadow, 139
Airola Peaks, 68
Alhambra Mine, 71, 72
Allen chipmunk, 42, 46
Alpine County Museum, 65-66
Alpine County, 65, 79, 87, 89
Alpine Meadows Ski Area, 31
Alpine Mine, 72
Alpine Walk Peak, 25
Amador County, 89
Amtrak, 27
Angels Camp CA, 80, 89
Angora Peak Fire Lookout, 35
Ansel Adams Wilderness, 3
Antelope Valley, 104
Archaeological Resources Act of 1979, 5, 105
Arctostaphylos, 90
Argemone muntia, 156
Armstrong Canyon, 177-184
Aspen, 46, 50, 55, 144, 157
Aurora NV, 93, 110, 115, 122
Austin, Mary, 175
Azurite, 16, 119
Babbit Peak Fire Lookout, 35
Baker Creek, 162, 164-166, 170
Baker Lake, 165-166
Baker Pass, 165
Baldwin Estate, 39
Banner Peak, 127, 139
Barker Creek Trail, 1
Barker Creek, 52
Barker Pass Road, 49
Barker Pass, 49, 50-52, 55, 58
Barker Peak, 51
Barney Riley Trail, 87
Basin Mountain, 154, 157
Beacon Point, 19
Bear Lake, 52, 55
Bear Valley Ski Area, 65
Beartrack Canyon, 125-128
Beavertail cactus, 193, 203
Belding Ground Squirrel, 36
Bend City CA, 175
Benecia CA, 101
Benson, Thomas Hart, 100
Big Meadow, 25-26
Big Pine CA, 167-168
Big Pine Creek, 165, 170
Big Pine Spring, 171
Bigelow coreopsis, 193
Billib, Emil, 110, 117
Birch Creek (Inyo County), 158
Birch Creek (Mono County), 151
Birch Mountain, 170, 172
Bishop CA, 148-149, 150-151
Bishop Creek Canyon, 145, 149, 158
Bishop Creek, 143
Bitter cherry (see Red cherry)
Blackrock Sawmill, 179
Blackrock Springs Road, 178
Blackwood Canyon Road, 49, 53, 55
Blackwood Canyon, 50, 55
Blackwood Creek Trail, 1
Blackwood Creek, 50, 55
Blackwood Middle Fork OHV Trail, 50-51
Bladder-sage, 193
Blazing star, 202
BLM, see Bureau of Land Management
Bloody Canyon, 145
Bloody Mountain, 147
Bloody Peak, 147
Blue Creek, 77, 79
Blue Lakes Road, 78
Blue Lakes, 79
Boca CA, 19, 27
Bodie CA, 109, 111, 122
Boise ID, 21
Boomtown NV, 26
Borda Ranch, 44
Bornite, 16

Index

Boundary Peak, 127
Bridgeport CA, 93-94, 95, 106, 107, 109, 108, 110
Bridgeport Valley, 108
Brockway Summit, 29-30, 32, 34, 38
Brown Lake, 165
Buck Lake, 58-59
Buckwheat, 202
Bull Ranch Creek, 15
Burcham Creek, 104
Burcham Flat, 102, 103
Bureau of Land Management, 4, 5
Buttermilk Country, 154-159
Buttermilk Road, 155
Cadillac Hill, 64
Cain, Ella, 109-110
Calhoun, Margaret, 128
California Department of Fish & Game, 4
California Department of Forestry and Fire Protection, 35
California Desert Protection Act of 1994, 3, 167
California Ground Squirrel, 36
California gulls, 118
California Wilderness Act of 1984, 3
Camp Independence CA, 175
Camp Nye NV, 44
Camp Richardson CA, 39
Cardinal Mountain, 170
Carson & Colorado Railroad, 149
Carson and Tahoe Lumber & Fluming Company, 46
Carson City NV, 13, 41, 43-44, 110
Carson Pass Toll Road, 69
Carson Pass, 67, 69, 74, 78, 89
Carson Range, 22, 25
Carson Valley, 42, 45
Carson, Kit, 100
Carson-Iceberg Wilderness Area, 68, 88
Carvin, Kennet, 43
Casa Vieja Meadows, 3
Castle Peak Mining District, 110
Ceanothus, 202
Centerville Flat CA, 65, 87, 88
Central Pacific Railroad, 11, 13, 18, 27
Cercocarpus betuloides, 181
Cercocarpus Ledifolius, 15, 127
Chain Lakes, 3
Chalmers mansion, 88-89
Chalmers, Antoinette, 88
Chalmers, Lewis, 88, 90
Chango Lake, 97
Charity Valley, 69, 75, 77
Chinquapin, 34, 42
Chipmunk, 36-37
Cholla cactus, 192
Chris Flat, 103
Chrysocolla, 119
Chrysothamnus nausesous, 156
Cisco CA, 13
Citellus beldingi, 36
Citellus lateralis, 36-37, 42, 46
Citellus, beecheyi, 36
Civilian Conservation Corps, 35
Clark, Thomas, 157
Clear Creek, 42
Cleopatra Mine, 14
Clover Valley, 3, 77
Clyde, Norman, 157
Colorado Hill, 72, 82, 87
Columbine, 202
Columbine, 46, 48
Commercial Row (Truckee), 28-29
Comstock mines, 27, 34, 44
Convict Creek Canyon, 145
Conway Ranch, 122-123
Conway Summit, 116, 117, 120
Copper Mountain, 116-122
Copper, 13, 83
Coreopsis bigelovii, 193
Corn lily, 202
Cottonwood Meadows, 105
Cow Creek, 165
Cow parsnip, 202
Coyote Creek Road, 162, 165
Coyote Creek, 160-163, 165, 178
Coyote Flats, 161, 165
Coyote Lake, 163

Index

Crater Flat, 132, 134
Crater Lake, 69-71
Crowley Lake, 151
Crystal Fire, 18-19
Crystal Peak, 18-19
Cuprite, 119
Currant Wildland Fire Information (website), 21
Currants, 43, 90-92, 204-205
Curtz Mine, 84
Dardanelles Peak, 68
Davidson, James, 43
Davis Meadow, 26
Deadman Campgrounds, 135
Deadman Creek, 131, 134, 136
Deadman Dome, 134
Deadman Pass, 137-141
Death Valley National Park, 167
Death Valley SUV Trails, 167
Death Valley, 117
Deep Creek, 103
Deer Creek, 80
Deer Mountain, 132
Deer Valley, 3, 77, 79-80
Deer, 170, 181, 193
Department of Water & Power (City of L.A.), 4
Desert aster, 193
Desert mahogany,15, 127, 156, 181
Desert peach, 203
Desolation Wilderness, 52, 56, 58-59
Devil's Gate, 101, 102, 104
Devil's Postpile National Monument, 129
DFG, see California Department of Fish & Game
Dinkey Lakes Wilderness, 3
Disappointment Peak, 170
Division Creek Mine, 182
Division Creek Powerhouse, 178
Division Creek Road, 178
Dog Creek, 18
Dog Valley Road, 18
Dog Valley, 19
Dogtown CA, 117
Dogtown Creek, 110
Domeland Wilderness, 3
Donner Pass, 27
Dorothy Lake, 145
Duane Bliss Peak, 46-47
Duncan Peak Fire Lookout, 35
Dunderberg Creek, 110
Dunderberg Mine and mill, 107, 110-113
Dunderberg Peak, 110
DWP, see Department of Water & Power
Eagle Station, 44
Earthquake fault, 135, 180, 181, 193
Earthquakes, 135, 140, 189
East Fork of Carson River, 85, 87, 88
East Walker River, 93
Eastern California Museum, 175-176
Eastern Sierra Jeep Trails, 2, 87, 88
Ebbetts Pass, 65, 77, 80, 81, 86, 87, 89
Egan, Ferol, 102
Ehrnbeck Peak, 97
El Diablo Mining Company, 163
El Dorado National Forest, 4, 39
Elderberry, 202, 204-205
Elephant's Back Peak, 76
Ellis Lake, 55, 59
Ellis Peak, 49, 52-59, 64
Ellis, Jock, 56
Ellis, Rod, 1
Emigrant Trail, 19
Enargite, 83
Ephedra viridis, 181, 208
Equipment checklist, 210-212
Erethizon, dorsatum, 7
Ershim-Dusy Jeep Trail, 3, 140
Eutamias nus, 36-37
Eutamias townsendi, 42, 46
Excelsior Range, 127
Exchequer smelter and furnace, 88-89
Faith Valley, 69, 77
Fales Hot Springs, 100, 101, 104
Firecracker Mine, 183, 184
Fireweed, 203
Fitzpatrick, Thomas, 101, 102
Floriston CA, 26

Index

Forest City Flat CA, 81
Forestdale Divide, 74, 76
Forsyth Peak, 97
Francis Lake, 153
Fravel Mine, 13
Fravel, H.H., 14
Fremont, John C., 65, 99-105
Fremont's "Lost Cannon", 99-105
Frogs, 63
Fuller, C.W., 11
Fuller's Crossing, 11
Funnel Lake, 165
Gains, David, 115
Galena Peak, 42
Gardnerville NV, 47
Gatekeepers Cabin and Museum, 39
Genevieve Lake, 145
Genoa NV, 82, 89
Genoa Peak, 45-47
Geologic Time chart, 200
Georgetown CA, 56
Georgiana Mine, 84
Glacial moraine, 108,
Glacier Lodge Road, 170
Glacier Mine, 184
Glacier View, 169-174
Glass Creek, 136
Glenbrook NV, 41-42
Gold, 82, 110, 111, 186
Golden Eagle Mine, 14
Golden Fleece Mine, 13-14
Golden Trout Wilderness, 3
Golden trout, 147
Golden-mantled Ground Squirrel, 36-37, 42, 46
Goleta Consolidated Mining Company, 117
Goodale Mountain, 170
Gooseberries, 90-92, 204-205
Grand Mine, 187
Grays Meadow, 187
Green Creek Road, 107, 110
Green Creek, 107, 110, 112
Green Lake, 165
Grizzly bear, 101
Ground Squirrel, 36-37
Grouse Meadows, 102
Grouse Ridge Fire Lookout, 35
Haiwee Pass, 191-194
Halford, Anne, 144
Hanging Valley Tungsten Mine, 156
Hangmans Bridge, 81, 87
Hard Point Prospect, 147
Harry Birch Springs, 179
Hawthorne NV, 119
Haypress Flat, 81, 84
Headlight Mine, 129
Heitz Meadow, 3
Heller Estate, 39
Hennes Pass Road, 19-20
Hermit Valley, 77, 80
Hidden Lake, 165
Higbie, Cal, 119
High Sierra SUV Trails Vol. II The Western Slope, 8, 140, 194
Hill, Thomas, 186
Hilton Creek, 143
Hindes, Margaret, 135
Homewood, 55
Hoover Wilderness Area, 97
Hope Valley Campground, 78
Hope Valley Mining District, 72
Hope Valley, 69, 70, 75, 77
Horseshoe Lake, 140
Horton Creek Canyon, 156
Horton Lake, 156, 157
Humboldt-Toiyabe National Forest 1, 3, 19, 39
Humphries, A.A., 157
Hunchback Peak, 163
Hunewell Lake, 106, 108
Hunter Creek, 25
Hunter Lake, 22-25
Hunter, John M., 25
Hunter's Crossing, 25
Huntoon Valley, 104
Hutchison, Edward and James, 158
Hyla regilla, 63

Index

Imperial Silver Quarries Company, 88, 89
Independence CA, 175-176
Indian paintbrush, 48, 145, 193, 202
Indian pond lily, 52
Inter Agency Visitor Center (Lone Pine), 189-190
Inyo County, 175
Inyo Crater Lakes, 131-133
Inyo Craters, 132-135
Inyo National Forest, 1, 4, 149
Inyo-Mono SUV Trails, 167
Ivins, Jon, 43
IXL Mine, 89
Jeep, 4
Jeffrey Pine, 34, 42, 46, 126, 151, 157, 179
John Muir Trail, 179
John Muir Wilderness, 3, 143, 153, 157, 165
Jordan CA, 117, 119, 122-124
Jordan Mining District, 117
Joshua tree, 192
June Lake Loop, 129
Juniperous occidentalis, 68, 79
Kaiser Pass, 140
Kaspian Campground, 50, 55
Kavanaugh Ridge, 110, 113
Kearsarge Mine and mill, 187-188
Kearsarge Pass, 185, 186
Kearsarge Peak, 187
Keeler CA, 149
Kenneth Lake, 153
Kern Plateau, 3, 147, 193
Kid Mountain, 172
King, Benjamin, 44
Kings Beach NV, 33
Kings Canyon, 41-44
Kingsbury Grade, 45
Kirkwood Ski Area, 65
Knee Ridge, 58
Konigsberg CA, 65, 88
La Siesta Press, 173
Labrador tea, 209
Lake Alpine Resort, 80
Lake Bigler Toll Road, 41
Lake Manly, 117
Lake Mary, 145
Lake Russell, 117
Lake Tahoe Basin Management Unit, 27, 33, 39
Lake Tahoe Hi-Lo 4WD Club, 1
Lake Tahoe Museum, 39
Lake Tahoe, 31, 33-34, 39, 41, 52, 54, 56
Lake, Myron, 11
Lake's Crossing, 11
Larkspur, 46, 48, 203
Laughton, Larry, 88
Laurel Creek Canyon, 145, 147
Laurel Creek glacier, 145
Laurel Creek, 143-144
Laurel Lakes, 142-147
Laurel Mountain, 145
Lava Springs, 104
Laws Railroad Museum, 148-149
Leavitt Peak, 97
Ledum glandulosum, 209
Lee Vining CA, 116, 121, 123, 125, 126
Lee Vining Canyon, 117, 126
Lekisch, Barbara, 56
Leviathan Mine Road, 81, 84
Lewis & Clark Expedition, 90
Lily Lake, 52, 58, 62-63
Lisbon Mine, 129
Little Pine CA, 175
Little Sister Mine, 155
Little Wolf Creek (Mono County), 97
Lobdell Lake, 104
Lodgepole pine, 50, 52, 55, 79, 139
Log Cabin Mine, 125, 128
Lone Pine CA, 189-190
Long Valley Caldera, 140, 151
Lookout Mountain, 162
Loon Lake, 58, 62
Loope CA, 82
Loope Canyon, 81-85
Los Angeles CA, 115, 139, 167, 189
Lost Cannon Peak, 104
Lost Cement Mine, 129

Index

Lost Lakes, 75
Lower Blue Lake, 73, 75, 77
Lower Laurel Lake, 145, 147
Lower Miller Lake, 64
Lower Rock Creek Road, 151
Lower Summers Meadows, 107
Lower Summit City, 75
Lucky Boy NV, 122
Lucky Strike Mine, 155
Lundy Canyon, 117, 123
Lundy Lake, 116, 119, 120
Lupine, 46, 48, 145, 188, 193, 203
Luther Pass, 67, 69, 74, 75, 78
Lynch & Faber, 14
Lyon Peak, 42
Machaeranthera tortifolia, 193
Malachite,16, 119
Malacosoma americana, 172
Malacosoma pluviale, 172
Mammoth City CA, 129
Mammoth Lakes CA, 129-132, 135, 137, 140, 145
Mammoth Lakes Visitor Center, 129, 143
Mammoth Mine, 129
Mammoth Mountain Ski Area, 131, 138
Mammoth Mountain, 127, 139
Mammoth Pass, 138
Mammoth Scenic Loop, 132
Manson, Charles, 175
Manzanita, 34, 42, 90
Mariposa County, 93
Marklee, Jacob J., 65
Markleeville CA, 65-66, 67, 69, 73, 77, 81
Markleeville Peak, 74
Marmot Lake, 157
Martis Fire, 21, 25, 35
Martis Peak Fire Lookout, 32-35
Martis Peak, 29, 32-38
Mason, R.H., 122, 124
Masonic CA 109, 122
Mattley Ranch, 119, 122-123
McGee Creek (Inyo County), 155, 157, 158
McGee Creek (Mono County), 143
McGlashan, Charles, 27
McKinney Creek, 52, 63
McKinney Lake, 58, 62, 63
McKinney-Rubicon Road, 57-58, 62
McKinney-Rubicon Trail, 52,58, 60-64
Meeks Bay CA, 50
Men To Match My Mountains, 103
Mentha arvensis, 209
Michigan Tunnel, 88
Middle Creek Campground, 75
Mildred Lake, 145
Mill City CA, 129
Mill Creek Power Plant, 119, 122-123
Mill Creek, 102, 117, 124
Miller Creek, 52, 64
Miller Lake, 58, 63
Minaret Summit, 137, 139
Minaret Vista, 137, 139
Minarets, 139
Minden NV, 45, 47
Mineral Peak, 42
Mint (wild), 209
Mitchell Scale, 8
Mogul CA, 65, 81, 82
Mogul Canyon, 83
Mojave Desert, 192
Mokelumne Corridor, 75, 76-80
Mokelumne River, 80
Mokelumne Wilderness Area, 3, 68, 74, 77, 80
Molybdenite, 147
Molybdenumn, 72, 143
Molzan, Julie, 1
Monache Mountain, 194
Monarch Wilderness Area, 3
Monardella odoratissima, 208
Monitor Ca, 65, 81, 82, 87
Monitor Pass, 65, 72, 81, 87
Monitor-Mogul Mining District, 72, 82
Monkeyflower, 202
Mono Basin Historical Society, 114
Mono Basin Visitor Center, 114-115, 119
Mono Chipmunk, 37

Index

Mono County Museum, 93-94
Mono County, 87, 93, 103, 109, 123, 145
Mono Craters, 127, 145
Mono Ditch, 124
Mono Lake, 115-119, 132
Monoville CA, 117, 124
Monte Cristo Mine, 129
Monterey CA, 101
Montgomery Peak, 127
Moore, James, 183
Morgan Creek, 154
Mormon tea, 208
Morningstar Mine, 82-84
Mosquito Ridge Fire Lookout, 35
Mound House NV, 149
Mount Abbot, 151
Mount Agassiz, 173
Mount Alice, 173
Mount Banner (see Banner Peak)
Mount Davis, 139
Mount Givens, 140
Mount Humphries, 154, 157
Mount Julius Ceasar, 151
Mount Mills, 151
Mount Morgan, 145, 151, 178
Mount Morrison, 145
Mount Patterson, 93
Mount Perkins, 184
Mount Ritter, 127, 139
Mount Rose Wilderness Area, 22, 25-26
Mount Siegel, 42
Mount Sill, 173
Mount Tom, 154, 157
Mount Watson, 29-31
Mount Whitney, 170
Mount Winchell, 173
Mountain Mahogany, 181
Mountain Warfare Training Center, 96
Mountain yellow-legged frog, 63
Mt. Bullion CA, 81, 87
Mule Ears, 50, 202
Munckton CA, 107, 109-112
Munckton Gold & Silver Mining Company, 110-111
Munckton, George, 110-111
Muntz, Phillip, 208
Murbarger, Nell, 109
Musser Street (Carson City), 44
Nadeau, Remi, 88, 109
National Antiquities Act of 1906, 5, 105
National Automobile Museum, 11
National Interagency Fire Center, 21
National Park Service, 4, 90
Negit Island, 118
Nevada Central Mine, 15
Nevada Historical Museum, 11
Nevada State Fair, 13
Nevada State Museum, 103, 105
New Coso Heritage Society, 189
New York NY, 27
Norman Clyde and the High Sierra, 173
North Crater (see Panum Crater)
North Logan House Creek, 46
North Palisade, 173
North Tahoe Society, 40
North Tahoe Trailbusters 4WD Club, 1, 50, 58, 62
Nymphaea polysepala, 52
Obsidian Dome, 135, 141
Obsidian, 135-136
Ogden UT, 27
Olancha CA, 191
Olancha Pass, 194
Old Mammoth, 143
O'Neal's Crossing, 18
Onion Creek, 170, 172
Onion Valley, 185, 187
Opuntia Basilaris, 193
Orange mallow, 193
Oregon Trail, 101
Owens River, 117, 139, 167, 189
Pacific Crest Trail, 4, 51, 55, 61, 64
Pacific Gas & Electric Company, 4
Pacific treefrog, 63
Paiute Indians, 101, 135
Paiute Pass, 157
Palisade Glacier, 165, 169-170, 172-172
Panum Crater, 127, 132

Index

Paoha Island, 118, 119
Parcher's Camp, 165
Parker Canyon, 117
Paymaster Mine, 14
PCT, see Pacific Crest Trail
Peavine Creek, 15
Peavine Peak Mining District, 13
Peavine Peak, 12-13, 15-16, 20
Pennsylvania Creek, 92
Pennsylvania Mine, 86, 87, 92
Penny Pines Project, 20
Pennyroyal, 145, 203, 208
Pentstemon monoensis, 193
Pentstemon, 76, 145, 193, 202, 203
Perkins Canyon, 184
Peterson Mine and Mill, 161-162
Peterson, A.H. (Salty), 161, 163
PG&E, see Pacific Gas & Electric Company
Phoenix Mine, 187
Pinchot Pass, 184
Pine City CA, 129
Pine Creek Canyon, 143
Pine Creek, 145
Pine Nut Range, 42, 47
Pinnacle Mine, 183
Piñon nuts, 81, 85
Piñon pine, 85, 126, 161, 206-207
Pinus albiculis, 56
Pinus monophylla, 85, 206
Pinus ponderosa, 126
Pinus, jeffreyi, 126
Pioneers of the Mono Basin,128
Plio-Pleistocene Ice Age, 117, 126, 141, 151, 158, 173, 201
Poe City, 13
Poe, John, 13
Poedunk NV, see Poeville NV
Poeville NV, 12-15
Ponderosa pine, 50, 55
Pope Estate, 39
Porcupine, 7
Potamogeton, 63
Powellite, 147
Preuss, Charles, 102
Prickly pear cactus, 193
Prickly poppy, 145, 156, 202
Promontory Point UT, 27
Prunus emarginata, 143
Pussy paws, 203
Putnam, Charles, 175
Rabbit brush, 145, 156, 181, 202
Rainbow Fire, 139
Rana muscosa, 63
Rawe Peak, 42
Raymond Meadows Creek, 90
Red cherry, 143
Red cones, 140
Red fir, 30
Red Lake Peak, 76
Red Lake, 73-74
Red Metal Mine, 16
Red Slate Mountain, 145
Red's Meadows, 139
Reno Evening Gazzette, 14
Reno Jeepers, 1, 52
Reno NV, 11, 15, 17, 18, 20
Reno, Jesse Lee, 11
Reusch, Ernst, 87
Rex Montis Mine, 187
Ribes, 90
Richardson Lake, 63
Rock Creek Canyon, 151-153
Rock Creek Lake, 154
Rock Creek, 143, 151, 178
Rocky Bottom Lake, 163
Roof pendants, 143
Roosevelt, Franklin D., 128
Roughing It, 119
Round Top Peak, 74
Round Valley Peak, 152
Round Valley, 157
Rubicon River, 52,
Rubicon Springs, 64
Rubicon Trail, 52, 56, 58-59, 62-64
Rudy Mine, 184
Sacramento CA, 13, 27
Saddleback Peak Fire Lookout, 35

Index

Sagebrush, 181, 188
Salazaria mexicana, 193
San Carlos CA, 175
San Francisco CA, 27
San Joaquin Ridge, 140
San Joaquin River, 139
Sand Canyon, 151
Sawmill Creek, 179
Sawmill Pass Trail, 178-179, 181
SCE, see Southern California Edison Company
Scheelite, 71, 147, 155, 178, 182
Schober Mine, 162-163
Schober, Harold, 163
Schumacher, Genny, 155
Scott, Edward, 36
Scotts Lake, 67-68, 69
Scotty Spring, 181, 182
Second Street (Carson City), 44
Sequoia National Forest, 3
Shadescale, 181
Shepherd Pass, 185, 186
Sherwin Creek Road, 143, 144, 145, 147
Sherwin Grade, 157
Shingle Mill Bench, 182
Shingle Mill Flat, 103
Shooting star, 203
Sidalcea oregana, 193
Sierra gentian, 203
Sierra iris, 203
Sierra juniper, 20, 35, 68, 79
Sierra National Forest, 35
Sierra Nevada batholith, 15
Silver Creek (Alpine County), 88, 89
Silver Creek (Mono County), 96-97
Silver Mountain CA, 65, 89, 90, 111
Silver Mountain Mining District, 87
Silver Peak, 92
Silver, 82, 186
Silverado Canyon, 121
Simpson Mine, 128
Simpson, Jim, 128
Sinnamon Meadow, 111
Sioux Indians, 101
Snowplant, 202
Snyder, Charles, 110
Sonora Pass, 95-98, 125
Sonora Peak, 97
Sourdough Hill, 63
South Lake Tahoe CA, 39, 42, 46, 49, 54-55, 57-58
South Pass WY, 101
South Sierra Wilderness, 194
Southern California Edison Company, 4, 123, 158
Southern Inyo Museum, 189-190
Southern Pacific Railroad, 149
Sparks NV, 11, 20
Spook Canyon, 178, 180
Spooner Summit, 41-42, 45-46
Spotted Dog Press, 173
Squaw tea, 208
St. Louis MO, 101
Stampede Reservoir, 19-20
Stateline Fire Lookout, 35
Stateline NV, 46
Stevenot Camp, 80
Stone, Irving, 103
Studebaker, John, 74
Sugar pine, 34
Sugarloak Peak, 165
Summit City CA, 74-75, 77
Summit City Canyon, 3, 74-75
Summit Meadows (Fresno County), 3
Summit Meadows (Mono County), 97
Sunflower Mountain, 25
Swall Meadows, 150
Sweetwater Range, 93, 97
Swift's Station, 42
Tahoe City, 39-40, 50-51
Tahoe House, 31
Tahoe National Forest, 19, 33, 35, 39
Tahoe phase, 183
Tahoe Pines CA, 49, 55
Tahoe Rim Trail, 4, 33, 46, 64
Tahoma CA, 55, 58, 62
Tallac Historic Site, 39
Tamarack Creek, 108

Index

Tamarack Lake, 106, 108, 153
Tamarack Mine, 107-108
Tamarack Trail, 106-108
Taylor Creek Visitor Center, 39-40
Temple Craig, 173
Tent caterpillar, 172
The Saga of Lake Tahoe II, 36
The Silver Seekers, 88
Thistle, 203
Thunder and Lightning Lake, 165
Thunderbolt Peak, 173
Tioga Pass Road, 115
Tioga Phase,143, 173, 183
Toiyabe National Forest, 107
Tollhouse Flat, 102, 103
Tom's Place, 143, 151, 152
Topaz Lake NV, 85
Tower Peak, 97
Tower Range, 95
Trichopitilium incisum, 193
TRT, see Tahoe Rim Trail
Truckee CA, 19, 27-30, 32-33
Truckee River Canyon, 15, 20, 23, 32
Truckee River, 11, 25, 35, 52, 63
Tungsten Hills, 155
Tungsten, 71, 72, 143, 145, 153, 155, 161-163, 178, 184
Twain, Mark, 119
Twin Lakes, 79
U. S. Forest Service, 4, 6, 7, 17, 32, 35, 39, 42, 50, 55, 87, 90, 96, 115, 128, 129, 139, 149
U. S. Geological Survey, 4, 163
U.S. Army, 100, 175
U.S. Department of Defense, 165
U.S. Marine Corps, 96
Union Pacific Railroad, 27
Upper Hoke Meadow, 20
Upper Laurel Lake, 145-147
Upper Sinnamon Meadow, 110
Upper Summit City, 75
Valley View Mine, 181-182
Valley Viewpoint, 185-188
Vanadium, 72, 143
Verdi NV, 12, 18-19
Verdi Peak Fire Lookout, 20-21, 35
Verdi Peak, 17, 19, 21
Verdi Spring, 20
Verdi, Giuseppe, 18
Villanueva, Garrett, 1
Vining, Leroy, 115
Vining's Gulch, 115
Virginia & Truckee Railroad, 149
Virginia City NV, 13, 18, 41, 47
Virginia Lakes Road, 113
Virginia Mine, 187
Volcanic eruptions, 132-135, 140
Warren Bench, 170
Warren Lake, 171
Washington DC, 78
Washoe County, 11
Washoe Indians, 44
Watson Lake, 30
Watson, Robert Montgomery, 31
Wentworth Springs CA, 58, 62
West Fork of Walker River, 100, 102, 103
Western mountain aster, 46, 203
Western Nevada SUV Trails, 42
Western Sierra Jeep Trails, 2
Western Sierra SUV Trails, Vol. II, 64, 194
Wheeler Guard Station, 104
Wheeler Ridge, 152
White alder, 50, 55
White Caps Mine, 155
White fir, 34, 50, 52, 55
White Hill, 46
White Mountain Ranger Station, 149, 151
White Mountains, 127, 140
White Pine Blister Rust, 90
Whitebark pine, 56, 59, 147
Whitney Portal, 189
Wildrose, 193, 203, 209
Williams, Laura, 1
Witcher Creek, 151
Wolf Creek (Alpine County), 3, 88
Wolf Creek (Mono County), 97
Woodfords CA, 67, 70, 74, 78

Woodpecker Meadow, 3
Woods Lake Basin, 179
Wyethia mollis, 50
Yellow Pine, 34, 126
Yellowheads, 193
Yosemite National Park, 93, 145
Yucca brevifolia, 192
Zaca Mine, 82
Zephyr Cove NV, 42, 45
Zindel, Louis, 101

The SUV Trails Series

High Sierra SUV Trails I
The East Side
$16.95

High Sierra SUV Trails II
The Western Slope
$18.95

High Sierra SUV Trails III
The Far North Country
$19.95

Death Valley SUV Trails
$19.95

Inyo-Mono SUV Trails
$19.95

So. Calif. SUV Trails I
The Western Mojave
Desert $19.95

Great Basin SUV Trails I
Southern Nevada $19.95

Great Basin SUV Trails II
Southwestern Nevada $19.95

Please add $2.50 media-rate shipping for the first book, and $1.00 for each additional book. (If you want Priority Mail shipping, add $4.00 for the first book and $1.00 for each additional book.) Orders sent to California addresses must include 7.25% sales tax. Allow adequate time for delivery. Send your check to:

Track & Trail Publications • P.O. Box 1247 • Oakhurst CA 93644

Check out our web-site: www.trackandtrailpublications.com